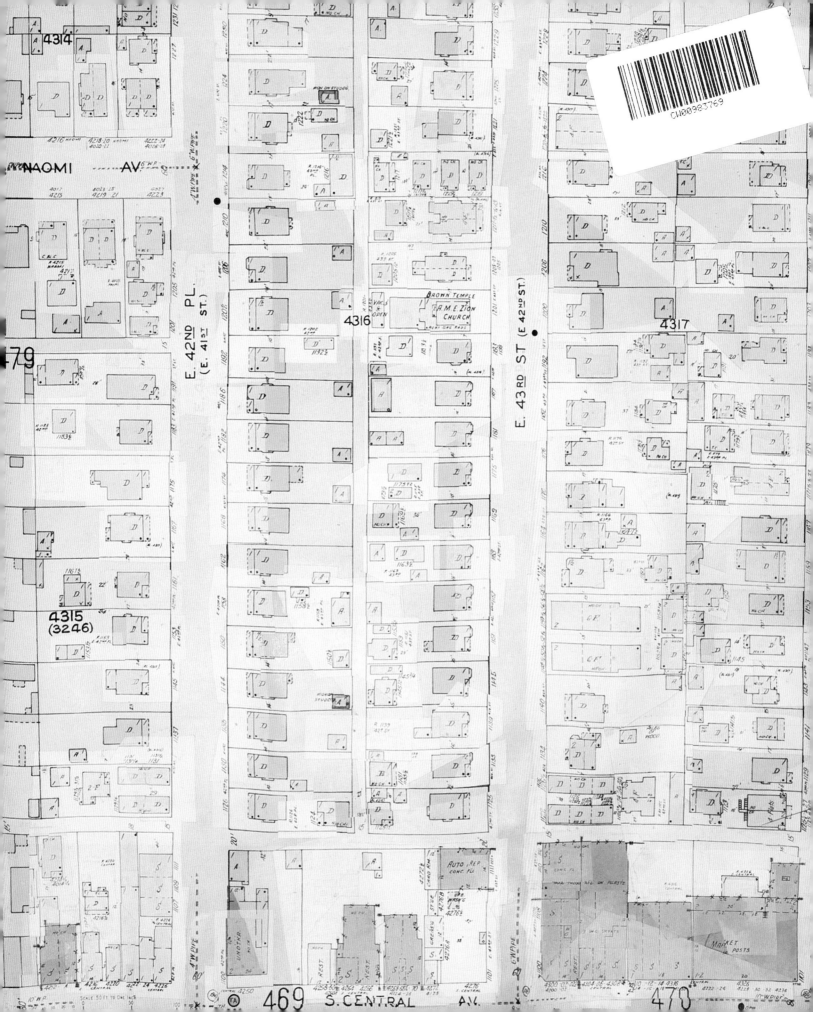

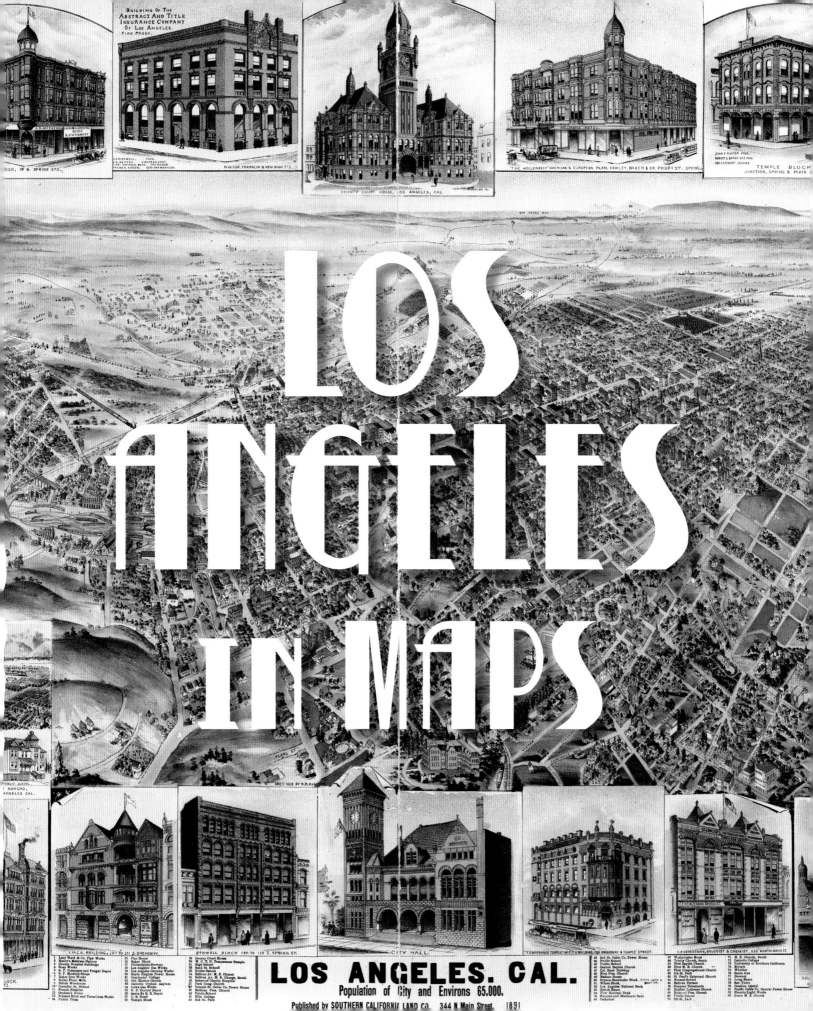

LOS ANGELES
IN MAPS

LOS ANGELES. CAL.

Population of City and Environs 65,000.

Published by SOUTHERN CALIFORNIA LAND Co.   344 N. Main Street.   1891

LOS ANGELES IN MAPS

GLEN CREASON

Foreword by D. J. WALDIE

with contributions by

DYDIA DeLYSER, JOE LINTON,
WILLIAM J. WARREN & MORGAN P. YATES

RIZZOLI

New York Paris London Mi

HE ELECTRIC POWER HOUSE
AL AVE. LOOKING NORTH.

To Charline Creason who put me on the map and Gloria Gerace who brought these beauties into the light. —G. C.

First published in the United States of America in 2010 by
RIZZOLI INTERNATIONAL PUBLICATIONS, INC.
300 Park Avenue South, New York, NY 10010
www.rizzoliusa.com

ISBN-13: 978-0-8478-3391-7
Library of Congress Control Number: 2010920884

Page 1: Panorama, 1891 (p. 52)
Pages 2–3: Pierce's Los Angeles, 1894 (p. 56)
Page 5: Map of Hollywood, 1887 (p. 128)

Designed by Aldo Sampieri

Distributed to the U. S. Trade by Random House, New York
Printed and bound in China

2010 2011 2012 2013 2014 2015/ 10 9 8 7 6 5 4 3 2 1

MAP OF HOLLYWOOD

Residence of H.H. Wilcox.

FOR PARTICULARS apply to H. H. WILCOX & Co.
34 N. Spring St.
LOS ANGELES, CAL.
October 1887

Contents

10 **Foreword** *by* D. J. Waldie

12 **Preface**
14 **Introduction**

Prehistory and Native American Presence
24 The Kirkman-Harriman Pictorial and Historical Map of Los Angeles County 1860 AD

Missions
26 Map of the Lands of the Mission San Gabriel

Ranchos
28 The Old Spanish and Mexican Ranchos of Los Angeles County
30 Map of a Portion of Los Angeles County showing the Abel Stearns Ranchos (for sale by Alfred Robinson)

Founding of the City
32 Ord's Survey

Early Growth
34 Kuchel & Dresel's California Views
36 Map of the 35 Acre Lots of the Los Angeles City Lands, Hancock Survey
38 Hansen Map
40 Ruxton Plaza
42 Bird's-Eye View of Los Angeles
46 Los Angeles in 1881
48 Map of the City of Los Angeles
50 Map of the City of Los Angeles — Compiled from Surveys Made by the City Surveyor During 1886
52 Panorama 1891

Land Booms

54 Ninth Street Tract

56 Pierce's Los Angeles

58 Official Map of the County of Los Angeles

60 Los Angeles 1909

62 Garland Atlas

64 Annexation Map

Social Life

66 Map of Lovers Lane Showing Proposed Lines of Alteration

68 Fort Hill Tract

70 Dakin Atlas

72 Business Property Map of Los Angeles

74 Baist's Real Estate Atlas of Surveys of Los Angeles

76 Branch Library Map

78 The Heart of Los Angeles

80 The Miracle Mile

Birth of the Suburbs

82 Sunset

84 Angelino Heights

86 Laughlin Park Tract Number 2099

The San Fernando Valley

88 Valley Historic

Water

90 Map Showing the Locations of the Old *Zanja Madre*, Ditches, Vineyards, and Old Town, etc.

92 Map of the Reservoir Lands in the City and County of Los Angeles

94 Topographic Map of the Los Angeles Aqueduct and Adjacent Territory

The River

98 "Mapping Los Angeles' Missing River" *by* Joe Linton

99 Map of the Los Angeles River from Los Angeles City Limits to the Pacific Ocean

Infrastructure
102 Map of the Proposed Sewer System for the City of Los Angeles
104 USGS Topo

Railways
106 Official Transportation Map of Pacific Electric Railway System
108 Go Places with the Los Angeles Transit Lines

Harbor
110 Map of Los Angeles County
112 Los Angeles Harbor and Vicinity

The Age of the Automobile
114 "Road Map of Eden" *by* Morgan P. Yates
120 Road Map of Los Angeles and Vicinity
122 Rueger's Automobile and Miner's Road Map of Southern California
124 The Panoramic Automobile Road Map and Tourist Guide Book of Southern California

Oil
126 Views of Oil Fields around Los Angeles

Hollywood
128 Map of Hollywood
130 Hollywood 1915
132 Hollywood 1925
134 Hollywood: Film Capital of the World

Tourism
136 "Mapping Tourism in Southern California" *by* Dydia DeLyser
138 The Travelure Map of Los Angeles and Vicinity
140 Greater Los Angeles
142 Official Sightseeing Map of Los Angeles City and County
144 Historical and Recreational Map of Los Angeles
146 Historic Roads to Romance

Olympics

148 Olympics Map

Maps to the Stars Homes

150 "Maps of the Stars Homes" *by* William J. Warren
152 Souvenir Map and Guide to Starland Estates and Mansions

Between the Lines: Stories of Los Angeles

154 Venice of America
156 Simon's Brick Company Yard No. 3
160 Chavez Ravine
162 Mesmer City
164 Barnes City
166 Nautical Map of Catalina Island
168 Arnold Schoenberg's Los Angeles
170 Bell Quadrangle
172 Central Avenue
174 Wrigley Field
176 The Goez Map Guide to the Murals of East Los Angeles
178 Literary Map of Los Angeles

Modern Maps

180 Los Angeles Area Freeway System
182 Interactive Map of the Chinatown Area of Los Angeles
184 Downtown Los Angeles
186 Map of Los Angeles Neighborhoods

188 **Bibliography**
189 **Index**
191 **Contributor Biographies**
192 **Acknowledgments**

Foreword

by D. J. Waldie

Geography of Home

Before Los Angeles began, there was a map—a sketch really—of house lots and a plaza adjacent to an unreliable river. The angle of that river and the high ground next to it prevented the proper orientation of the lots and plaza, which should have been 45 degrees askew from north and south as required by the Laws of the Indies for all the settlements of *Nueva España*. The non-existent streets of the not-yet-city in 1781, as drawn by Governor Felipe de Neve, were cocked an imprecise 36 degrees.

Even after almost 230 years, the streets in the city's core still point in directions not quite true. Such is the shaping power of a map.

The city imagined into existence by de Neve drew its future on larger and larger sheets of paper after 1850, platting a newly American city, the boomtown of 1888, the city of middle-class leisure at the turn of the twentieth century, and the suburban immensity that working-class Los Angeles became—and still is—in the years after World War II. Maps of Los Angeles—even those designed to evoke a nostalgic past—always seem to project the city somewhere else: into a topography of longing, into the fiction that tomorrow's city will finally assuage desire, or into a place that might be called home.

Homes are this city's cultural monument. Maps sold them by tens of thousands, each tract of houses a dream of health and happiness in the sunshine, their gridded streets efficiently subdividing a presumed paradise. But Angeleños are apt to be disoriented. They have come to a place so new, so free of associations. Los Angeles needed maps to orient buyers on the anonymity of the plain that descends from the plaza south to the ocean and within the bowl of the San Fernando Valley, empty of landmarks. Until the advent of GPS, just about every driver in Los Angeles owned a copy of *The Thomas Guide* street atlas, its page references half-memorized.

Maps of rail lines, streetcar lines, boulevards, and finally of freeways deny the legend of this city's unplanned sprawl. Those networks preceded the stages of the city's growth, and accelerated it. Los Angeles has many centers of power as a result, and they are located at sites summoned from the movement of people and goods along routes that planning made possible.

The imagination of Los Angeles is still in its maps, in their reach and aspiration. It is an imagination that appalls some, whose disorientation is not resolved by reference to tourist guides and maps to the homes of the stars. Los Angeles, whose streets are familiar to every moviegoer in the world, still baffles. The uniform urban grid of the city, which can be seen as a spectacle of democracy, isn't enough to overcome the sunshine and noir iconography that is the concealing screen that hides the real Los Angeles.

Maps assure me (even as I doubt it) that "here" on the Los Angeles Plain is connected to "there" across the many divides of the city. Because a map links my neighborhood to the vast grid of Los Angeles, my place is more real to me, if not more comprehensible.

All maps are fictions, but maps of Los Angeles, as you will see, are more fictive than most. They led us into the future with the conviction that mere lines on paper can make a city. They did once, to our wonder and sorrow. Having finally run up against its limits, both geographical and psychological, that city of the imagination waits to be remapped as the geography of home.

Preface

"I perhaps owe having become a painter to flowers."
– Claude Monet

I t may be akin to a veteran carpenter having an epiphany while finishing a doorframe and getting moony over the grain of the wood but after decades of using maps to answer questions as a reference librarian I found myself becoming enamored of the variety of cartographical renderings of my home town. This love of the maps of Los Angeles eventually morphed into two exhibits that led to a much more serious study of the way these old beauties demonstrate the journey of Los Angeles to the present. Just as Monet owed being a painter to his need to express his love for flowers I will try here to take some of the essential maps along with some that give local flavor and just connect a few dots of Los Angeles' past. Choosing maps to represent the cultural and geographical vastness of Los Angeles can only be done with vignettes, anecdotes, and cartographical snapshots of the little pueblo become metropolis. It is perhaps impossible to incorporate all the stories of this area under one cover although that aim certainly has been a day to day struggle for me. To view this sprawling, unpredictable landscape you need Cinemascope squared or a very vivid imagination. It is hoped that the images here while baring their stories will demonstrate a history of L.A. without too many wasted words.

Unlike some other American places, Los Angeles has taken more than its share of raps, but the locals seem to take it all in stride. While sports fans chant "beat L.A." and wits knock the city of the angels, we just get back on the freeway and continue our pursuit of paradise. Unfortunately much of the literature on the city has come from visitors not firmly rooted in the southland soil—thus the reams of the cynical nonsense that paints Los Angeles as null and void. Anyone who chooses to dig into this soil will find treasures of historical proportion.

Still, some of the tourist siren songs are true; there are snow-capped mountains and movie stars and the Pacific Ocean just thirty off-ramps away. *Los Angeles in Maps* is a reflection of the place and people, a tale not told enough of the bounty of this land. The stories of this history are truly fascinating and if you look closely enough at this cartography you may glimpse a portal into Los Angeles' past. While the panorama of Los Angeles' history is a richly textured tapestry, the maps shown here may give some insight into how the big city sprung from humble beginnings as a pueblo. This is not the final directive in that journey; thousands of other maps sit in drawers across the country ready to tell their story. Despite the somewhat pedestrian intentions of many of the popular forms of cartography used to illustrate points here, the plebian maps tell a tale that needs less explanation than the most thorough survey. Many aspects of the history of the city and the accompanying maps can and have had entire books devoted to their study. Indeed, most of the broad topics are wonderfully researched and great scholarship abounds in the city. There are many more roads to be traveled to find the entire saga of Los Angeles, probably somewhere between Nathaniel West's "dream dump" and Phil Och's thought that "the final story, the final chapter of western man, lies in Los Angeles."

I grew up here and saw my home town begin the acceleration toward big league in the 1950s when the city of the angels was so flush, the money flowed out into the suburbs and made the place the four thousand plus square miles of colorful, crazy, and somewhat eccentric landscape of today. It was a city without a center, as downtown slumbered and drifted in the doldrums, until resurgence in the 1970s, when skyscrapers sprouted and the megalopolis just sort of materialized in places stretching from downtown to a wider swath across the southland. The pueblo, founded in 1781 has progressed through many phases of waxing and waning, with booms causing growth like a pubescent kid whose pants are suddenly five inches short. The reasons for these spurts vary from the dispersal of water, the establishment of order, the coming of the railroads, the lure of the weather, glamour seeking tourists, plentiful jobs in the factories of Vernon, the sudden rise of the movie business, oil, aircraft, automobiles, and sundry other fresh opportunities in paradise.

My personal journey began in the post-war, blue-collar suburb of South Gate, but continued across the basin, over to the West Side, around to the Northeast and East along with much time spent in South Central. As a boy, I rode the J-Car from the loop in Huntington Park over to Slauson, where we jumped on the V-car to Vernon and Figueroa, offering us that adventurous walk to the Coliseum where we sold programs at football games. I was a delivery boy in the 60s driving a VW beetle around the valley of the smokes, taking fruitcakes, hams, and assorted sports and theater tickets to places ranging from Hollywood to the San Fernando Valley to the stately/seedy Alexandria Hotel in downtown. I learned the topography of the city the hard way: by getting lost in every neighborhood in town. As a native there was only one college I yearned to attend and my rather undistinguished academic career at UCLA did not interfere much with the unbelievable adventure of attending university during the Summer of Love and the Wooden years. After some wandering in the cultural desert of being a salesman, hippie freelance writer, janitor, ticket broker, and researcher at the old *L.A. Herald Examiner*, I found myself at the Los Angeles Public Library in the history department. It was there that my true education began, including the study of maps about the city going back to the establishment of *El Pueblo de Nuestra Señora la Reina de Los Angeles de Porciúncula*. For thirty years these maps have been my tools in answering questions about the city's roots and inspirations for my own questions regarding my native stomping grounds.

Too often I have read wildly misguided descriptions of this place and its people, written by those who believe the city is some kind of amalgamation of movie sets, gang strongholds, grimy slabs of concrete, and endless stretches of sun washed beaches filled with dim-witted but spectacularly built blonde people. In truth, Los Angeles is one of the most difficul-to-explain places on the planet. The sprawling metropolis has been reviled, written off, and overlooked as a place of culture and vitality for almost as long as it has existed. The history of the region seems to be forever misunderstood as movies and sunshine that sprang out of the smog-filled basin during the Eisenhower administration. L.A. is surprisingly beautiful, in parts, and deeply fascinating in places, but the story is rarely told of how we came from adobe huts to an international city in just a couple of hundred years. The town that was once a sleepy, little pueblo by the Porciuncula River, has boomed, expanding across the landscape, in a 50-by-30 mile swath of intense, unbounded growth. From the original eleven families who hiked up here from Sonora, there are now over twelve million counted who inhabit the metropolis surrounding the city of the angels.

Introduction

The great Roman philosopher Seneca once wrote that "every new beginning comes from some other beginning's end" and we must begin our map journey with the first surveyed map of the city that really is not a beginning at all. Two solid frameworks made it possible for Los Angeles to exist in the first place. The Native American presence is purported to date back thousands of years and is graphically delineated by the Kirkman–Harriman map (p. 24), which demonstrates the strength and variety of indigenous settlement. The early village of Yangna was the initial center of population that served as a model for the first pueblo. Before the stouthearted eleven founding families found themselves on the banks of the new settlement of la ciudad de Los Angeles, the Tongva tribe had enjoyed the abundance of the southland for countless generations. When the Spaniards first sailed past the pristine coastline the die was cast for European settlement, but the process was slow and somewhat difficult.

The missions provided satellites and a backbone of guidance, supplies, and personnel, while the Rancho system used by both Spain and Mexico here connected the land to some kind of government and, depending on the point of view, development or desecration. These two institutions were early civilizing factors, but both were severely flawed and made for tremendous complications in creating a city. The Title Insurance pictorial map (p. 28) of the Ranchos paints a rosy picture of the Spanish and Mexican era, but behind the colorful façade there were a thousand stories of heartbreak and disaster. The early advertisement of the Abel Stearns Ranchos (p. 30) is a prime example of the dissolution of this old world solution and the commencement of the Americanization of the area. The secularizations of the missions was also a rapid and dizzying process that permanently disenfranchised the Gabrieleno and Fernandeno Indians in this area, which is a story told by the map of the San Gabriel Mission lands (p. 26). The egalitarian settlement and free systems of government provided an early multi-lingual city that in many ways continues today.

Despite the efforts to homogenize the place, Los Angeles has always been one American city that expanded the definition of metropolis. One of the reasons Los Angeles has survived the many crises it has endured lies in this flexibility and an ability to utilize the creativity of a great variety of people from all over the world. In fact, the Ord Survey (p. 32), which represents the start of mapping of the city, only represents a point in time when the pueblo of Los Angeles began its internship with the United States and moved away from preceding eras toward the megalopolis of today. By the time of the survey in 1849, the old plaza at the center of the Ord map had already existed for sixty-eight eventful years, but cartography had been either not needed or was sadly neglected before Lieutenant Ord and his assistant roamed the saw grass spreading their chains. Certainly, there are sketches of the area done before this date, but none that include street names and points of interest. The maps included here will show some of the growth outward along with certain aspects of the cultural life in the southland that make the modern city of the angels unique.

One could argue that the cartographic chronicle of Los Angeles is a story of subdivision upon subdivision. The first slicing up of the land can be seen on several maps, especially Hancock's survey (p. 36), which sees the old city lands being dispersed along with the "35 Acre Lots" that break up the real estate east of the river. The early, decorative plat maps, created as land value increased due to rail connection to the city—such as the Henry Stevenson of 1884 (p. 48) and Rowan and Koeberle's of 1887 (p. 50)—show in fine detail how the ownership of plots slowly passed from the pioneers to the new generation. As the real estate booms waxed and waned the center could not hold, and the old plaza began to fade as the heart of the city. By the time Ruxton made his map of the Plaza in 1873 (p. 40) its days were numbered, and a business district was taking place on far away 2nd and Spring. By the mid 1870s, the city began to flourish despite a national economic downturn and public buildings appeared, including St. Vincent's College, the new High School near Fort Moore Hill, and St. Vibiana's cathedral. The Southern Pacific Railroad connected the city to San Francisco in 1876 and the population climbed to 12,000 in 1881. The *Los Angeles Times* celebrated that year with a model and map fifty years later, which recreates that scene remembered easily in this preservation of Los Angeles. In the model used for the map we can see the city poised to experience the most rapid growth in its history with the land booms of 1887 and 1888.

While the population increased in leaps and bounds after the railroads opened up the city, the need for a proper infrastructure became tantamount to joining other major American urban centers. Water, and all the related ramifications of having concentrated populations gathering here, was at the center of Los Angeles' earliest struggles. Demand, water use, water treatment, and flood control were all parts of the equation. It is a huge story, but one just glimpsed in the quest for, and battle to keep pure, this liquid gold.

City surveyor Michael Kelleher shows the early Zanja system in a map (p. 90) and the early attempts to collect and distribute water can be seen on the *Map of the Reservoir Lands* by William Moore (p. 92). Water in this semi-arid climate was as essential as oxygen and when the Los Angeles River began to be overtaxed by the booming city other solutions were sought. Joe Linton discusses the long and winding tale of that river and the crucial role it played in the history of Los Angeles in his essay (p. 98). The battle with nature is graphically shown on the *Map of the Los Angeles River* (p. 100) done by county engineer James Reagan, which looks at the constant conflict people had with the watercourse and the struggle to tame the flooding they suffered over the years. Water and the river is a story not only of usage for homes, industry and agriculture but also a tale of sewage and flood control. The fascinating story of the creation of a sewage system and the political wars that were fought over this daunting task are seen at the beginning in the *Map of the Proposed Sewage System* (p. 102) done by the famous Frederick Eaton, who appears all over the canvas of Los Angeles history. Water, the precious elixir of change gushes into local history with the Los Angeles Aqueduct, detailed by the topographic map of 1908 (p. 94), done by the Water Department of the City of Los Angeles, led by the towering figure of William Mulholland. Mulholland changed the city like few before or after with this one grand engineering accomplishment.

Los Angeles, like New York, was not a city planned for its beauty but put together mostly with regards to pragmatic commerce. The great economic possibilities of the area were unknown in the beginning, when cattle was the main source of income; but when oil, automobiles, airplanes, railroads, the harbor, and movie making took hold, the city blossomed and made lots of money. Maps reflect the commercial appeal of the city at almost every look, but some views focus on specific areas of enterprise. Transportation aside we can see the huge influence of oil in C.S. and E.M. Forncrook's *Views of Oil Fields Around Los Angeles* (p. 126), which shows the city at the tail end of a boom that placed it amongst the world leaders in this industry. Edward Doheny made the first discovery of crude oil in 1892, but the petroleum giants scoured the landscape for every available drop in the ensuing century.

Of course, industry on the coast was tied directly to the creation of a deep water harbor, which began as a battle between the cities of Santa Monica and San Pedro that can be glimpsed in three maps including the old 1877 bird's-eye map (p. 42) by E.S. Glover, splitting the possibilities in one view and then progressing forward to the modern shipping powerhouse, with the all-important port thriving at the end of World War II as seen on the Board of Harbor Commissioners *Los Angeles Harbor and Vicinity* (p. 112). To accomplish the harbor connection to the city, the shoestring configuration was worked out as seen on Chadwick's simple map of the city limits (p. 110) done in 1912. Without the harbor, or oil, or the rail hubs, Los Angeles would have remained static and unable to expand as it did throughout the nineteenth and twentieth centuries. As the cash and water flowed, Los Angeles gathered up communities around it and grew richer and more powerful. The annexation map of the city created by R. L. Merget in 1928 (p. 64) offers a jigsaw puzzle look at how the many small pieces joined for a myriad of reasons but eventually became the big city.

This growth coincides with the golden age of panoramic maps that encouraged newcomers to flock to the land of unlimited opportunity. Once L.A. took on pretensions to big city status, the maps featuring it began to flow and boosterism flourished. Panoramic or bird's-eye maps returned to vogue in the Victorian era. This was a style of mapping that had been part of national movement in the mid-nineteenth century as exemplified by an early example of this city by Kuchel and Dresel done in 1857 (p. 34) when Los Angeles was taking baby steps toward civility with a bank, several schools, and a water company. Glover's often-reproduced look at the entire spread of Los Angeles (p. 42) was done in the watershed year of 1877, straddling the pueblo and boom city in time. These grand views offering unlimited possibilities in the city of the angels are beautifully executed in the 1891 panorama (p. 52) by Elliot and the amazing duel view by Pierce (p. 56) done in 1894, which served real estate promoters bent on populating every inch of the basin. Oil had been discovered and places of prestigious higher learning now appeared, including Throop University (later known as California Institute of Technology), while the street railways reached as far north as Mount Lowe above Pasadena. By the time Perry created a wide-scope look at the county in 1898 (p. 58), the harbor had begun expansion, Griffith Park became the largest municipal park in the nation, and the first automobiles appeared on Los Angeles roads.

Besides the major chapters of cartographic history shown here there are the small nuances of everyday life in the old pueblo and the developing metropolis that exist in the details. Some of the maps featured show lurid detail and some peek in the windows of the city streets. A look at "Lovers Lane" shown in 1871 (p. 66) is merely light-hearted but the Fort Hill Tract map (p. 68) where the earliest burials took place has a sad back-story. The same could be said about a Dakin atlas sheet (p. 70) that describes the houses of ill repute and street life of early days as the old pueblo gave way to the modern city. On the other hand a Baist atlas page (p. 74) from the early '20s takes a detailed examination of the phenomenon of Boyle Heights, a neighborhood that was home for many ethnic groups of Angelenos who left their mark on the city from that small community east of the river. The growth and power of downtown's business center can be seen in two fine maps: the superb Robert Marsh business properties map of 1913 (p. 72) and Payne's *Heart of Los Angeles* from 1931 (p. 78), wherein every business in town can be seen and studied. In the same vein, the spread of retail power can be seen in the Nirenstein Atlas sheet of the Miracle Mile (p. 80) done in the 1953 during a flush period when the city once again embraced a blooming of the local economy. Finally, to remind everyone that Los Angeles is not the city of sun-baked airheads, there is the unique Branch Libraries map of 1930 (p. 76) offering pen and ink proof that the locals read books and have always been literate.

While the population expanded at an astounding rate, doubling in a decade three times, the first suburbs began to appear then sprouted quickly, aided by memorable maps that marked their inception. Out in the sticks, places like Hollywood, Sunset, and later Westwood, started to take shape, while closer to town, developments such as Angeleno Heights and Bunker Hill created impressive neighborhoods. The 1887 map of early Hollywood by H.H. Wilcox (p. 128) sets the standard for the spread of the city but the Sunset map done by the Los Angeles and Santa Monica Land and Water Company (p. 82) hints at a place in the sun where residents would gaze out at the Pacific Ocean and be free from the hurly burly of big Los Angeles with its 50,000 residents. In town, the quality increased with the quantity and places like Angeleno Heights drawn up on Fielding J. Stilson's map (p. 84) offered genteel spaces and the beginnings of an architectural standard in the city. Such striving for domiciles equal to the Eden of the land also led to developments of distinction such as Laughlin Park laid out by visionaries like Fremont Ackerman. Los Angeles is a city of such neighborhoods where residents bond over a name and take pride of ownership to another level. Even dreamed of places like the 9th Street tract demonstrate the grand ideas of a beautiful place despite the purely commercial intent of the real estate peddlers. While the Semi-Tropic Homestead Company may have been trying to sell real estate to the working class they did leave behind an impressive look at the landscape of that part of the city around 9th and Alameda in 1894 (p. 54), ironically a year when labor riots shook Southern California. The mother of all suburbs in Los Angeles is the San Fernando Valley, where rolling wheat fields were eventually replaced with rolling tract home developments, which is also featured. The Lankershim Ranch map of 1887 (p. 88) shows the vast expanse that was soon to become the American dream for generations of Angelenos. In the beginning this flat plain suggested the perfect agricultural cornucopia for Southern California, but businessmen saw real estate. After World War II the area was flooded with hopefuls who escaped the city to create an area so diverse and prosperous that it has often flirted with its own cityhood. While only one separate map is included here the San Fernando Valley is an essential part of the true city of Los Angeles and is included in almost every bit of cartography that extends beyond downtown.

Nothing aided the spread of the metropolitan area across the county more than the network of streetcars that were begun as early as 1873 and flourished with the electric cars after the consolidation of numerous companies by Henry Huntington, who created the Pacific Electric Railway at the turn of the century. The groundbreaking Laura Whitlock map (p. 106) of that system pictures this extensive coverage in a tidy single look after the great merger of 1911 when the Southern Pacific Railway took over all the lines. Once this rapid transit system was the envy of the nation and provided citizens of Los Angeles a mobility that really could not be matched by the freeways with their congestion and pollution. Even into the post-war years the Pacific Electric lines continued to provide the people with transportation seen in the Los Angeles Transit Line map of 1945 (p. 108), when internal combustion engine buses battled the electric cars for space; of course, both were to be swamped by the automobile. The age of street rails set the pace for the future automotive city and this look at all-important transportation systems that connected Los Angeles and presaged the megalopolis provides a base for the automotive city that started taking shape in the late 1930s.

The entire history of the city could be framed by the annals of road building that seems to have taken place in every era dating back to the original dwellers of Southern California. While the Kirkman-Harriman map shows the logical trails in and around Los Angeles, the first freeways seemed to have followed well-worn paths that had served as trails for the settlers or stage routes for visitors of just the place where the mountains parted just enough to let horses and wagons into the basin. In the early days of the internal combustion engine there was an immediate necessity of mapping that is evidenced in the early Rueger map of 1903 (p. 122). Speed "limits" then rested at 8 mph and local newspapers were dotted with tales of accidents involving citizens being mowed down by the speeding autos that, despite the racket they caused in this expansive city, surprised pedestrians and caused quite a few fatalities. Morgan Yates' essay (p. 114) perfectly describes the beginnings of the automotive age, detailing the role of the Automobile Club of Southern California and their early efforts to make this an auto-civilized place by getting roads identified, paved, thoroughly mapped, and made safe for drivers. The availability of affordable cars made leisure in the southland suddenly accessible for the middle-class. The assembly line cars brought mobility and flexibility to the social network but also changed the landscape forever. Pages from the charming and informative Panoramic Auto Guide (p. 124) show just how motorists took to the roads and expanded the city. Ironically, the 1937 Auto Club map (p. 120) lays out the grand landscape of the county at the very beginning of the surge toward freeways. The other Auto Club map shown (p. 180) jumps ahead seventy years and finds Los Angeles as part of a concrete grid that stretches in every direction and provides a handy freeway on-ramp to almost anywhere within miles to the citizens of Los Angeles. Of course, the freeways offer other things, too—but that's another story. Not seen here but most certainly essential to all who travel the maze of Los Angeles are the street guides that connect the people and places. Jack Renie was the trailblazer with his Renie Guides, followed by the fine Gillespie guides, and all gathered under the umbrella of the sweetly familiar *Thomas Bros. Popular Atlas of Los Angeles County*, the bible of drivers hereabouts.

While newcomers have seen Los Angeles as many things good and evil, the myth and magic of Hollywood has been an irresistible lure for generations of visitors from across the world. Once a rather prim and spiritually bent settlement, Horace Wilcox's Hollywood was to be kept apart from the dens of downtown iniquity. Ironically, the town began as a dream of another sort shown on the Wilcox map (p. 128), when the pepper trees lined the streets and demon rum was not allowed within the city limits. Yet, when we see the place after annexation in S.B. Reeve's 1915 *Map of the Central Locations of Studios* (p. 130), the die had been cast and movies were being made daily in places like Gower Gulch, beneath the 300-plus days of sunshine. By the time Security Trust and Savings Bank drew up a map with the old city limits of Hollywood in 1925 (p. 132) the area was a major part of the Western economy and an identity for the area that continues today. By the post-war years the studio system was at full steam and cute tourist maps like *Hollywood Film Capitol of the World* (p. 134) sent out a siren song to dreamers all over the globe. When newcomers got to Hollywood, it wasn't always roses and sweet oranges, of course; still, beyond the silver screen, there was an industry that put thousands to work in Southern California. One of the truly unique cartographic creations in the city, of which Bill Warren writes (p. 150), were the ubiquitous maps to the stars homes that became a genre all on their own. People are still buying them and collectors are chasing them down all over America. Many of the stars might not even be recognizable today, but the art involved makes them well worth remembering as maps.

Along with heavy industry, shipping, oil, and the film industry, Los Angeles from the beginning made itself attractive as a tourist destination and in this guise the tourist map was developed here like few other places in America. As Dydia DeLyser points out in her essay (p. 136), the maps may have fibbed a bit but the spell they cast drew millions to Los Angeles and many stayed for the sunshine or the work. Still, the visitors spent money on hotels, amusements, restaurants, traveling by rail, car, airplane, and boat. Some of the most memorable maps of Los Angeles were created with this purpose in mind. The appropriately named *Travelure Map* (p. 138) and *Greater Los Angeles: The Wonder City of America* (p. 140) were both created in the "golden" year of 1932 as the country suffered through the depression. While money was scarce, graphic artists seemed to be thriving in the area, evidenced by the fine all year sightseeing map of 1940 (p. 142), drawn at the behest of the great tourism inducing All Year Club of Southern California, which did more than any other organization to establish the city as a big time travel destination. Two of the greatest pictorial works existing stem from this motivation including the work of the map maestro Jo Mora, who finished his masterpiece of pictorial mapping on Los Angeles in 1942 (p. 144). Lastly the wonderful "Roads to Romance" series kept up the call to tour the southland into the 1960s, and while they stretched the geographical truth a bit the maps remain things of beauty forever.

Sports might not seem like a front page story in the entire history of a great city like Los Angeles, but no event set the city on a path for national recognition quite like the 1932 Olympics and Union Oil's fine map of the event (p. 148) captures some of the bravado of the little city trying to stand up with the big boys. Sports also figures in the early days of the Pacific Coast baseball league with a Sanborn atlas sheet of the beloved old Wrigley Field (p. 174), where the minor league Angels thrilled Angelenos like few teams, including today's Dodgers and Lakers. Despite its early depiction, Chavez Ravine as seen on a 1910 Baist atlas (p. 160) carries much intrigue and drama about the ground where Dodger Stadium now stands.

The maps here cannot tell the entire saga of this complex city, of the thousands of crises passed, of the millions of simple stories of the sons and daughters of those early pioneers who struggled up here from Sonora, or of the lucky strokes that led Los Angeles to become one of the great cities of the world. Some might mistakenly think the mystery of the place is a blank space, the "72 suburbs in search of a city," but there are some maps included that tell just a sliver of the texture of the history here. Tom Waits once sang "the dreams ain't broken down here, they're just walking with a limp," and this is most certainly true about many of the fantasies Angelenos attempted to bring to life. Certainly, Abbot Kinney's Venice was such a chimera—shown here in the *Map of Venice, America* (p. 154)—which tantalized many but was not really delivered. The same story can be told for the possibilities of Mesmer City, done by the optimistic realtor George Bray, offering a sort of Camelot but showing more vacant lots than mythology (p. 162). There are darker tales from Los Angeles history marked by dots on the map like the place called "Sleepy Lagoon" where a fight amongst teenagers ended in murder and a chain of events that saw racism in its most raw form on the streets of downtown and in the courtroom (p. 170). Also the little rail stop called "Simons" on the Jacobs and Rock map (p. 156) of the city in 1908 distills the epic story of a company town of imported Mexican laborers right in the heart of Los Angeles County. Other stories might be more light-hearted like that which accompanies *Barnes Square Tract*, where clowns, acrobats, and a ringmaster shared the acreage with a huge menagerie including a 12 foot, 8 inch, "seven ton" elephant named Tusko (p. 164). The charming island known as Catalina to locals is described on a nautical chart done by the fascinating Frank Jansen in the 1920s as the resort prepared for the golden days of big bands and a romance with Hollywood on shore. In some cases the maps might capture the glory of multi-cultural Los Angeles where disenfranchised ethnic groups rose above prejudice and made essential contributions to the cultural vitality of the city. The sheets of a Sanborn Fire Insurance Atlas (p. 172) are prime cartographic examples of the glory of Central Avenue where African-Americans created one of the most remarkable cultural achievements in all of America. The same must be said about the Goez gallery map guide of the murals of east Los Angeles" (p. 176), which preserves the blossoming of the Chicano art movement in Los Angeles that continues to this day.

Of course, each map seen here incorporates in essence the contributions of hundreds of characters from Los Angeles history playing their parts behind the scenes that make the story interesting. Not just the mapmakers or publishers but the forces in society

Following pages:
Lithograph by Charles Koppel of Los Angeles, California, c.1853
From Robert S. Williamson's Report Upon the Routes in California to Connect
with the Routes near the Thirty-fifth and Thirty-second Parallels,
33d Cong., 2d sess., Senate Executive Document 78

German artist and engineer Charles Koppel published this full-page lithograph
of the pueblo of Los Angeles as part of a survey of possible railroad routes from
the Mississippi River to the West Coast. This view, looking east out across the
plaza, is purported to be the first published rendering of the area.

that created the necessity to create such documents. In looking at the maps of Los Angeles you will meet many engaging characters that are unique to this place and their time. The names percolate out of the histories: Pio Pico, Abel Stearns, Phineas Banning, Arcadia Bandini (aka Arcadia Bandini de Stearns and Arcadia Bandini de Stearns Baker), Hugo Reid, Horace Wilcox, Isaac Lankershim, Prudent Beaudry, Henry and Collis Huntington, Frederick Eaton, Biddy Mason, Edward Doheny, William Mulholland, Harrison Gray Otis, Abbot Kinney, William Garland, Aimee Semple McPherson, G. Allan Hancock, Mary Foy, Simon Rodia, Charles Lummis, Lucky Baldwin, Griffith J. Griffith, William Workman, Upton Sinclair, John Fante, Roz Wyman, and on and on. The mapmakers while different in styles and purpose created geographical guides that in many cases were much more art than direction. Starting with Edward Ord and continuing with Henry Hancock, William Moore, Henry J. Stevenson, V.J. Rowan, B.W. Pierce, G. William Baist, George Kirkman, Robert Marsh, James H. Payne, Jo Mora, the United States Geological Survey, the Automobile Club of Southern California, Jack Renie, right on up to the present work of James Rojas, Los Angeles has been defined but never restrained by mapmakers who dreamed as they drew. The name Sam Behrend should be mentioned as the preeminent private collector and archivist of Los Angeles maps. He was one of the first and foremost insurance brokers for the film industry and made a fortune writing policies for the early pioneers. Behrend was a Los Angeles native and from an early age he collected data, anecdotes, photographs, and many maps. For decades Mr. Behrend created one of the finest archives ever in Los Angeles and when he died in October of 1940 he bequeathed much of these treasures to the Los Angeles Museum and some other institutions. Many of the best original maps on the city can be found with the tidy stamp on the back saying "Sam Behrend." A few of those maps can be seen in these pages.

The maps of the city that appear here should direct readers off on paths to local history enlightenment, to places and stories particular to the many historians searching the city for the truth. Los Angeles is different things to different people. It can be Zubin Mehta conducting Mahler or Dick Lane shouting "whoa Nellie!" while broadcasting the Figure Eight jalopy races from Ascot Park. It can be the bright lights of "L.A. Live" or the open air used auto bazaars on Florence Avenue in South Central. It can be LACMA or MoCA or the Getty unless one prefers the Swap Meet at the La Mirada Drive-In. L.A. might be the sound of a basketball bouncing on a Sherman Oaks driveway in autumn or the crash of the waves of the mighty Pacific in Malibu. It can be the Rose Parade on January 1st or symphonies under the stars at the Hollywood Bowl. The experiences can include a Laker parade down Figueroa or the great high school football rivalry game between Roosevelt and Garfield. It is a Range Rover with a Che Guevara decal on the tinted windows. It's a punk rock band blasting away in a garage in Highland Park, a kid's art class at Plaza de la Raza; it's the reading room at the Huntington Library, the Chinese New Year's parade in Chinatown, or an orthodox Jew walking up Pico with his shtreimel covering his head. The glittering and stupendous dream of Los Angeles cannot be found in one book or archive or library but in the long journey that begins at the Porciuncula River's edge.

The Kirkman-Harriman Pictorial and Historical Map of Los Angeles County 1860 AD

T he Kirkman-Harriman map was an ambitious cartographic undertaking by Major George W. Kirkman in which he attempted to weave many levels of Los Angeles history onto one grand tapestry. While his scholarship is admirable and cartography mostly accurate, the thrust of this creation was to draw folks to colorful landmarks of Los Angeles with historic facts that the city fathers had not heretofore provided to visitors. A brochure written in stilted but brisk paragraphs that call to mind the prose of Edward Bulwer-Lytton accompanies the map. Kirkman was a local historian and rather bombastic columnist for the *Los Angeles Times* in the 1920s, but he was also a real estate man at heart, describing the profession as a "highly honored extremely attractive absorbing interesting widely ramified and superlatively profitable occupation."

Yet the map seems to have been his crowning achievement. As he said, "it is a pictorial map but is preeminently a historical map, as is evidenced, for instance, by the ancient roads and highways of this section as they were in 1860." Despite the eccentricity in its creation, the Kirkman-Harriman map is very valuable to historians for several reasons. Most important is the location of the many camps of the Native American tribe Tongva, including the central village of Yangna, where eventually the pueblo was located when the *Pobladores* (the 44 original settlers) arrived in 1781. Although downplayed in the grand scheme of the map, the sizeable presence of these Indians, later called the Gabrielinos by the Mission settlers, is the subtext of the purported origin of the city. The Tongva, a peaceful and thriving tribe probably five thousand strong, was one of the most successful settlements in Alta, California, that hunted, fished, and existed here contentedly for thousands of years.

Kirkman also included the thirteen battle sites around the county, the army posts, the mines where gold was found a full six years before Sutter's Mill, the old salt pond at Redondo, and the "asphalt works" of the La Brea Tar Pits. He showed the discoveries of Cabrillo and Vizcaino, and the route of Portola that set up the eventual settlement at the pueblo. Of great interest also are the Indian trails that very often trace the routes of modern highways and today's freeways, like the Hollywood, the Pasadena, the Harbor, and the Santa Monica—the most traveled road in the world.

William R. Harriman, listed here as coauthor, was the Los Angeles County Superintendent of Charities for a short time and long-time head of Rancho Los Amigos, sometimes known as the Los Angeles County Poor Farm. He was also endlessly active in civic organizations and was a pioneer in the humane treatment of the indigent. He is not mentioned at all by Kirkman in the lengthy descriptive notes, nor does his name attend to any part of the drawing of the map. It is unclear exactly what role Mr. Harrington played here but it warranted equal billing.

1938
George W. Kirkman and
William R. Harriman
Colored lithograph
48˝ x 37˝
Los Angeles Public Library

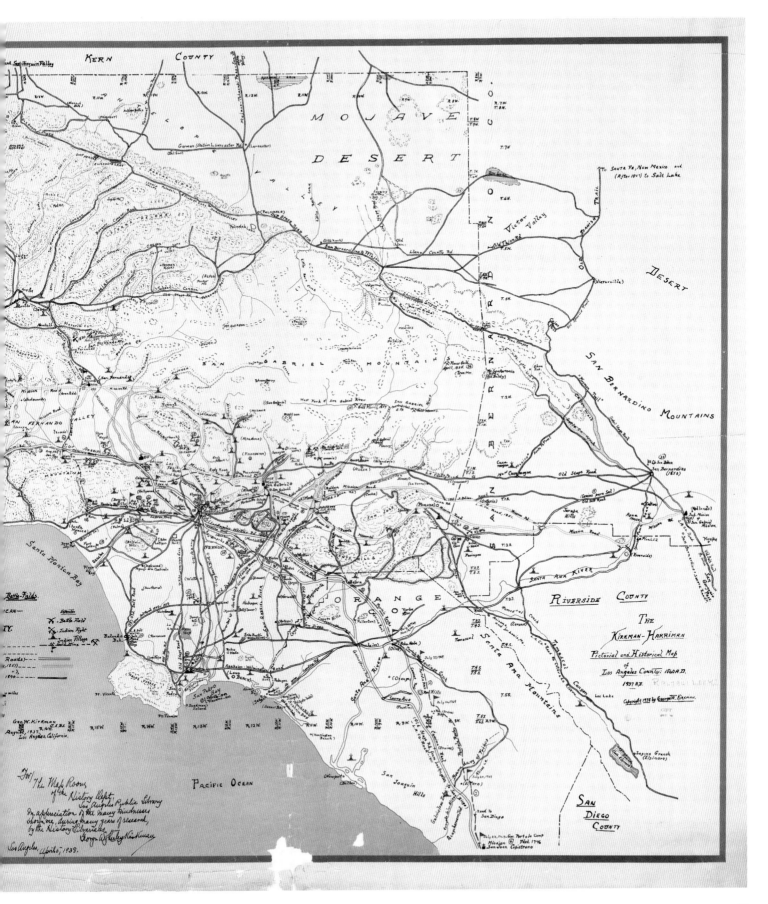

Map of the Lands of the Mission San Gabriel: situated in Los Angeles County, California, originally sold to Mssrs. Workman and Reid, now owned by Mssrs. Workman, Howard, Brannan, and others

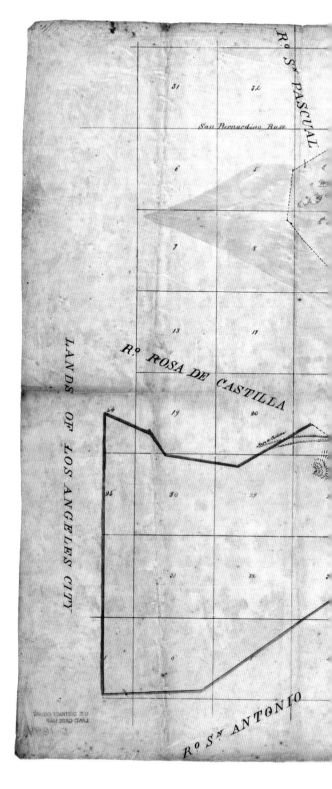

This map, concerning land case 345, is another chapter in the turbulent history of San Gabriel Mission and an example of the confusion and bureaucracy that marked the changeover to American rule in Los Angeles. Known as land case maps, these were created to prove legal claim to property purchased by Californios and Mexicans or granted to them by previous Spanish and Mexican governments. Despite their utilitarian and legal purposes, they are important records of land ownership in Los Angeles County. This map was surveyed by Henry Hancock and submitted to the United States District Court as cartographic evidence on behalf of William Workman and his new partners to demonstrate the land he had possessed and improved.

Workman was an Englishman who had come to Southern California in 1841 from Taos, New Mexico, supposedly drawn west by tales he heard from Kit Carson. He took the grueling, 1,200-mile journey following the Old Spanish Trail with business partner John Rowland, friend Benjamin "Benito" Wilson (later mayor of Los Angeles), and forty other brave souls. After surviving the trip and admiring the landscape, Workman and Rowland petitioned governor Juan B. Alvarado for land in the San Gabriel Valley. They were granted the 48,790 acres of "La Puente" in 1845 upon the promise that they would care for the Indians living on the land. Both men built ranchos and honored a pledge they made to the padres of the recently secularized Mission San Gabriel on this land. In June 1846 Workman and Reed (actually Hugo Reid) were able to purchase the mission estate, including the land and buildings, for past aid and service. They also had to assume $7,000 in debt accrued after secularization. Later the title was declared invalid in the changeover to American rule, and Hugo Reid died in December 1852. So Workman had to go to the district court to prove title to what had been his all along. The case dragged on until 1867, and finally the land was divided between Rowland and Workman the following year. Due to poor investments and the failure of his Los Angeles bank, a distraught Workman committed suicide in May 1876.

The stories of the missions of Alta California are filled with struggle, hardship, and much controversy. Never intended to be permanent settlements, they were used by the Spanish government to populate colonies in this new world that was little known to the far-away viceroys who were supposed to govern the establishments. The Spanish and Mexican governments used the religious aspect to achieve some foothold in the new empire. Perhaps the most successful of the missions, San Gabriel ("the Queen of the Missions") was a spiritual and cultural hub for the area, greatly influencing the establishment of *El Pueblo de Los Angeles* just eight miles away.

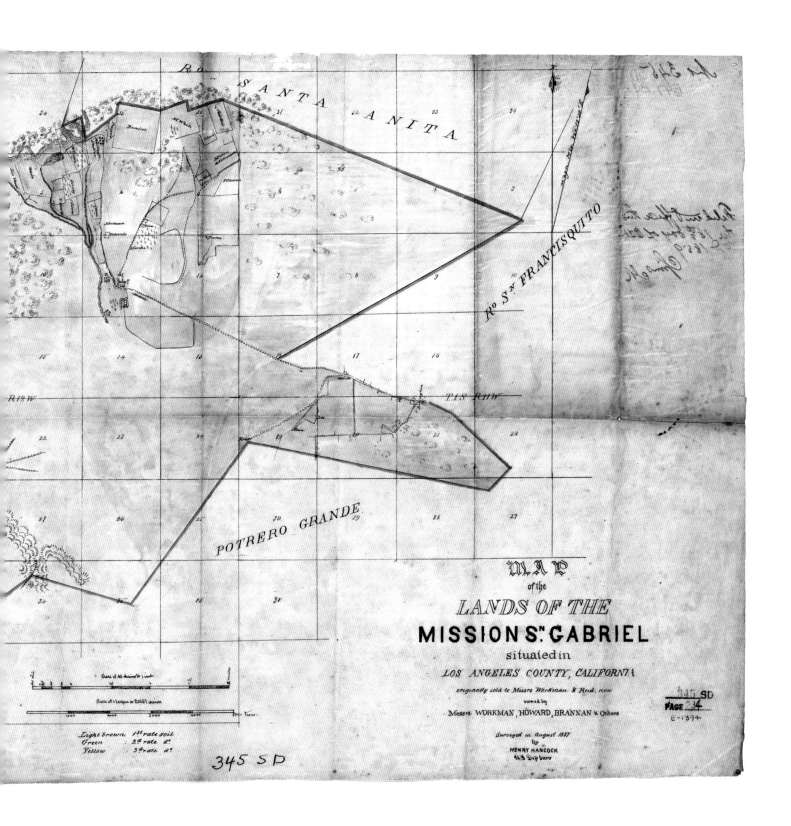

MAP
of the
LANDS OF THE
MISSION Sn GABRIEL
situated in
LOS ANGELES COUNTY, CALIFORNIA
originally sold to Messrs Workman & Reid, now
owned by
Messrs WORKMAN, HOWARD, BRANNAN & Others

Surveyed in August 1857
by
HENRY HANCOCK
U.S Dep Surv

345 SD
PAGE 234
E-1394

Light brown 1st rate soil
Green   : 2d rate do
Yellow   : 3d rate do

345 SD

1857
Henry Hancock
40 chains to one inch
Manuscript
18.5" x 28"
Bancroft Library University of California

The Old Spanish and Mexican Ranchos
of Los Angeles County

The romantic days of the old ranchos that encircled the pueblo of Los Angeles are evoked in this simple but very engaging map that harkens back to the Spanish and Mexican rule of California. The first land grant in Southern California in 1784 was merely the product of Don Jose Dominguez asking Pedro Fages, governor of the Californios, for grazing land near the pueblo for his two hundred cattle and receiving a portion that ranged from today's Compton to the ocean. As was the case in most such transactions, this permit was granted to Dominguez in his retirement because of his military service guarding the missions for Spain. These first distributions led to a small number of similar petitioners who followed suit in the area. When Spain relinquished governmental control to Mexico in 1822, official land grants were given and the process became slightly more complicated, demanding a formal petition, a drawing of the *diseno* or proposed piece of land, and one year of provisional ownership if the reply from the governor was positive.

The ranchos spread across the landscape, from the Santa Susana pass in the mountains to the entire coastline, from Long Beach up to Malibu, and from the San Fernando Valley to Whittier. Due to political instability back in Mexico City and the lack of a strong Mexican government presence, the rancheros were forced to become completely self-sufficient. Most had their own provision stores, blacksmiths, carpenters, wineries, dairies, teachers, and security. They eventually contained four times the population of the pueblo, but many traveled great distances to enjoy the more urban experience of Los Angeles.

Drawing a composite map of all the ranchos is not an easy task due to the rudimentary surveying techniques used by applicants for the grants and the hand-drawn *disenos*, but the Los Angeles–based Title Insurance and Trust Company, a leading American company providing accurate land title abstracts and selling title insurance, was up to the task. This Art Deco pictorial gives an excellent picture of the approximate locations of the land grants in the county along with present communities and topography. Eventually, Title Insurance entered into the escrow business and was instrumental in developing the San Fernando Valley. As the company thrived it took great interest in local history and geography, creating superb maps on a variety of subjects and amassing one of the best collections of photographs, maps, and real estate documents in the country. This map is just one version of its highly popular, uniquely colorful, and informative real estate promotional sets for the ranchos.

c.1937
Gerald Eddy
Title Insurance and
Trust Company
Colored lithograph
18˝ x 16˝
Los Angeles Public Library

THE OLD
SPANISH AND MEXICAN
RANCHOS
OF LOS ANGELES COUNTY

Prepared and Copyrighted by
Title Insurance
and Trust Company
Los Angeles

Scale of English Miles
Spanish Leagues
Spanish Varas

Map of a Portion of Los Angeles County
Showing the Abel Stearns Ranchos
(for sale by Alfred Robinson)

The sale of the real estate holdings of Abel Stearns announced on this attention-getting map of the time is a perfect example of the disassembling of the old Spanish and Mexican ranchos and a cautionary tale about the disastrous effect title claims and taxation had on many Californios. A native of Massachusetts, Stearns moved to Mexico in 1826, gained citizenship, then headed north to Los Angeles, where he used his business acumen to trade manufactured goods from the East with the local Angelenos and amass a large fortune. Don Abel Stearns—at one time probably the largest landowner in the area—held title to more than two hundred thousand acres and had a reputation for being a shrewd businessman. He was the first to connect the city to the harbor at San Pedro, via a stagecoach route, and ship gold, hides, and tallow from Los Angeles to the commerce capitals on the East Coast.

But the Land Act of 1851 required all landowners to prove title and pay taxes, which involved great legal costs and became a huge financial burden. When a devastatingly long drought lasting from 1862 to 1865 wiped out fifty thousand of Stearns's cattle, he attempted to save his holdings through large mortgages. One of these gave over the great Rancho Los Alamitos, where Stearns kept a summer home with his young wife, Arcadia Bandini, to northern California financier Michael Reese, who held the mortgage. Bankruptcy followed in 1865, and in an attempt to pay off debts Stearns sold 177,000 acres to the land syndicate named here as the Los Angeles and San Bernardino Land Association. Stearns died in 1871 after recouping much of his fortune, but the land was eventually subdivided by the company. Five of the ranchos formerly owned by Stearns were put up for sale, divided into one square mile each—an astounding two hundred square miles in all.

1873
Geo. H. Baker
Colored lithograph
18"x 20"
Los Angeles Public Library

MAP OF A PORTION OF

NGELES COUNTY Showing the

TEARNS' RANCHOS

n square miles in blocks of 1 mile square
each side. For sale in sections or fractions

ALFRED ROBINSON Trustee at the
.S & SAN BERNARDINO LAND OFFICE

St. corner of Montgomery St. San Francisco
OR APPLY TO THE
NCY. LOS ANGELES OR ANAHEIM

EDITION MAY 1873

LITH. BY GEO. H. BAKER, 408 CALIFORNIA STREET, SAN FRANCISCO CAL.

FARMING LANDS

Early selections, under Grants from Mexico, in 1784 or 1834, confirmed by the United States Courts; Titles perfect. Distant six miles E. of the San Pedro and Los Angeles Railroad, now in operation; ten miles E. from Wilmington Port. Twelve miles S. E. from Los Angeles; 2 miles from Anaheim Landing, where the steamers regularly deliver and receive cargo.

The River New San Gabriel runs along the west side, the Santa Ana on the east, and the Pacific Ocean forms the southern front.

This large tract, nearly level, with a gentle slope southward towards the Ocean, comprises a variety of soil, rich and fertile, well adapted to wheat, barley, oats, potatoes, etc., and choice tracts for the culture of the lemon, orange, olive, fig, mulberry, grape, and tropical and northern fruits generally; also, cotton, hops, castor-oil beans, hemp, flax, and tobacco.

The large southern portion consists of bottom lands of rich alluvial and sandy loam, with water three to seven feet under and moistening the surface—especially appropriate for the cultivation of CORN on a large scale, without irrigation, from which land eighty to one hundred bushels per acre may be produced.

The famous German Settlement, "Anaheim," is on these lands.

For health and comfort the climate is excellent, as well known.

Steamships leave San Francisco every six days for San Pedro, Wilmington and Anaheim Landing—running time, forty hours.

Freight from Anaheim Landing or vicinity to San Francisco, (by sailing vessels) $3 per ton.

The Government system of survey has been extended over these Ranchos for convenience and certainty of description.

TERMS—One-fourth cash; balance in one, two, and three years, with interest, payable at the end of each year, at ten per cent.

THE SHADED TRACTS ABOVE ARE SOLD.

PROPRIETORS:
E. F. NORHAM;
EDW. MARTIN;
C. B. POLHEMUS;
EST. OF A STEARNS;
GEO. H. HOWARD;
A. W. BOWMAN,

Ord's Survey

T he Ord Survey dates back to August 29, 1849, and represents the start of mapping in Los Angeles. Despite the existence of *El Pueblo de Los Angeles* for more than sixty years, there was no official survey taken of the city until statehood appeared imminent. With the gold rush drawing fortune seekers up north, California was quickly becoming the land of opportunity. Yet the city of Los Angeles had little or no cash, since up to that time the economy was based on bartering, with agreements made by handshake. L.A. did have land and needed to sell lots to pay the taxes that would follow with admission to the union. To survive as a municipality, the *Ayuntamiento* or City Council sought to create a map, showing boundaries and preparing lots for sale. The Military Governor Bennett C. Riley recommended young lieutenant Edward O. C. Ord for the job, and after some negotiating over payment Ord accepted, hiring an assistant, William Rich Hutton. The two headed out into the city in July 1849. Los Angeles had been without an official map for sixty years when the two men covered the heart of the old pueblo extending from the Porciuncula River to the hills of Elysian Park and from the Old Calvary cemetery down to near where Pico Boulevard stands today. While this only covered a small portion of the original "four square leagues" of the Spanish pueblo, it did reflect the main area of population and commerce. This Ord map or City Map No. 1, then described as "a very pretty one," was finished in September and given to the City Council with very little explanation and few block dimensions and street widths. Yet it stands as probably the most important cartographical document of the early city, since it spells out the street names in both English and Spanish and provides the central point from which the great city spread. Many of the names survive today, including Spring, Main, Flower, and Hope. Appropriately, the long street that led to the city's Catholic cemetery was known as *Calle de Eternidad* or Eternity. The city radiates out from the plaza, and the top of the map is oriented northeast, unlike the normal grid of American cities. Although the City Map No. 1 did not survive, this version was created to replace the tattered four-sheet original and hung on the wall of the council chambers.

Plan De La Ciudad
de Los Angeles
City Map No. 1
1849
Surveyed and drawn by Edward
O. C. Ord Lt USA and
Wm. R. Hutton Asst.
Colored lithograph
29˝ x 31˝
Los Angeles Public Library

Explanation of the Signs

PLAN
De la Ciudad
DE LOS
ANGELES

Surveyed & Drawn by

Wm. R. Hutton

August 29th 1849

Scale of 16 Inches to the Mile

Compass Course of Main Street from corner opposite Jose Antº Carrillos House S 24° 45′ 91″
Compass Course of Main St. North of the Church N 9° E.
Variation of the Needle 12° 44′ E.

Kuchel & Dresel's California Views

The calm, idyllic pueblo portrayed on this early panoramic map may have been more a fantasy of those thumping the tub for the burgeoning city than a reflection of reality. The scene focuses on the picturesque setting with the San Gabriel Mountains in the backdrop and peaceful prosperity obvious in the quaint city streets; the only sour note is the brick jail on the hill at the extreme left. Despite the obvious growth and the addition of two-story and brick structures amid the old adobes, the place was pretty much a Wild West town with little of the order and civility depicted here. Just eight years after statehood, the plaza was still a place of single-story adobes, unpaved streets, orchards, and open horse corrals. We glimpse a domestic scene with ladies doing the laundry in buckets out of doors, a beehive oven ready for cooking, and gents conversing amiably by storefronts.

Main Street, also known as *Calle Principal*, is a broad thoroughfare along the left border, with horses and carriages moving north and south. At the far end of this road is the Plaza Church with the bell tower visible, and to the right of that the old plaza where Olvera Street stands today. Around the borders are vignettes of prominent citizens' homes and public buildings. Also shown is the first hotel, the Bella Union, where visitors could rent the six-by-nine-foot rooms, and the grand showplace of the residential area, *El Palacio* of Abel Stearns, which was once besieged by an unruly mob of criminals during a celebration. In the area of commerce we can see the store of dry-goods purveyor Solomon Lazard in the early shopping center Mellus Row, the blacksmith John Collier, and the always-welcome saloon *Los Dos Amigos* with gracious host Don Filipe Riehm.

This map is one of about forty-two in a series called *California Views* produced by immigrants Charles Conrad Kuchel and Emil Dresel, the former Swiss and the latter German, both based in San Francisco. Dresel was a trained architect who tried his hand first at gold mining, then, after partnering with Kuchel, traveled all over the state sketching scenes or making drawings from daguerreotypes, which were later made into these panoramas. In many cases the sketches in the borders of the maps were more valuable than the maps themselves, due to the accuracy of styles and the structure of the buildings. The company did not last long, as Dresel settled down to become one of the first viticulturists in Sonoma County. Kuchel continued to pursue lithography and eventually retired in San Francisco.

Los Angeles, Los Angeles County, Cal
1857
Kuchel and Dresel. Printed by Britton and Rey
Published by Hellman Brothers
offset lithograph. 22˝ by 18˝
Huntington Library

DON JUAN RAMIREZ.

TIMMS & CO. COMMISSION & FORWARDING BUSINESS, SAN PEDRO.

STEPHEN C. FOSTER.

DON JOSÉ SEPULVEDA.

McFARLAND & DOWNEY.

BADEFAURE & VIDAL.

TIN SMITH.

DON VICENTE GUERRERO.

Entered according to Act of Congress, in the year 1857, by Kuchel & Dresel, in the Clerk's Office of the U.S. District Court for the Northern District of Cal.

TEMPLE.   FRANCIS MELLUS.   SOLOMON LAZARD.   DON FELIX RIEHM.   BACHMAN & CO.

JOHN GOLLER.

Printed by Britton & Rey.

LOS ANGELES,

LOS ANGELES COUNTY, CAL. 1857.

Published by Aitman & Bro.

Map of the 35 Acre Lots of the Los Angeles City Lands, Hancock Survey Official Map No. 2 of Los Angeles City

T his official map was commissioned by wise city fathers, particularly former mayor Damien Marchessault, who hoped to achieve "the liquidation of a portion of the indebtedness of the city," which had grown to over eighty thousand dollars by 1868. The map was officially endorsed by the Common Council and signed by native Californio mayor Cristobal Aguilar, along with council president John King, who paid the mapmaker $492 for his laying of the chains. The methodical and precise county surveyor George Hansen, with the help of his deputy captain William Moore, drew up Official Map No. 2. The two men, over just two summer months in 1868, created this extremely accurate and important cartographical document that crosses the divide in Los Angeles. The Ord Survey had covered the center of the newly Americanized city, but there was much more to subdivide and claim to bring money into the municipal coffers. Hansen and Moore's map shows one portion of the original Spanish pueblo land's four square leagues east of the Los Angeles River, including roads, watercourses, land ownership, topography, and the structures built by early pioneers who settled there before statehood. There are familiar names appearing on the plat, like Hellman, Childs, Hancock, Beaudry, and Downey, alongside the house and barn of Andrew Boyle, who later gave his name to much of the area surveyed as Boyle Heights. The lots for sale are listed in pencil on the left margin and were sold from two to six dollars an acre. The recorder of the document, Thomas Dillingham Mott, was Los Angeles's county clerk and later state assemblyman who at one time held the property that became Bunker Hill.

Basically, the city was selling the land that stood along the river but placed their marker on the very water flowing across the basin. In the line of succession of the Spanish pueblo, the city of Los Angeles had "preferential" rights to the Los Angeles River, which was legitimized by the California Supreme Court. The town's boundaries stayed static for more than thirty-five years, but when it came time to grow, the local government held the most valuable commodity in Los Angeles: water. The ultimate enticement to join the city became that water that was essentially city property until 1902, when it took over all water service. Many of the largest annexations came about because of the desire for this water.

George Hansen came to Los Angeles in 1853 and thrived in the southland until his death in 1897. He was, among other things, a planter of vineyards, an engineer-builder of the flume that connected the San Gabriel River to Wilmington's Drum Barracks, an early proponent of establishing Elysian Park, and "the father of Anaheim," which he laid out for immigrant Germans and Austrians under the auspices of the Los Angeles Vineyard Society in 1857.

1868
George Hansen, assisted by
William Moore
City of Los Angeles
Hand-colored parchment
Los Angeles City Archives

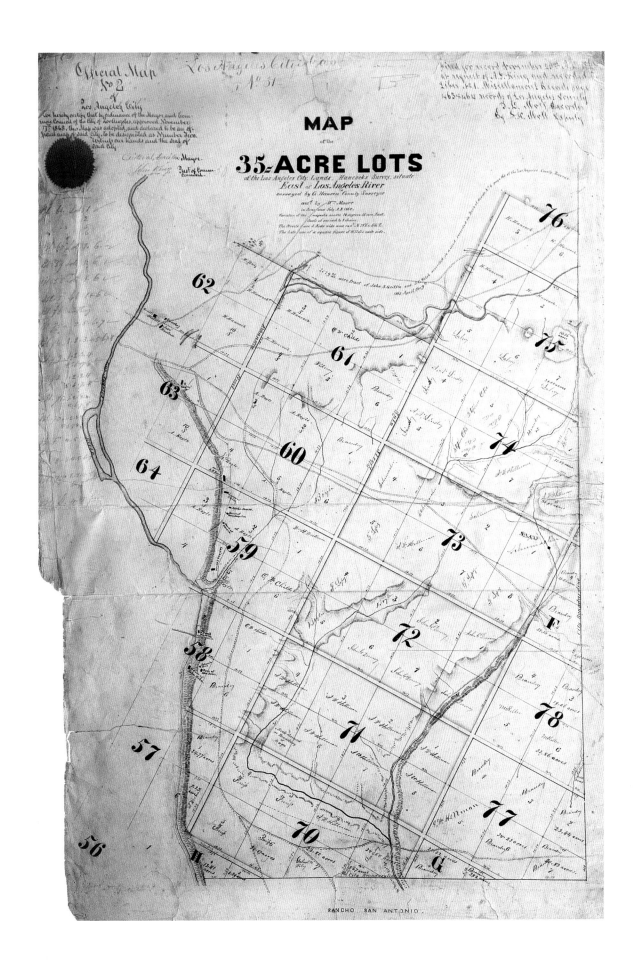

MAP

of the

35 ACRE LOTS

of the Los Angeles City Lands, Hancock's Survey, situate

East of Los Angeles River

surveyed by G. Hansen County Surveyor

RANCHO SAN ANTONIO

Hansen Map

T his remarkable map was published in the Spring Street offices of the real estate firm Bancroft and Thayer and sent all over the country to lure possible buyers to the limitless opportunities in Southern California. It is really a hybrid of two works on one sheet: the Ord Survey at the center, which covered just the more populated civic center, and the Hancock and Hansen surveys showing the property out to the boundaries of the four square leagues of city lands. After statehood Los Angeles had to prove its title from the original Spanish pueblo, and after much digging by J. Lancaster Brent, an attorney hired by the City Council, the proper documents were located describing the city's lands covering four square leagues—more than seventeen thousand acres. The United States Board of Land Commissioners certified the title of this public land to the city on February 5, 1856. Still, the actual boundaries of this area needed to be drawn up on a map, and that job was given to Henry Hancock, one of the city's first surveyors, owner of Rancho La Brea, and father of George Allen Hancock, one of the area's first oil tycoons. (The same illustrious family gave its name to the oldest and most exclusive neighborhood in Los Angeles: Hancock Park.) Henry completed the job in September 1858, showing an approximate square, starting at the Plaza and extending a league on each side, about three miles. Other surveyors broke this area into parcels, seen here numbered. Chief among these cartographers was George Hansen, whose boundaries extended out to the ranchos on the perimeter. The tireless Hansen, an Austrian immigrant, had much to do with early development, including the digging of the Echo Park reservoir. The donation lots mentioned in the survey were subdivisions amounting to thirty-five-acre parcels that were sold at rather spirited auctions. Bids started at about one dollar per acre for the larger lots but sometimes dipped much lower. The Hancock and Hansen surveys begin to place the city into a logical grid, as opposed to the early Ord map, which reflected an old pueblo-style layout radiating out from the Plaza without much regard to uniformity. This composite of the surveys was widely used in the mid-1870s and was the first appearance of the printed Ord Survey, which had previously only existed as a four-piece manuscript. The boundaries demarcated by Hansen remained basically unchanged for thirty-six years, but this map is a watershed from the pastoral days of the far-flung ranchos to the building of the American metropolis.

Map of the City
of Los Angeles
c.1875
O.C. Ord, Henry Hancock,
and George Hansen
Bancroft and Thayer, Publisher
Lithograph
28" x 28.3"
Los Angeles Public Library

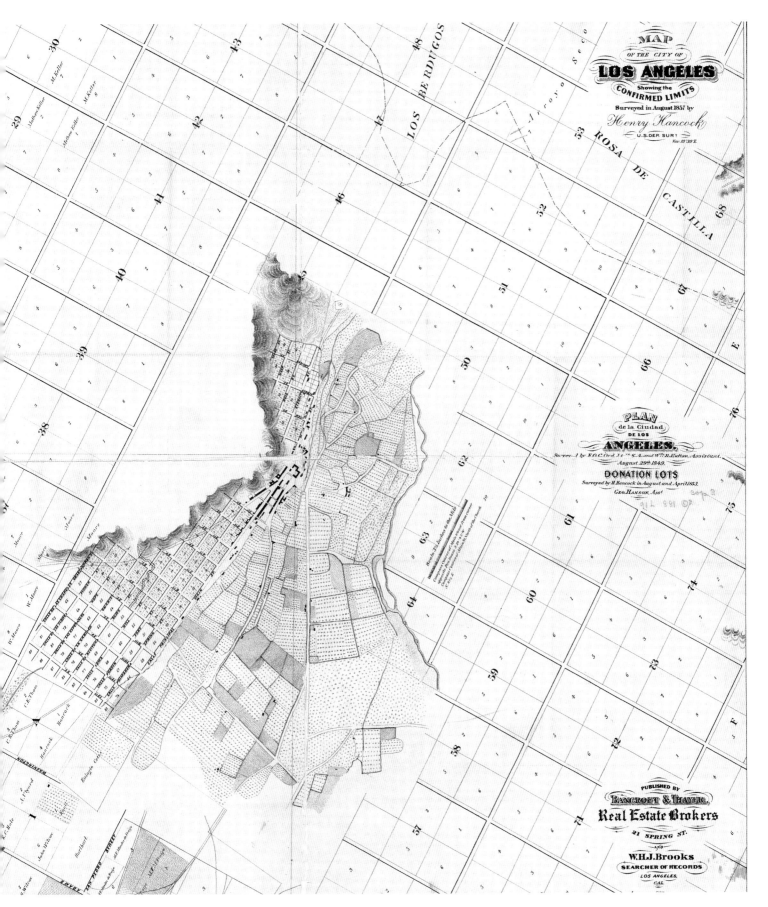

MAP
OF THE CITY OF
LOS ANGELES
Showing the
CONFIRMED LIMITS
Surveyed in August 1857 by
Henry Hancock
U.S. DEP. SURY.
Var. 13 30' E.

PLAN
de la Ciudad
DE LOS
ANGELES,
Surveyed by E.O.C. Ord, Lt. U.S.A. and Wm. R. Hutton, Assistant.
August 29th 1849.
DONATION LOTS
Surveyed by H. Hancock in August and April 1853.
Geo. Hanson, Asst.

PUBLISHED BY
Bancroft & Thayer.
Real Estate Brokers
21 SPRING ST.
AND
W.H.J. Brooks
SEARCHER OF RECORDS
LOS ANGELES,
CAL.

Ruxton Plaza

There were a number of maps of the Plaza created as the uneasy growing pains of statehood started to change the old pueblo and uproot its pioneer residents. County surveyor Frank LeCouvreur, city surveyor M. Kelleher, A. J. Stahlberg, and A. G. Ruxton produced various maps of the Plaza area, all with some nostalgia for a part of history that was fading from the old city. In some cases the intentions were good, in others there was some sentiment toward moving the city away from its Mexican roots toward a more homogenized, American settlement. Ruxton's map remains interesting on several historical levels, both intended and accidental, but the Plaza seen here is about to undergo a transformation. The streets still bear the old names like *Calle Alta*, *Calle Principal*, Republic, Alameda, Marchessault, Bath, and Wine (sometimes identified as Vine). Wine was evolving into Olvera Street, after Superior Court Judge Augustin Olvera, who lived opposite of the square. This block would later face the headquarters of the Los Angeles City Water Company. The center of the settlement is still the old Plaza Church, *La Iglesia de Nuestra Senora La Reina de Los Angeles*, and the little graveyard next door is identified as "garden." There are numerous old adobe homes, identified with such familiar Californio names as Avila, Lugo, Mascarel, and Sepulveda. The streets appear in both English and Spanish but would soon be overtaken by the Yankee versions: Upper Main, North Main, Los Angeles, and High Street. The Zanja Madre, the main water source, can be seen making a diagonal across the landscape, passing the Bath Street School at a halfway point on the map. It is surprising to see such a large number of female property owners: Juana Redona, Maria Lisoldo, Pilar Quintera, Ascension Navarro, Maria Sylvia, Serafina Uribe, Maria Figueroa, and several others.

This is the Plaza as it was laid out sometime between 1823 to 1830, with the rectangular central plaza featuring a reservoir at the center that was to be changed to the more American circular design in later years. To the south of the Plaza is the new Pico House, the grand hotel built by Pio Pico in 1869 and opened for business in 1870; it was the destination for travelers arriving in San Pedro and brought by stagecoach to the civilization of Los Angeles. Pico had hoped to maintain the central position for the old Plaza in the growing city, but with new developments like the first gas works next to the Plaza Church, the decline had already begun. Eventually, this area became the gathering place for the disenfranchised and immigrant populations and was marginalized by the establishment of the late nineteenth century. The originally innocent name *Calle de los Negros* was merely a description of the dark-skinned residents hailing from Sonora, Mexico, but later was twisted into a racist epithet that lasted way too long in the area.

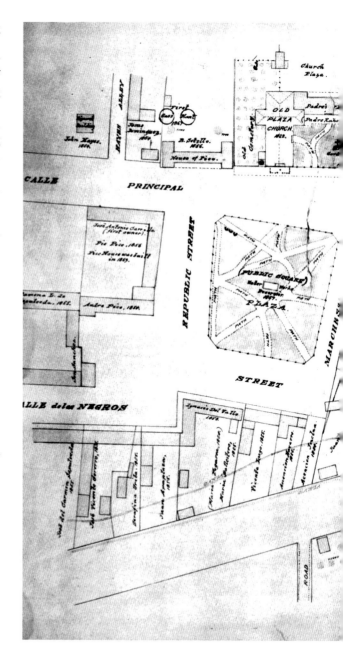

Map of the Old Portion of the City Surrounding the
Plaza, Showing the Old Plaza Church ...
March 12, 1873
G. Ruxton, surveyor
Solano-Reeve Collection
16˝ x 10˝
Los Angeles Public Library

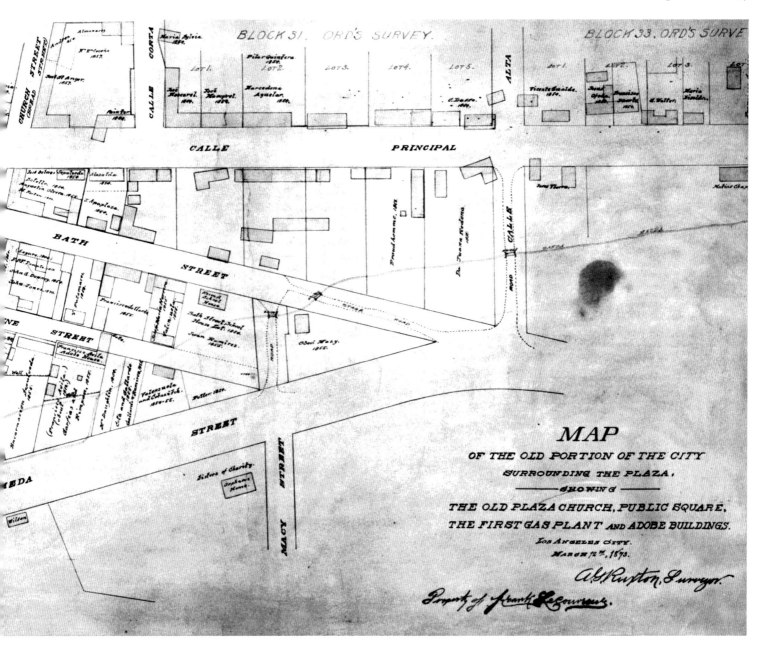

Bird's-Eye View of Los Angeles, California, Looking South to the Pacific Ocean, Twenty Miles Distant

This three-scene panoramic map shows the burgeoning city spreading out from the Plaza all the way to the coastline, which would be around San Pedro from this vantage point. Popular in the nineteenth century, the bird's-eye map was not drawn to scale but maintained the same perspective to landmarks and physical features. Because of recent advances in lithography processes, these panoramic maps could be printed in great numbers and sent to the other thirty-seven states and beyond. Eli S. Glover, one of the most active cartographers in Southern California, created bird's-eye maps on behalf of the Brooklyn Land and Building Company to lure interested buyers to the beautiful and temperate climes of the southland, where Glover not too coincidentally owned acreage. Many such maps were created using oblique-angle photographs taken from hot-air balloons, allowing a view of the landscape while capturing the vitality of the area. This exaggerated view demonstrates two rather unique characteristics of Los Angeles: its proximity to the mighty Pacific Ocean and the clean air that would allow such a vista. Ironically the view compares the city's two possible ports, Santa Monica and San Pedro, which would compete fiercely some twenty years later to supply the entire area.

Although it is most certainly a map to be placed on walls for the enticement of new settlers, its subtext is one of railroads in Los Angeles. Easily visible is the Plaza with the oval that had replaced the original rectangle by 1870, the grand new cathedral of St. Vibiana finished in 1876, St. Vincent's

College at what appears to be Bunker Hill, and the spanking new Southern Pacific Railroad Terminal. The same railroad had just connected Los Angeles with San Francisco in September 1876, and the influx of visitors was increasing the population rapidly, from five thousand to more than eleven thousand in that decade alone.

The scene of Wilmington looking north toward Los Angeles and the Sierra Madre Mountains shows the historic Drum Barracks and harbor where the rail terminus of what was the very first rail line in Los Angeles was established. Phineas Banning built the first connector railway from downtown to Wilmington, a city named after his hometown in Delaware. Banning saw the harbor as essential to commerce and made the connection several years before this map was produced, but eventually had to give it over to the powerful Southern Pacific, whose wharf and depot are easily discernible.

The third image shows the recently founded Santa Monica in 1875, giving a glimpse at the ocean front with several boats and a ship in the bay, and the Los Angeles and Independence Railroad line with its wharf extending like a pier. By July 4, 1877, the Southern Pacific bought out the Los Angeles and Independence, adding eighteen miles of track toward Los Angeles and achieving a rail monopoly in the area. In this new age of rail, faraway places like Wilmington and Santa Monica—the "port and pleasure resort"—were less than an hour's travel from Los Angeles.

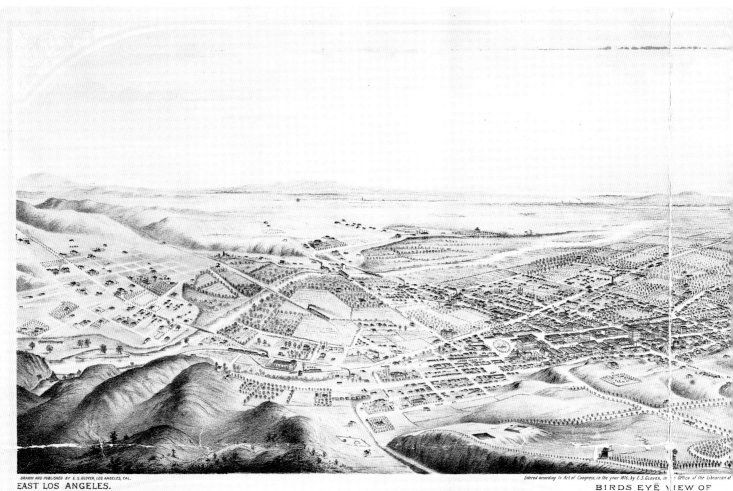

DRAWN AND PUBLISHED BY E.S.GLOVER, LOS ANGELES, CAL.

EAST LOS ANGELES.

Entered according to Act of Congress, in the year 1876, by E.S.Glover, in the Office of the Librarian of

BIRDS EYE VIEW OF

LOS ANGELES
CALIFORNIA.

Looking South to the Pacific Ocean
Twenty Miles Distant.

1877.

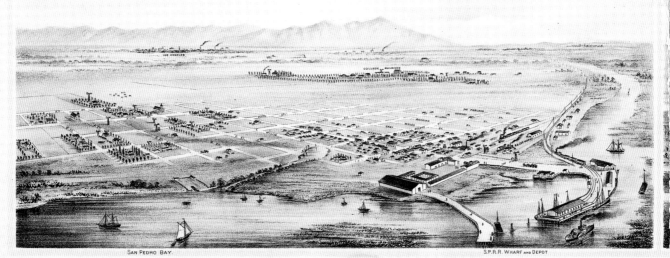

SAN PEDRO BAY.

S.P.R.R. WHARF AND DEPOT

Birds Eye View of WILMINGTON Los Angeles Co. Cal.

Looking north from Wilmington Harbor to the SierraMadre Mountains, thirty miles distant.
Ocean terminus of the Southern Pacific R.R. Twenty three Miles from Los Angeles.

A.L.BANCROFT & CO. LITH. SAN FRANCISCO, CAL.

WEST LOS ANGELES

South SANTA MONICA.   CENTRAL ADDITION.   SANTA MONICA.

Birds Eye View of **SANTA MONICA** Los Angeles Co. Cal.

Looking south to the Pacific Ocean and Santa Monica Mountains to the right.
Sea Port and pleasure resort, Seventeen Miles from Los Angeles.

1877
E. S. Glover
A. L. Bancroft, Publisher
Lithograph
20″ x 17″
Los Angeles Public Library

Los Angeles in 1881

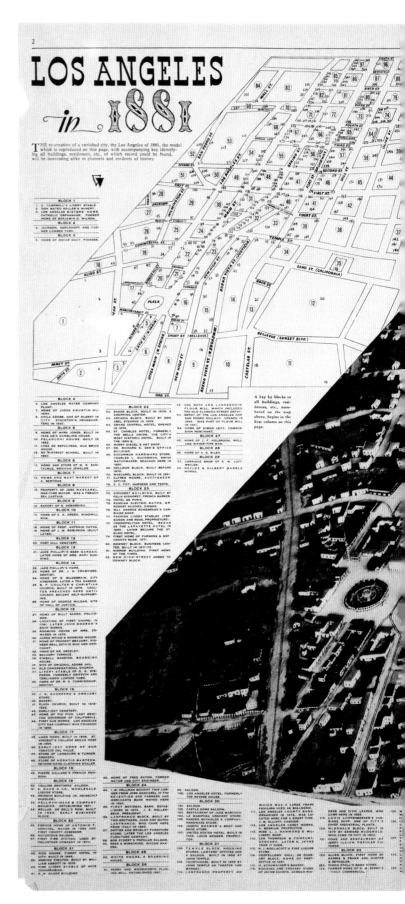

What began as a celebration of the fiftieth anniversary of the *Los Angeles Times* in the form of a scale model became one of the most detailed looks at the topography and street layout of the city in the nineteenth century. Model maker Robert H. Sexton Jr. was charged by the paper in 1931 to create an exact miniature replica of the city as it looked in 1881 when the *Times* began publishing. For six months he labored to re-create the place as if it had been photographed from a blimp floating over the basin. On an eight-by-five-foot rectangle Sexton built the city, using photographs, maps, drawings, recollections from citizens, and engineers' surveys. The details are minute, including picket fences, tiny tombstones, streetcar lines, and flagpoles, along with every building, street, and park in town. The job took considerable historical research, and at its completion, the final product was advertised, then unveiled at the Los Angeles Public Library on the last day of November 1931. Some three thousand visitors filed through the library rotunda to view the model the first day, and a total of twenty-five thousand during the two-week exhibition. The model was moved around the city to places like the Los Angeles Athletic Club and City Hall, but it mysteriously disappeared in the ensuing years. Fortunately it had been photographed, published in the *Times*, and made into this map with the streets drawn in for perspective. The map portrays the city before the onset of an intense real estate boom as a place still rather quaint and peaceful compared to the colorful past. Every home and public building is delineated, 369 in all. Notable landmarks include the Baker Block, Mellus Row, where John C. Fremont had his headquarters, the old adobe jail, the round house, and the gas and waterworks of the city of eleven thousand people.

1931
Created by Robert H. Sexton Jr.
Los Angeles Times
Huntington Library

A SCALE MODEL PREPARED BY THE LOS ANGELES TIMES IN COMMEMORATION OF ITS FIFTIETH ANNIVERSARY

Prepared as a reminder of other days and as a mark of fifty years' service to Los Angeles by The Times, this model of Los Angeles, in 1881, serves to introduce the Fiftieth Anniversary Edition of The Times. Therein you will see the photographs used in constructing this model and will read the interesting story of how Los Angeles and The Times grew up together.

Map of the City of Los Angeles

The very active cartographer H. J. Stevenson, a U.S. Department Surveyor, originally produced a version of this map and published it in 1876 at the beginning of a surge in population brought on by the connection of the Southern Pacific Railway and the ensuing real estate boom. This updated work in full color is a beautiful and extremely valuable historical document: a true plat map showing individual tracts and property ownership covering the original four square leagues. It provides divisions of the first subdivisions along with street names, topography, the water source of the Zanja Madre, cemeteries both Hebrew and Catholic, plus reservoirs that would later become Echo Park and Silver Lake. Downtown boasts two places of higher learning—St. Vincent's and the Normal School—while the rectangle marked "Plaza" denotes a park that would later become Pershing Square. On this plat are names of settlers that would later be given to streets and neighborhoods all across the basin: Scott, Heller, Solano, Prager, Workman, Beaudry, Lankershim, Sepulveda, Mott, Glassell, Avila, Chavez, and Vignes, among others. The city is portrayed accurately, with the Los Angeles River offering the easily recognizable landmark dividing Boyle Heights and East Los Angeles from a central hub at the Plaza, then extending out to Agricultural Park, where the University of Southern California was established just five years before. The southern limits are expressed at the south end of the city's charter boundary line, and to the northeast is Highland View and Highland Park, which together would become the city of Los Angeles's largest land annexation when joined eleven years later.

1884
Henry J. Stevenson
Colored lithograph
26″x 35″
Los Angeles Public Library

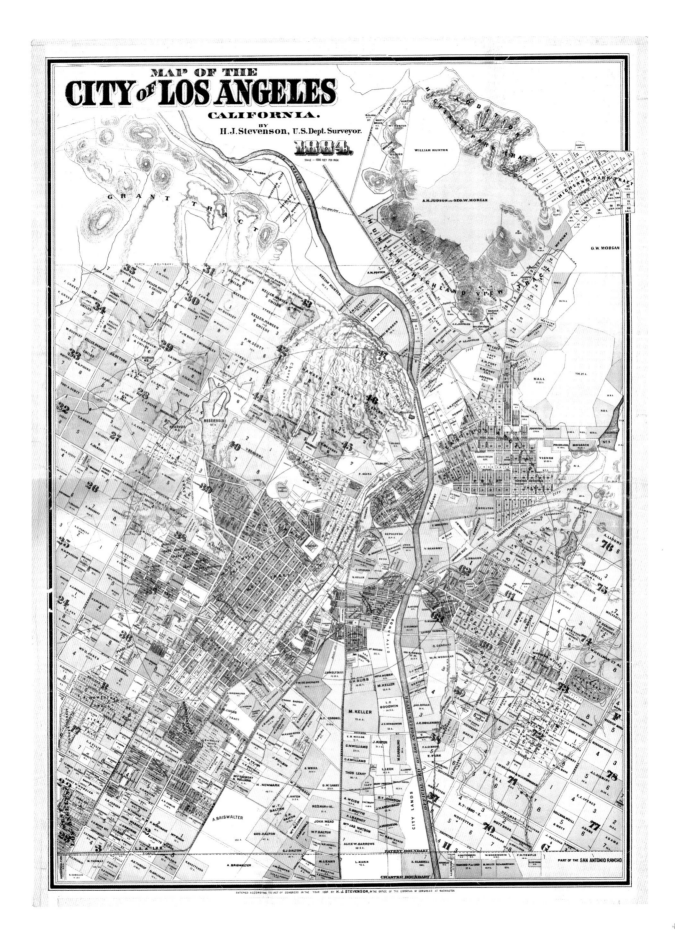

MAP OF THE
CITY OF LOS ANGELES
CALIFORNIA.
BY
H. J. Stevenson, U.S. Dept. Surveyor.
1884
SCALE—1000 FEET PER INCH

49

Map of the City of Los Angeles. California. Compiled from Surveys Made by the City Surveyor During 1886

While similar to the Stevenson Map of 1884, this rare example of an authentic plat map tells Los Angeles history with amazing detail and colorful cartography that includes the identification of land owners, tract names, locations of water, rail lines, township numbers, subdivisions, and even the long-forgotten Los Angeles and Ostrich farm trolley. The year 1887 was the peak of the great real estate boom of the eighties, and the rush to acquire land in the new Eden was reaching a fever pitch, with thousands of people flooding into Los Angeles on the newly connected railroads. Excursion trains left downtown constantly, shuttling possible buyers out to the places named on this map. In a cutout is the literature-inspired suburb of Ivanhoe, where one could buy land with just 20 percent down. Some of the earliest movie studios, including Walt Disney, began in this area. The nearby "LA City Res site" would someday be the Silver Lake Reservoir that graces the gently rolling hills near the eastern line of the grant to the canal and reservoir company, which was bringing precious water from the river in that direction. Elysian Park, named just the year before, can be seen here for the first time, and Reservoir Number 4, which would later be called Echo Park, gives a familiar landmark along with forgotten tract names like Orange Slope, ELA Hills, Nob Hill, and Colina Park. Also seen for the first time is the romantic-sounding subdivision called Sycamore Grove in the northeast, where locals would enjoy rustic picnics and celebrate Independence Days. The ten-year-old Evergreen Cemetery is visible east of the "official bed of the Los Angeles river," which tells a tale in itself since the city owned the rights of that bed, which later drew the San Fernando Valley into the bosom of Los Angeles.

Cartographer Valentine James Rowan was the son of Mayor Thomas E. Rowan, a successful pioneer who sent his son off to San Francisco to study engineering as a teenager. V. J. came back, established offices downtown, and commenced a great career as surveyor that included the creation of this map when he was just twenty-three years old. It was said that "he surveyed more property and laid out more subdivisions than any man in city history." In his rather spectacular cartographical career he surveyed all of the city's streets and bridges, mapped Catalina Island and much of the San Fernando Valley, and created a monumental map of Los Angeles County for which he was paid the whopping sum of ten dollars.

1887
V. J. Rowan and Theo. G. Koeberle,
Surveyors. Formerly of the City Surveyor's
Office.
Schmidt Label & Litho. Co.
San Francisco
59″ x 48″
Colored lithograph
Collection of Barry Lawrence Ruderman

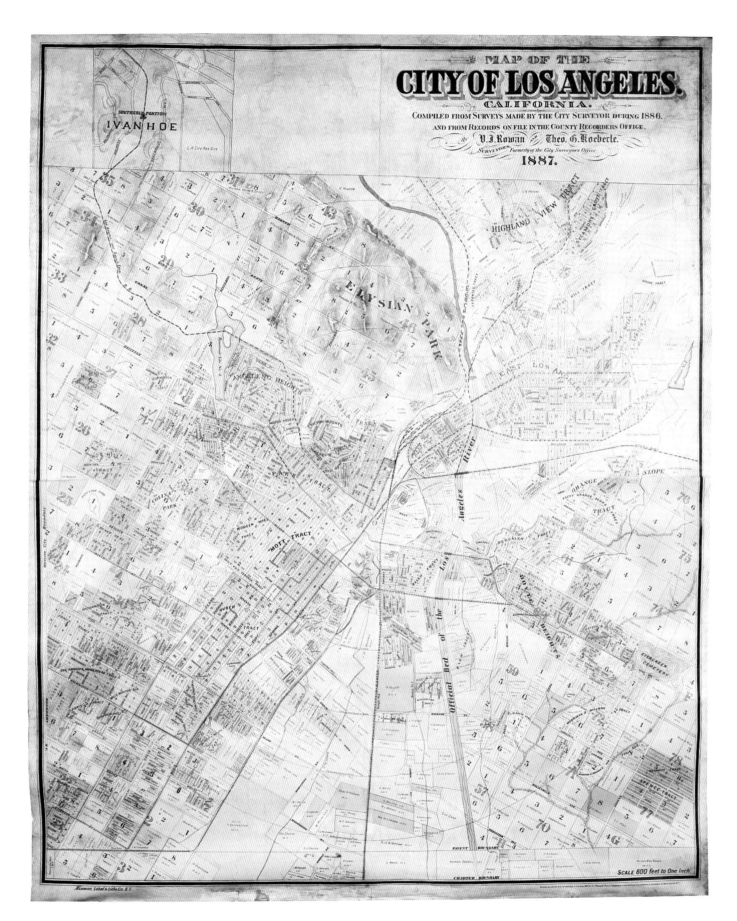

MAP OF THE
CITY OF LOS ANGELES.
CALIFORNIA.
COMPILED FROM SURVEYS MADE BY THE CITY SURVEYOR DURING 1886.
AND FROM RECORDS ON FILE IN THE COUNTY RECORDERS OFFICE.
By V. J. Rowan and Theo. G. Roeberle.
SURVEYORS, Formerly of the City Surveyors Office.
1887.

SOUTHERLY PORTION
IVANHOE

ELYSIAN PARK

HIGHLAND VIEW TRACT

Scale 600 feet to One Inch.

Schmidt, Label & Litho Co. S.F.

CHARTER BOUNDARY

Panorama 1891

While this panoramic map of the city presents a rather loose projection of the local geography, it vividly and minutely describes the commercial establishment and potential for those wanting to participate in a city of opportunity. The Southern California Land Company had offices in the Baker Block and sold real estate in the market after the boom and bust of the 1880s. It focused on lots in "South Los Angeles: the garden spot of the county" and provided maps to interested buyers. The approach on this map was to stress the well-populated capital city of Southern California and show the established businesses, well-developed infrastructure, and impressive architecture in the center of the city. The map cleverly restricts the view to the developed sections near present-day downtown but offers vistas that stretch to a perspective-bending gaze past San Pedro to the recently developed Catalina Island, which appears to be a few hundred yards off the coast. The model seems to have been a photo or sketch made from a hot-air balloon looking from the northeast and portraying a city expanding from the original plaza toward the southeast, where orchards, vineyards, and hills are occasionally interrupted by blocks of development, including large structures like the newly opened high school on Fort Moore Hill or the huge City Hall building at 2nd and Broadway. Elysian Park is in the lower left-hand corner, and faraway Santa Monica in the upper right. As much as the landscape paints the picture of a growing city, the impressive buildings frame the topography and demonstrate that the place has all the amenities of any major city. There is government in the form of the County Courthouse and City Hall; transportation in the headquarters of the Santa Fe Railroad on the Phillips Block and the depots of the Southern Pacific and Santa Fe; the U.S. Hotel; several banks, including Farmers and Merchants; the Normal School; the Gas Works; French Hospital; churches of several denominations, including Lutheran, Presbyterian, Baptist, and Catholic; the new University of Southern California; the YMCA; Ernest Fleur Wholesale Wine and Liquor Merchant; and, appropriately, the headquarters of the Women's Christian Temperance Union. The color here adds to the aesthetic appeal, and maps like this one were displayed like art with the not so subtle commercial appeal. Maps like this one might have been hung on parlor walls, where proud residents could point out their neighborhood to visitors. While the Southern California Land Company wished to drum up business in 1891, prints of this work still hang on walls in Los Angeles today.

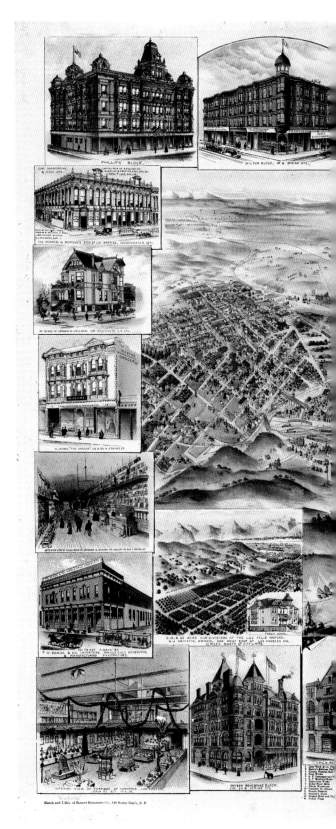

Los Angeles, Cal., Population of City and Environs 65,000
H. B. Elliot
Southern California Land Company
Colored lithograph, 31″ x 44″
Library of Congress

LOS ANGELES. CAL.
Population of City and Environs 65,000.
Published by SOUTHERN CALIFORNIA LAND CO., 344 N. Main Street. 1891

Ninth Street Tract

This real estate advertisement map for some choice land near the rapidly widening downtown is fanciful but compelling. Being sold as the wide-open spaces of an "eighty-foot wide" street near the modern electric streetcar routes along Central Avenue, these parcels are just one-and-a half miles from the business center that young commuters could travel to in minutes by the streetcar or horse car available on nearby Santa Fe Avenue. Many Easterners had already started a trend that continued for one hundred years: coming west to escape the congestion of the urban centers on the East Coast and seeking either residence or investment. The open, bucolic look of this map would have had great appeal to those from high-density population centers and enticed speculators who might buy and subdivide. To add to the possibilities, backyard oil wells were starting to appear all across the city, including the southwestern portions, where a strike might pay for the land all by itself.

However, Mr. Pierce's map shows the windmill and vast orchards right in the middle of the tract, creating a picture of idyllic domesticity and easy Southern California living. To sweeten the deal, the Semi-Tropic Homestead Company offered no-interest loans and just ten bucks down to own this land. Interested buyers could take a horse and carriage from the 2nd and Main Street offices to look at 117 building lots, which they could pay off at another reasonable ten dollars a month. The population was standing at 75,000 and rapidly increasing, with a land lust spreading southwest toward the far-off West Los Angeles area that we now call Exposition Park. Yet the country was suffering one of the major economic crises in its history involving the gold standard, and suddenly it was a buyer's market. So the Semi-Tropic Homestead Company hoped this colorful siren song about affordable land might just get dreamers on a train heading for Los Angeles

This view looking north positions the tract in a strategic position according to the real estate brokers, with the new court house and high school with the clock towers visible in the foreground and smokestacks of industry belching smoke that would translate into money for the businessmen moving into the area. The cartographer makes the one and a half miles look like shouting distance here. The orchards and agricultural land are visible, mixed in with the public buildings and residences, while the upper right-hand portions of the map show the Los Angeles River looking as robust as the Mississippi, flowing under several bridges that connect East Los Angeles to the rest of the city. This map does not show the place where the highly contentious Ninth Street Bridge was placed across the river, but the close-up look at the tract does show the spot where the Southern California Brewery Company set down roots as well as the not-so-idyllic area that became known as "the warehouse district," a far cry from the walnut and orange groves of the 1890s.

*A Portion of Los Angeles as Seen from
the Ninth Street Tract; and Map of
the Ninth Street tract
1894
B.W. Pierce, Lithographer
Semi-Tropic Homestead Company
Colored lithograph, 9.3" x 12.4"
McBride Press
UCLA Special Collections*

A PORTION OF LOS ANGELES AS SEEN FROM THE
NINTH STREET TRACT.

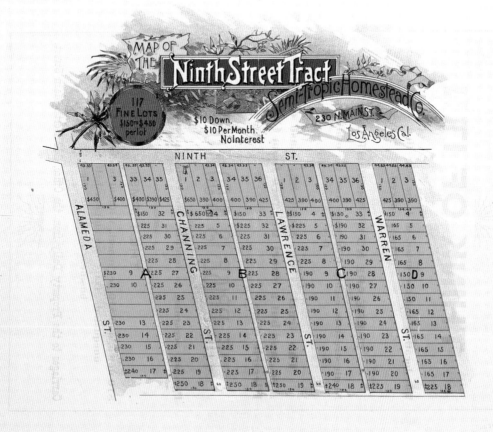

Pierce's Los Angeles

At first glance B. W. Pierce's bird's-eye pictorial of the city in 1894 looks typical of the Victorian style with the wide orthographic landscape ringed by productive factories and prominent public buildings presenting a grand picture of a big city. Yet Pierce went one better with two looks at Los Angeles on one map, gazing north toward the San Gabriel Mountains and south past Agricultural Park, all the way down to the Pacific Ocean, where Catalina Island peaks out of the mist. It amounts to a 360-degree look at the city in a peculiar time between booms, when a slumping economy threatened the rapid growth that is evident in both directions. The Semi-Tropic Homestead Company, for whom the cartographer drew this gem, was selling land around the county and wanted to show all the available wide-open spaces. Despite being created only a few years after the earlier Stevenson and Rowan panoramic views, Pierce's map demonstrates great variety in the chosen subjects. A rather robust-looking river divides the city, with the east side already showing plenty of development, including the impressive Prospect and Hollenbeck parks and a pond that appears big enough to offer fishing and boating. Westlake Park at the lower right was a vacation destination by this time, with its picturesque lake surrounded by very nice hotels for visitors. The southern exposure is filled with agricultural land and orchards, especially in the southeast, where the Southern Pacific tracks cross the river through miles of open land and the Los Angeles Terminal railway offers passage to San Pedro, past some oil wells that began to appear in such far-flung locations after the initial discoveries two years earlier.

Despite the cosmopolitan intent, the city was still struggling with its frontier roots and in 1894 created the *Fiesta de las Flores*, sponsored by the Merchants Association, to help revive the slumping economy and improve relations in the already multicultural city. Griffith Park was still two years away from being presented to the city; electrical streetcars were also two years down the track. The automobile was being developed, and the population of the entire county had zoomed to 129,000 from 60,000 a decade before.

Bruce Wellington Pierce was a jack-of-all-trades in the early city, arriving in Los Angeles in 1884 and finally retiring from the City Engineers in 1938. He took on many tasks, from surveyor, road-cleaning inspector, cartographer, and draftsman, to graphic art sketcher, the creator of bird's-eye maps, and pamphlet illustrator from his studio on the Downey Block. He also seems to have been an accomplished bicyclist, winning prizes for the middle distances in a sport that was very popular in Los Angeles in the late nineteenth century.

1894
B. W. Pierce
Semi-Tropic Homestead Company
Colored lithograph
Library of Congress

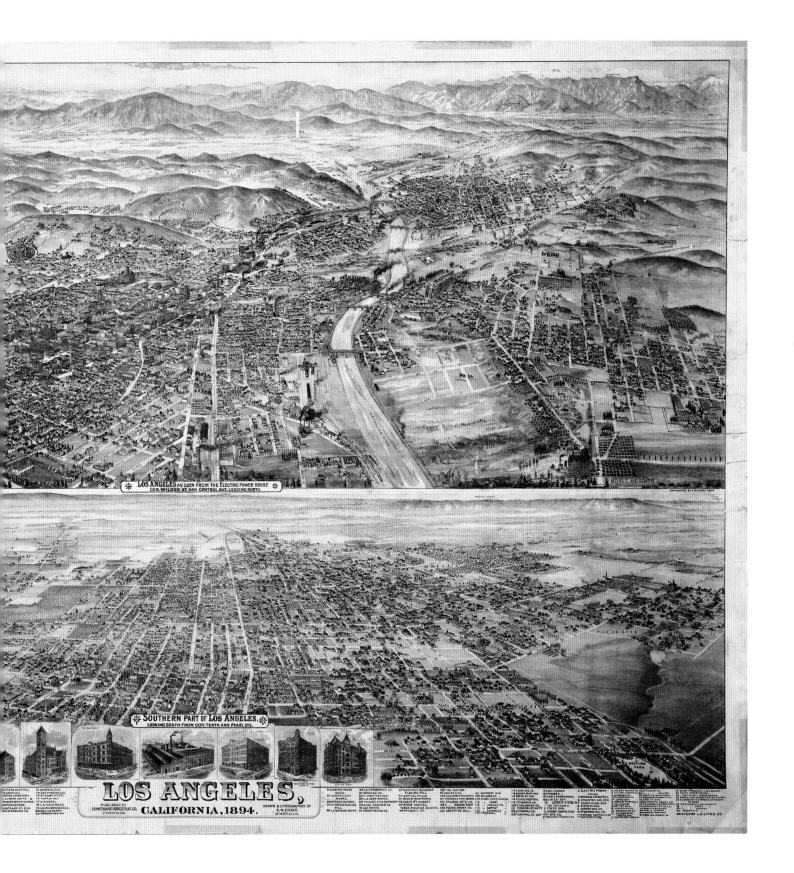

LOS ANGELES AS SEEN FROM THE ELECTRIC POWER HOUSE
COR. WILDER ST. AND CENTRAL AVE. LOOKING NORTH.

SOUTHERN PART OF LOS ANGELES.
LOOKING SOUTH FROM COR. TENTH AND PEARL STS.

LOS ANGELES,
CALIFORNIA, 1894.

PUBLISHED BY
SEMI-TROPIC HOMESTEAD CO.
STIMSON BLOCK.

DRAWN & LITHOGRAPHED BY
B.W. PIERCE.
STIMSON BLOCK.

Official Map of the County of Los Angeles

One of the last true cadastral maps of the entire county, this official version contains surprising details and brilliant color that take it above a mundane tax assessor's survey. The topography of the area is cleverly illustrated by peaks and valleys expressed with hachures and marks of altitude. The mostly agricultural lands to the west and southwest of the civic center are already chopped into lots and ready for sale with property owner listed, like E. J. "Lucky" Baldwin's vast holdings or Isaac Lankershim's huge ranch north of the Santa Monica Mountains or Griffith Park with Cahuenga Peak drawn standing boldly over the city. Many of the names on this map passed into contemporary usage with no changes, including La Cañada, Tujunga, Malibu, Cerritos, Los Alamitos, La Puente, Los Felis, and Altadena. Yet others did not pass the test of time, such as Montezuma, Sunset, Howard, Manzana, and Santa Maria. The inset contains U.S. Coast and Geodetic Survey maps of Santa Catalina, and San Clemente Island containing the telltale landmark "Smuggler's Cove."

Endorsed by the four county supervisors whose names appear in handsome longhand in the upper left-hand corner, this map was drawn up by C. N. Perry for county surveyor E.T. Wright not just to show property lines but to demonstrate the changes that would transform the basin into a modern metropolis in the not-too-distant future. With the old pueblo's four square leagues at the center surrounded by the rapidly dividing rancho lands, this map shows the bones of the Spanish and Mexican city that would vanish altogether in the coming decades. The Spanish-American War was on the front page of the city's four newspapers, and the Gilded Age was taking hold in Los Angeles, with industrialists sizing up the Promised Land. Los Angeles was converting the streetcars to electricity, oil wells were popping up all over the map, the population was approaching 100,000, railroad depots were in place, and even a few automobiles were appearing on the dirt roads of town. This map shows where the ranchos once spread in the time of cattle raising and dry agriculture, but that land was becoming something quite different to the fewer and fewer names printed on the tracts.

1898
C. N. Perry, Draftsman
Los Angeles Lithographic
E. T. Wright, County Surveyor
Colored lithograph
UCLA Department of Special Collections

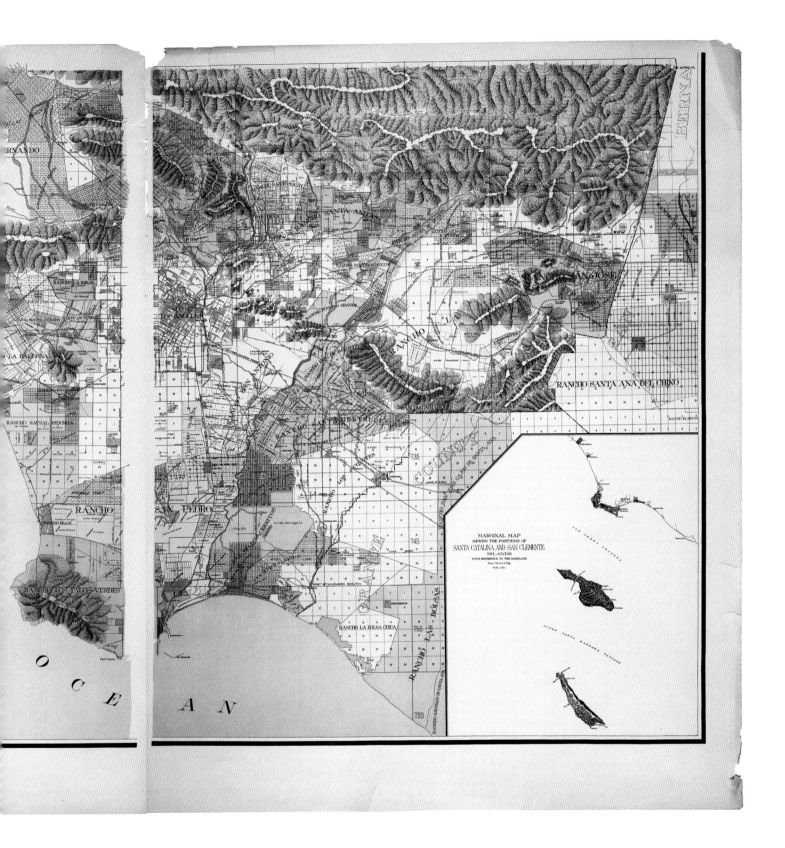

MARGINAL MAP
SHOWING THE POSITIONS OF
SANTA CATALINA AND SAN CLEMENTE
ISLANDS
WITH REFERENCE TO THE MAINLAND

Los Angeles 1909

Certainly the finest example of a classic bird's-eye map of Los Angeles is this 1909 masterpiece, created appropriately by the Birdseye View Publishing Company, portraying a place that would change rapidly in the next twenty years. The map is like a city directory, tour guide, road map, business advertiser, and topographic map all rolled into one. The work was amazingly accurate and rendered meticulously by Danish artist Francis Lawrence, who spent fifteen months walking the streets and sketching the layout of the area until he had every detail perfect. It was announced in the *Times* on October 3, 1909, as "a map showing Los Angeles as it would appear from a balloon in flight." The broad scope encompasses the western portion of the basin and the edges of East Los Angeles as seen from the southeastern part of the city. Lawrence was able to show the land in relief, including the San Bernardino and San Gabriel mountains with local peaks Mt. Baldy, Mt. Wilson with its observatory, Mt. Lowe with railway in place, and far-off Mt. San Bernardino. Seen to the west is the barely developed community of Hollywood that would be annexed the following year. Worthington Gates added the touches that made the map into a statement of civic pride and a call to visitors from across the continent.

The city was shaking off its Victorian trappings and readying itself for a push into the twentieth century with the Los Angeles Aqueduct, another oil boom, the first movie studios, the Pacific Electric Railway, and a flood of newcomers on the horizon. Yet this map shows a complex place, home to 300,000 people and a civic center with beautiful architecture, grand theaters, fine hospitals, a growing presence of automobiles, several colleges, ten separate newspapers, a telephone company, and more than twenty large hotels. This delightfully detailed map not only shows individual buildings in their actual architectural style, but also identifies neighborhoods and scenes of commerce like no other map before or since. Bunker Hill, with its famed funicular railroad "Angels Flight," is visible, as are Angelino Heights, Central Park with heavy landscaping, the Echo Park reservoir, the optimistically named Edendale, Chinatown, and an untouched Elysian Park—all drawn in precise detail. The exhaustive index to the map, created by Mr. Gates, gives not only the location of each site on the map but the address of the establishment or the building where they did business (such as the Grosse Building at 4th and Broadway, where the Birdseye View Publishing Company set up shop). The huge number of boarding houses and apartments listed beside a paucity of restaurants shows the city as a stop on the way toward the major leagues but not there quite yet.

1909
Francis Lawrence
Worthington Gates, Editor
Birdseye View Publishing Company
Colored lithograph
72″ x 38″
Library of Congress

LOS ANGELES
-1909-

Garland Atlas

The real estate atlas can be a Technicolor movie of local history, and while certain companies dominated the trade nationally, there were local producers of fine, limited editions with a somewhat smaller scope. *The Garland Atlas of Los Angeles* is a very rare example from this kind of cartographic source, but it is no less interesting and can be useful in the study of urban development. The atlas was produced by a fascinating and unsung Los Angeles entrepreneur and philanthropist, William May Garland, who created these colorful and precise map books to sell real estate, mostly in the downtown area. Garland claimed to have coined the term "realtor" and managed to somehow lure the Olympic Games to Los Angeles in 1932. He came to the city from Maine by way of Chicago in 1890, and during his impressive career in the city of the angels he was the first member of the school board, the board of library commissioner, president of the realty board, and president of the Los Angeles Athletic Club. He was even lauded at the men's grillroom of the Broadway department store as "the most useful citizen in Los Angeles for 1923." From his offices at 749 S. Spring, Garland sold millions of dollars of commercial real estate, began the development of Wilshire Boulevard, built the Los Angeles Memorial Coliseum, and commissioned the *Garland Atlas*, which gives a fine picture of the city at the end of World War I. The famed Garland population predictions, posted grandly on billboards and in the papers, were all part of boosting the city of Los Angeles in the eyes of the world.

This sheet from the atlas focuses on one of the real chameleons of the downtown landscape, seen here as "Central Park." Actually the space went through dozens of transformations, as evidenced on maps dating back to the old Ord Survey of 1849. Possibly due to its proximity to a rather troublesome arroyo that produced a sort of bog (and the accompanying mosquitoes), this lot 15 in the survey was not sold to any private party and was declared a public square by Mayor Aguilar in 1866. It was called by many names over the years: *La Plaza Abaja* by Spanish speakers, Los Angeles Park, Central Park, 5th Street Park, 6th Street Park, St. Vincent's Park, and, in a fit of "Armistice day fever" at the end of World War I, Pershing Square to commemorate the hero of the American Expeditionary Forces. Many landscaping schemes and configurations followed over the years, including the design seen here by architect John Parkinson, with the central fountain and criss-crossing walkways. In the 1920s many impressive buildings were erected in the vicinity, such as the Biltmore Hotel in 1923, the Oviatt Building in 1927, and the Title Guarantee and Trust Building in 1930. Pershing Square was for years a place of vitality, featuring soapbox orators, newsstands, and even a mobile library stalls maintained by the nearby Central Library.

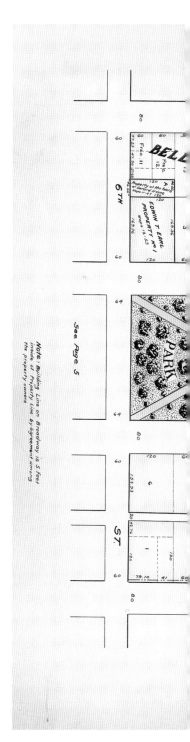

1917
W. M. Garland
William Garland Company
Colored lithograph
24" x 28"
Los Angeles Public Library

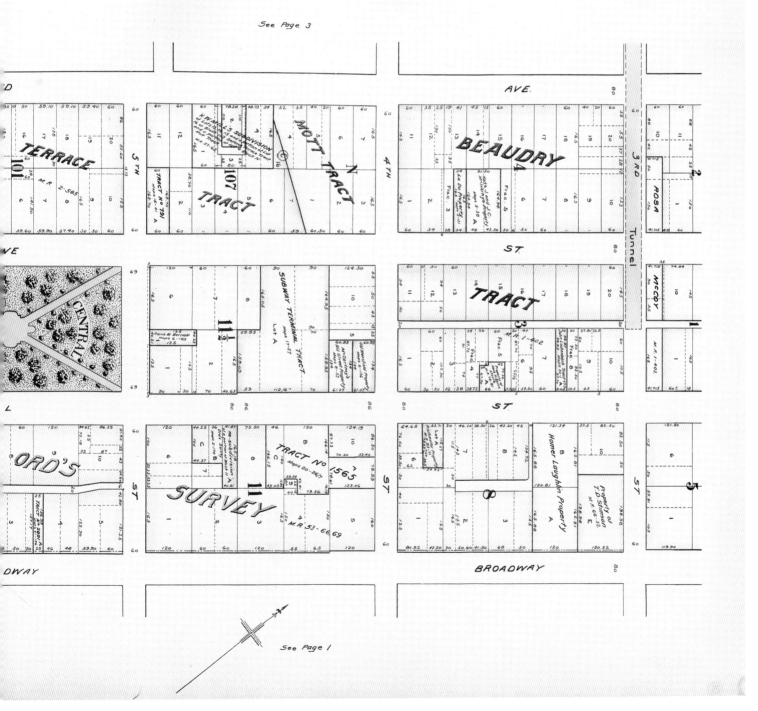

See Page 3

See Page 1

63

Annexation Map

W̲hat appears to be a geographic jigsaw puzzle is one of the most telling maps in all of Los Angeles cartographical history and the answer to a million versions of the same question: how did Los Angeles grow? Here the Bureau of Engineering offers a simple progression, by date and number, of how the city gained territory and traded services and many cases of water for property and taxes. This map shows the journey to megalopolis, up to the Great Depression, when oil, movies, aircraft, agriculture, shipping, and railroads created an economic juggernaut that would continue throughout the twentieth century. There are still many holes in the metropolitan fabric, and independent cities like San Fernando, Pasadena, Santa Monica, Glendale, and Beverly Hills stand like bastions against the big city, but soon many of the gaps were filled as the place grew from four square leagues to almost five hundred square miles.

This map named the cities swallowed up by Los Angeles City and includes the key acquisitions: Highland Park in the northeast with more than nine hundred acres; the University Park District with little land but lots of people in 1899; the critical shoestring of Harbor Gateway in 1906, linking city limits with the harbor cities of San Pedro and Wilmington, which joined the following year as acquisition numbers seven and eight. Many of the earliest annexations really gave an identity to the area, like Colegrove, Hollywood, and East Hollywood, with Griffith Park in tow, along with the 1915 San Fernando Valley addition, containing a whopping 108,732 acres of good agricultural land, thirsty for Los Angeles Aqueduct irrigation.

While the size of the acquisitions vary from the eight-acre Holabird to massive places like Tujunga, Chatsworth, and Calabasas, this halfway point in the development of the city shows the patchwork quilt that comprises the municipality. Part of the reason why Los Angeles is a city of distances reached mostly by automobile is this annexation process that reached many miles from the center. Hidden in arcane names of consolidation are the destinations that make up the modern city: Westwood, where UCLA stands; Leimert Park; the Fairfax District; Eagle Rock; the Venice boardwalk; Hollywood Boulevard, Mid-Wilshire; and the vast San Fernando Valley, another kind of Los Angeles.

Annexation Map of the City of
Los Angeles
1928
R. L. Merget
Police Printing Bureau
Board of Public Works
Engineering Department
John C. Shaw, City Engineer
24″ x 17″
Los Angeles Public Library

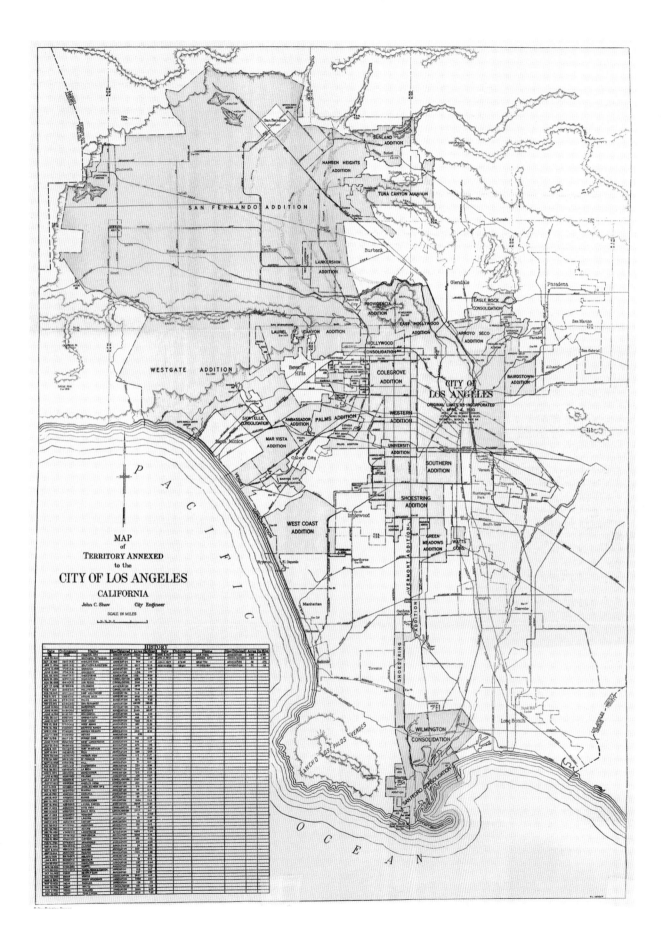

MAP
of
TERRITORY ANNEXED
to the
CITY OF LOS ANGELES
CALIFORNIA

John C. Shaw   City Engineer

SCALE IN MILES

Map of Lovers Lane Showing Proposed Lines of Alteration

Despite its romantic title and depiction of a street that suggests courtship and evening assignations, this map is a document created by the city with the proper numeration and placed into official records. City Map No. 85 shows the small street that branched off Alameda Street just a couple of blocks to the east of the plaza, where it continued toward its conclusion near the Los Angeles River. It was one of the small, tree-lined lanes that paralleled Aliso Street, the main road to San Bernardino from Los Angeles. The same area is shown on William Moore's 1868 map of the Zanja Madre but there the lane is marked only as a "road." Lovers in their finery could certainly have strolled or rode horses over to the privacy of this lane within minutes and commenced any manner of wooing. Yet Harris Newmark in his *Sixty Years in Southern California, 1853–1913* describes the place as "willowed and deep with dust," which would certainly have discouraged placing blankets on the ground and would diminish the picture of early Angelenos seeking what more modern folks found on Mulholland Drive. There was some debate, but Lover's Lane was eventually renamed Date Street in 1877. Date survived until Union Station and Terminal Annex were built in the late 1930s and obliterated many small roads in that area.

William P. Reynolds, the county surveyor, drew up this precise map, including the names of property holders and identifying the Sisters of Charity Hospital, the first in the city. The institution was first established in an old adobe in the pueblo in 1858 by the Sisters of St. Vincent de Paul but moved to this five-acre parcel when they outgrew those quarters and included an orphan's home. Considering the street name it seems a rather unusual location for a Catholic organization. The sisters eventually became known as the Sisters of Charity, due to their work with the poor, and occasionally were called God's Geese because of their winged-looking habit. There were frequent problems with flooding in the area, which might explain why the road was being altered. During rainy periods the nearby Aliso Street, where the stage line ran, became impassable; such was often the case for our Lover's Lane, spoiling the intentions of young swain in the City of the Angels.

City Map No. 85
1871
Surveyed by William P. Reynolds
Laminated parchment
22″ x 19″
Los Angeles City Archives

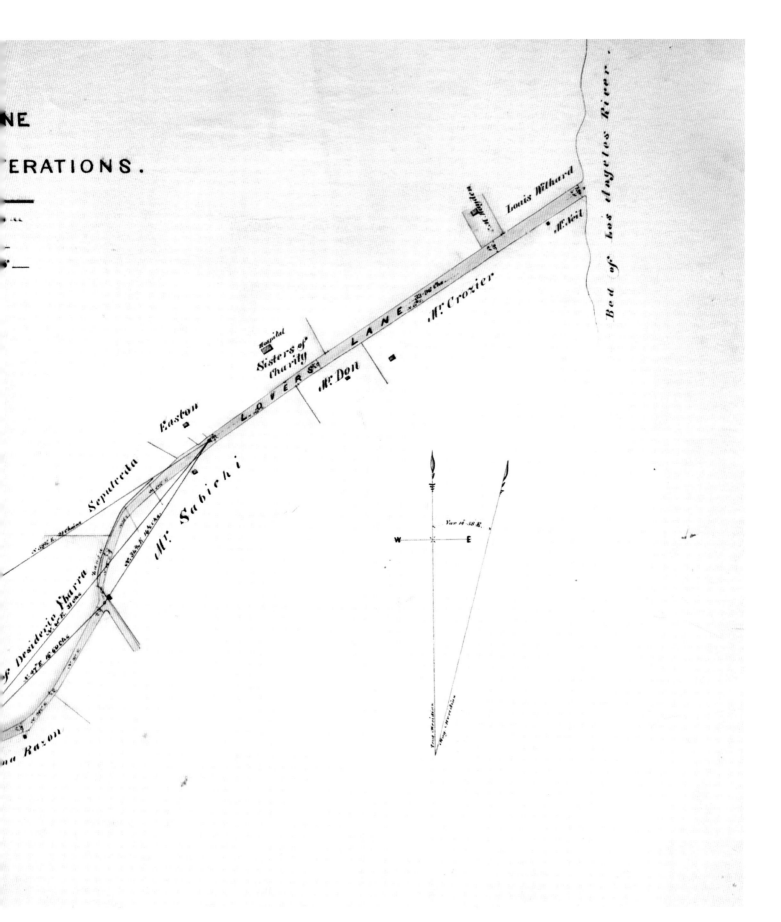

NE

ERATIONS.

Bed of Los Angeles River.

Louis Withard

Mc. Neil

Mc. Crozier

L O V E R S   L A N E

Hospital
Sisters of
Charity

Mc. Don

Easton

Sepulveda

Mr. Sabichi

of Desiderio Ybarra

na Razon

Var 14.58 E.

W — E

67

Fort Hill Tract

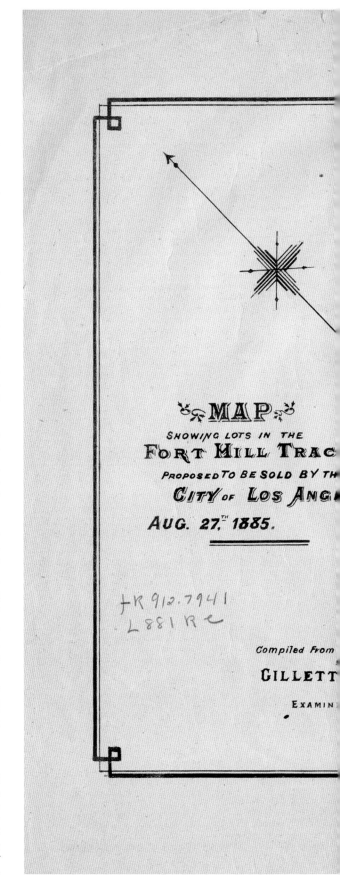

Then his simple auction announcement map contains a lurid undertone from a rather dark chapter in early Los Angeles history. The cemetery at the center had a rather colorful history starting in 1853 with the burial of a local rustic killed by a bear in the Santa Monica Mountains. It seems to have had several names, but Fort Hill Cemetery, the Los Angeles City Cemetery, Fort Moore Hill Cemetery, and the Protestant Cemetery were the most common. Many of the earliest pioneers were buried here even though the place did not have a real caretaker until 1869. As seen on the map, the ground was divided into sections, including plots for fraternal groups in the city such as the Odd Fellows, the Masons, Los Angeles Firemen, and the United Order of Red Men. Also included were segments for the Knights of Pythias, the Olive Lodge, Societé Française, temporary Chinese graves, and individual plots for soldiers of the Mexican War. However, at first there was no official oversight and the deceased were just placed in the ground with no title, staying in the graves by "squatter's rights." The place was poorly maintained and considered somewhat remote and forlorn, so when Evergreen and Rosedale cemeteries were opened in 1877 and 1884 it was mostly abandoned and went completely to seed. Further burials were forbidden unless the deceased were members of the organizations that maintained space there.

At the time this advertisement was published, the city was content to sell the land without much concern for those under the earth, since a major land boom raged following the Santa Fe Railroad's arrival in town. Fort Hill suddenly became quite fashionable, and the cemetery was expendable. Turn-of-the-century historian Horace Bell described the sordid event: "A recital of the various forms of rascality perpetrated by the boomers would fill a volume. But the one greatest piece of rascality of all, to my mind, was the desecration of one of the city graveyards. It was a small pioneer graveyard covering ten acres. Some of the most honored California pioneers and officers of the army were interred there, but it was no longer used for burials. The city allowed promoters to map it, cut it up, and sell it off in small building lots. In building streets through it, human remains were excavated and scattered and to-day wagons rattle through streets built up over buried human bodies. Houses stand on graves. The city of Los Angeles sold "... this cemetery plot, a municipal burying ground, without pretending to remove and re-inter elsewhere the bodies resting there."

Eventually the Los Angeles Board of Education took over the property and finally annexed the main cemetery ground. A portion of the remains did find their rest at Rosedale or Evergreen or even the Hollywood cemeteries, but many just ended up underneath buildings, streets, and parking lots.

Map Showing Lots in the Fort Hill Tract Proposed to Be Sold
by the City of Los Angeles
Compiled from the county records by Collette and Gibson
Robert Renshaw, Engraver
1885
Printed map
17″ x 12″
Los Angeles Public Library

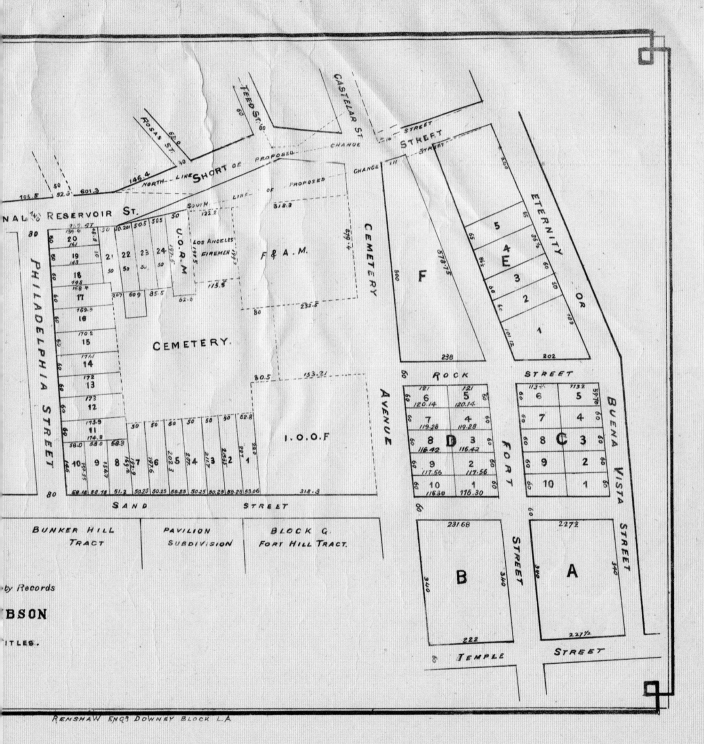

69

Dakin Atlas

The early fire insurance atlases are gold mines of information about the urban development of any city, especially the city of Los Angeles, that grew quickly and in some cases haphazardly. Some darker stories of the old city may not be detailed in print, but often these maps give hints as to the wild side of the City of Angels. The *Dakin Atlas* was an early rival of the Sanborn Company in the fire insurance information business and a beautiful example of cartography created to protect insurers but collected by institutions as vaults of historical knowledge. The detail supplied reaches into many levels of the infrastructure, including the quality of the buildings, the availability of fire suppression, the width of the streets, water sources, the location of public buildings, and descriptions of property use. Since the maps were created to inform insurance companies, there is some emphasis on that aspect, especially in a city with just four engine companies, one hook and ladder company, and three hose companies.

Perhaps more interesting is the description of the buildings in the areas around the historic plaza in what was the original Los Angeles Chinatown. The area was long established within the frontier town of early statehood days and maintained a Wild West atmosphere, including all the temptations of the flesh known to man. In the late nineteenth century prostitution was permitted in Los Angeles in this general vicinity per City Ordinance 224, and much of that activity took place in the area depicted on this sheet of the Dakin Atlas. Large portions of the railroad-building workforce were Chinese bachelors who were unable to bring women to the new world and prohibited by law to marry "natives." Houses of prostitution were alternatives for these men, who were far away from home and desperate for companionship. Yet the makeup of both the houses and the customers was as mixed as the gathering places of the very multiethnic population of the city. Chinatown was a lively place full of street merchants, curio shops, and outdoor farmer's markets, but it also contained several streets where houses of "Ill Fame" existed, as seen designated here by "I.F.," along with other sordid descriptions such as "Opium Joint," "Gambling," and "Sal." for saloon. This old Chinatown continued to be a wide-open district well into the 1920s but eventually became respectable before being demolished to make way for the Union Station Train Terminal.

Map of the City of Los Angeles, California
Showing the water service, distributing reservoirs, and
districts supplied by each street index, fire limits. Location
of fire department and fire patrol buildings, etc.
1888
Containing corrections to 1893
Dakin Publishing Company
San Francisco
Atlas sheet
Los Angeles Public Library

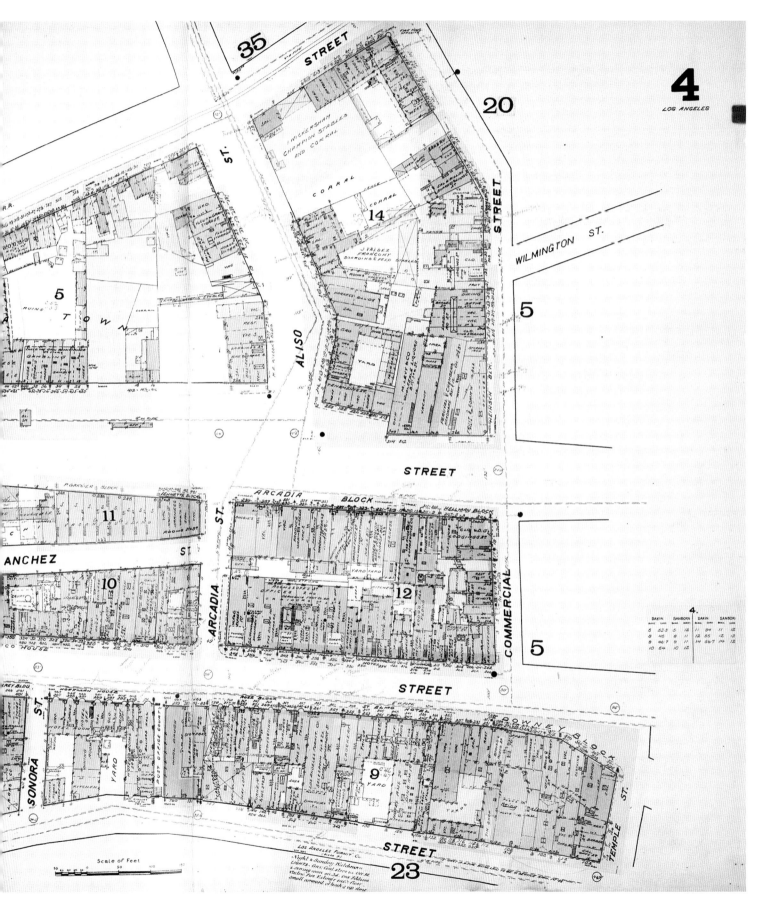

Business Property Map of Los Angeles

obert Marsh's axonometric map of the downtown Los Angeles business district was decades ahead of its time. Created with street-level studies and rudimentary orthographic projection, the map shows the pre-skyscraper skyline of the city, with height and placement of structures popping out of the drawing with amazing vibrancy. The size and location of every major structure in what was then a fairly centralized commercial area could be used for myriad reasons, especially for the promise of large-scale real estate transactions.

Since Marsh was one of the major players in commercial real estate, he seems to have been sizing up possible developments and giving desirable clients a clear look at the exciting money center of a city ready to reach toward unlimited prosperity.

In 1913 the Los Angeles Aqueduct was completed, bringing water to the dry climate of Los Angeles and dramatically expanding the economic potential of the entire metropolitan area. Money was flowing into the city, and this map gently guided prospective buyers toward the Marsh-Strong offices

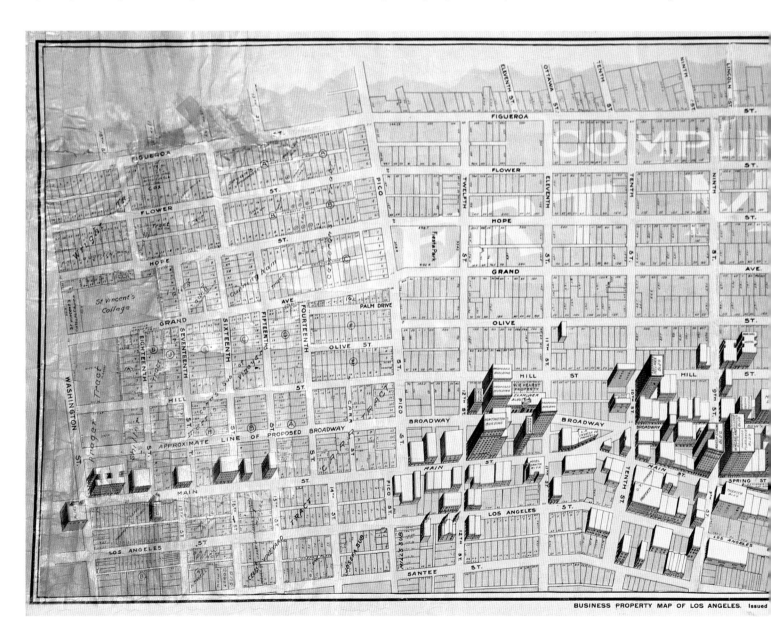

BUSINESS PROPERTY MAP OF LOS ANGELES. Issued

appearing on the map at Main and 9th. While it excludes anything west of Grand Avenue, "the Business Property map" stretches from the showpiece Hall of Records building and Post Office on the northern end to the Prager tract on the southern tip, where Angelenos once found amusements at Chutes Park then Luna Park—so-called trolley parks at that time. The destination contained a zoo, a baseball field where the Pacific Coast League Angels played, an expansive garden, and a theater. Two of the city's newspapers are shown, the *Los Angeles Times* at 1st and Broadway, just three years after the bombing in a labor dispute, and William Randolph Hearst's *Examiner* at 11th and Broadway. Also prominent on the landscape are the magnificent six-story Beaux Arts–style Hamburgers Department Store with its "moving stairway" at 8th and Hill and Oliver Morosco's Orpheum theater on Broadway near 6th, where locals could see shows like Percy Bronson and Winnie Baldwin's vaudeville act. Yet the talk of the town was about the Orpheum acquiring Thomas Edison's newest invention called the kinetophone, which could broadcast talking pictures.

Marsh was an energetic entrepreneur and land developer who had engineered the subdivision of Mt. Washington near downtown, where he built a beautiful hotel and a funicular railway that scaled the steep hills of that hillside community. At first he wanted to create an enclave for "those of artistic tendencies to the dreamer, to people of imagination" but later decided that he would rather appeal to "hard-headed, wide-awake, everyday people."

1913
Robert Marsh & Co.
Colored lithograph
Seaver Center for Western History

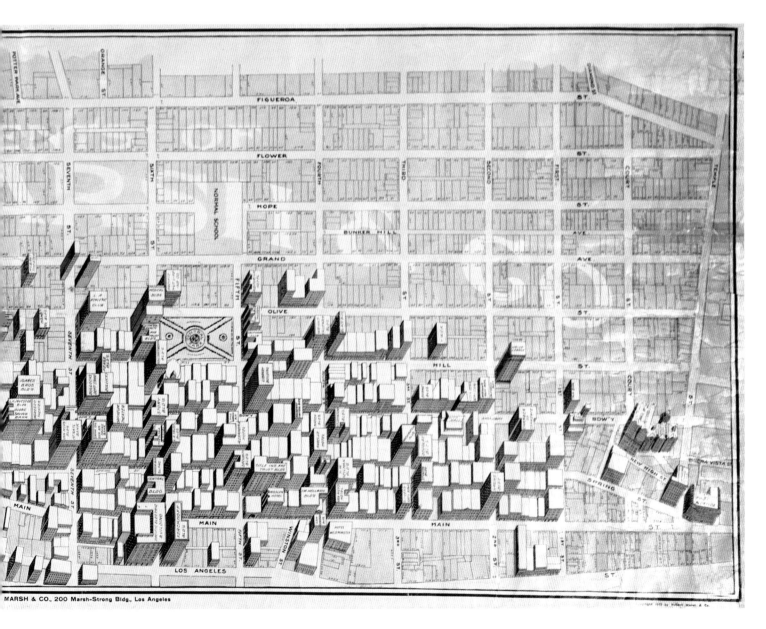

MARSH & CO., 200 Marsh-Strong Bldg., Los Angeles

Baist's Real Estate Atlas of Surveys of Los Angeles

Just as the Lower East Side of New York was always an entry point for various immigrants and ethnic groups, Boyle Heights on the eastern side of the Los Angeles River has held the lantern up to those groups trying to establish themselves in this city on the opposite shore. Back in 1858 Andrew Boyle purchased land in the area called "the white bluffs," or *Paredon Blanco*, and took up residence near what is now Boyle Avenue. It remained rather remote until the 1870s, when bridges were built across the river allowing horse-drawn streetcars to connect the area to the rest of the city. When Boyle died in 1871 his son-in-law, William H. Workman, subdivided the area, naming it Boyle Heights in his memory in about 1876. Development was rapid, and at the dawn of the twentieth century settlement there had increased from a mere forty homes in 1877 to a vibrant neighborhood exemplifying the melting pot with Russian Molokans, Yugoslavs, Mexicans, African Americans, Japanese, and, by the 1920s, the largest Jewish community in the western United States. Streets were also named for places in the Midwest or East, like Chicago, Brooklyn, or St. Louis, to lure settlers to familiar-sounding surroundings. To accommodate this great influx of population, Roosevelt High School was constructed in 1924, becoming one of the first truly integrated educational facilities in the city, and, in a progressive move, an adult education center was created in the mid-thirties, teaching English to the recent arrivals. Roosevelt set a good example of racial harmony that sadly did not reach all neighborhoods in Los Angeles. Unfortunately, many of longtime Japanese-American residents were displaced by internment and lost what they had built up over generations.

The center of the area was always considered Brooklyn and Soto, but Breed Street, with its famous Breed Street Synagogue (then called Congregation Talmud Torah) completed in 1923, was the hub of Jewish life in "Boyle Yeights," as the youngsters called it because of the prominence of Yiddish language on the streets. Hollenbeck and Prospect parks are Los Angeles landmarks seen on maps from the earliest days. The Evergreen Cemetery is one of the city's oldest and largest, established in 1877 and operated as the only integrated place of burial in the city. By the 1940s Boyle Heights became mostly a proud Mexican-American neighborhood and has remained so to this day.

The area is shown in a 1921 real estate atlas by the G. William Baist Company of Philadelphia, one the very best producers of atlases in the United States. Surveyor and cartographer G. William Baist directed the production of these atlases from the late nineteenth century to the mid-1930s and for Los Angeles from 1910 to 1921. They present a wide view of the neighborhoods. The scale was set at 1:300, which allowed a look at a sixteen-street swath of development, as opposed to the 50 to 100 of fire insurance maps.

1921
G. W. Baist
Philadelphia
Sheet 25
Boyle Heights
Atlas plate
31″ x 21″
Los Angeles Public Library

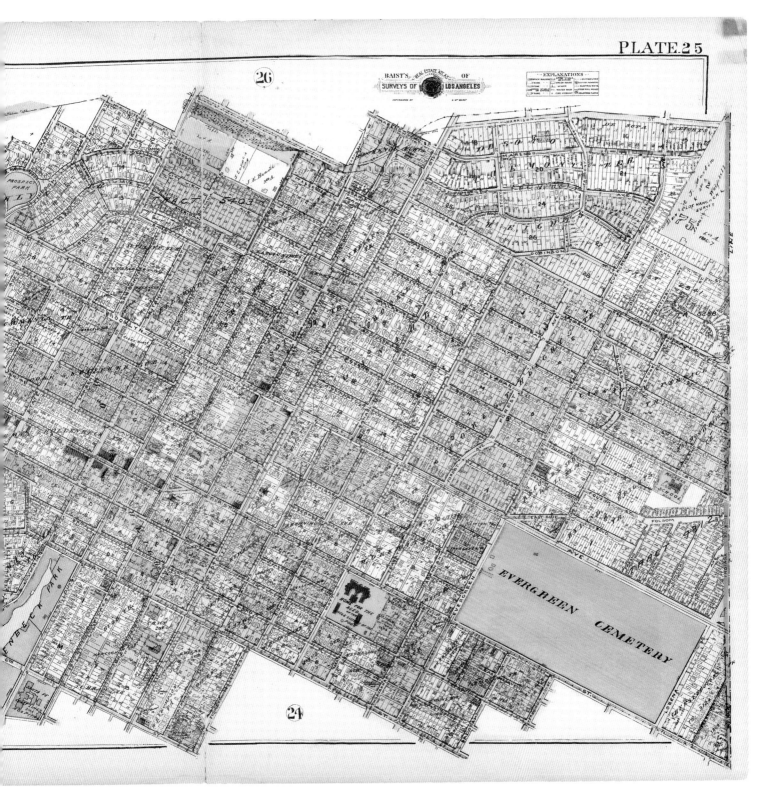

Branch Library Map

This jewel box of a pictorial map represents many things about the cultural vitality and ambition of the city of Los Angeles, which was finding ways to make progress toward a national leadership in the arts during tough economic times. The idea for this work was originally submitted to the art committee of the Public Works of Art Project, which was part of the national program created by the Roosevelt administration to put artists to work bettering the national cultural literacy. Gail Cleaves was a very talented Los Angeles artist who specialized in bookplates and decorative maps, so she was the perfect choice to create a celebration of the recent blooming of the library system with thirty-six buildings constructed since May 1929. She created this five-by-seven-foot oil on canvas of the forty-nine branch libraries in the system that ranged far across the city, from the harbor city of San Pedro to the San Fernando Valley, and from west to east Los Angeles. The project was endorsed by the Board of Library Commissioners, and the library paid for the materials while the Public Works of Art Project remunerated the artist. At a ceremony on April 5, 1934, the work was mounted on a wall at the Central Library and Cleaves was thanked by city librarian Althea Warren.

The map portrays in pristine detail each of the varied architectural styles of the branch libraries, built and named to reflect their unique neighborhoods and places in the city. Arroyo Seco, Boyle Heights, Vernon, Cahuenga, Lincoln Heights, and Vermont Square libraries were original Carnegie libraries shown on this map; the latter three still exist.

Despite a misconception about the hedonistic Angelinos, the city had long been one of the biggest users of the public library in the world, ranking second in books circulated (some thirteen million) and first in amount read per capita in the 1930s. Reports from the American Library Association saw Los Angeles reading ten books for every man, woman, and child in the city, a remarkable feat during any year. Thirty percent of the population owned city library cards. Due to their great popularity, the city libraries were shown great generosity by the Public Works programs, and the new Central Library, completed in 1926, was decorated with murals, statuary, and canvasses that still exist today. Sadly, Cleaves's wonderful map disappeared, but this copy still retains the magic of that time of great hope.

1930
Gail Cleaves
Photograph of oil painting
5' x 7'
Los Angeles Public Library

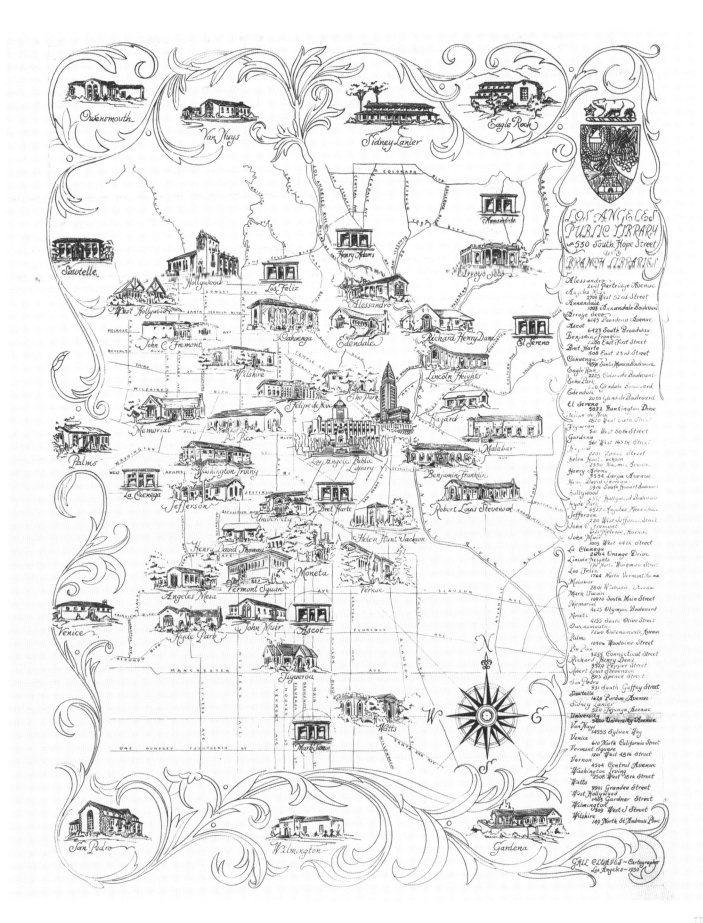

The Heart of Los Angeles

James H. Payne was a construction engineer who put together this four-in-one map of the downtown area, full of vitality and enticing amusements despite the city being in the grip of the Great Depression. Payne was practical but lent some history to the street scene, adding original names to the ones in current usage, like *Calle de las Flores* for Flower, *Calle de Caridad* for Charity (which became Grand), *Calle Occituna* for Olive, and *Calle Chapulos* or Grasshopper Street for Figueroa. One year away from the 1932 Summer Olympics, downtown was very much the nerve center of the metropolitan area, including the financial district of Spring Street, the theater district of Broadway, and the wholesale and industrial districts that existed on the southern edge in a commercial section. There were numerous grand scale department stores that dotted the downtown landscape along a designated shopping district, including May Company, Bullocks, Broadway, Walkers, and J. W. Robinsons, along with many fine hotels like the Biltmore and Alexandria.

In the upper right corner we see the original Ord Survey for comparison to the first street layouts; on the bottom right are the city limits as they existed that year, with the early four square leagues of the Spanish pueblo delineated; and at the bottom left a clever transportation legend describes the routes of the Los Angeles Railway Yellow Cars and the Pacific Electric Red Cars with appropriate car designations. There are also the much ballyhooed but never completely realized subway proposals that were to travel under 7th, Broadway, and out West Pico Boulevard. The fully functional Pacific Electric Subway opened in 1925 and ran from 1,045 feet under 4th and Hill Street beneath the Subway Terminal Building to a portal near Beverly and Glendale boulevards.

What appears to be a thriving metropolis was suffering with the rest of the country in the first stages of a depression that saw five million Americans out of work and bank failures taking place every day. Stern, tea-totaling mayor John Clinton Porter was a reformer, but Los Angeles was plagued by xenophobia that saw more than ten thousand Mexican laborers repatriated and a police scandal that shocked the nation. Still, the city soldiered on toward its glorious Olympics triumph, and as one local newspaper wag wrote some twelve years before the end of the nation's economic disaster, Los Angeles would come out of its economic troubles by just finding "the return of mental poise."

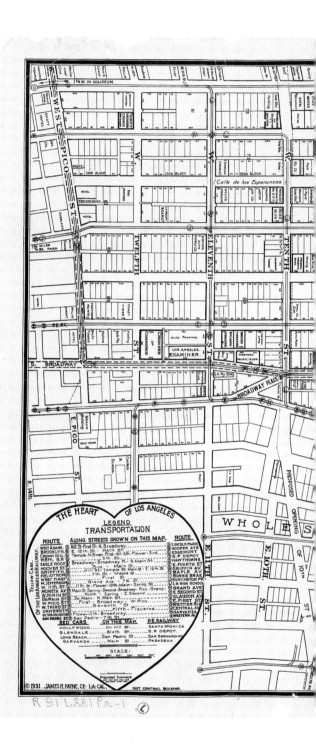

1931
James H. Payne
Printed map
24″x14″
Los Angeles Public Library

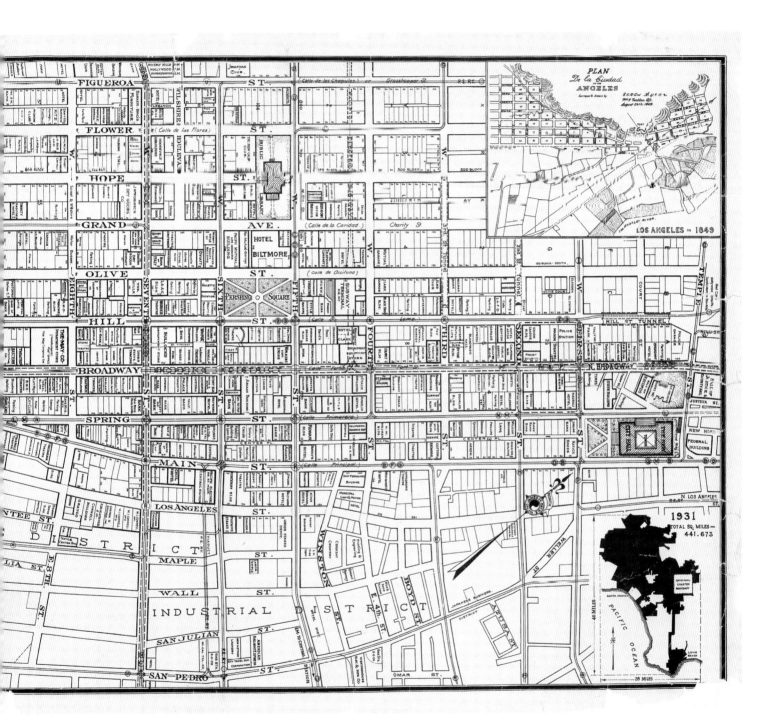

The Miracle Mile

The Nirenstein atlases seem like the perfect measure of 1950s cities and suburbs, particularly the West Coast towns that were gaining population rapidly. The Depression was finally over, soldiers were returning home victorious, and the American dream was in full flower in Southern California. The decade ushered in an unprecedented era of urban growth and prosperity especially reflected in a robust and mobile middle class. Postwar Los Angeles was a place of unlimited possibility and free-flowing cash to spend on businesses, homes, or just the good life that defined the beginnings of the Baby Boomer generation. Money was being spent at "America's most colorful shopping centers" around the county on boulevards like Lankershim in the Valley, Colorado in Pasadena, Brand in Glendale, Long Beach, Hollywood, and Wilshire, sometimes called the "Miracle Mile."

Nathan Nirenstein was a product of the American dream himself, emigrating from Russia in the early 1900s and starting his real estate atlas business in the mid-1920s from Springfield, Massachusetts. Nirenstein recognized the move toward metropolitan suburbs early on, focusing on eleven Western states where suburban communities grew two and a half times faster than the old urban centers. The Nirenstein atlases described businesses and gave in-depth information on shopping centers while providing demographics, an aerial photo, and these information-packed maps with the names of all businesses on a block. Nirenstein playfully described his volumes as "the mishnayot of the real estate world," pointing out the study of the subject that almost reached rabbinical thoroughness. The atlases were virtual business almanacs, giving information on population, number of banks, newspapers, number of registered automobiles, availability of public transportation, existing chain stores, and big shopping days. With a unique numeration system the maps offer the names of property owners, the tenant, the assessed value, the square footage, and the height, as well as a clear view of the neighbors. This particular time capsule shows a shoppers Shangri-la on Wilshire Boulevard, lined with high-end stores like Mullen and Bluett, Orbachs, Silverwoods, and a couple of grand department stores: the May Company and Desmonds. There is an obvious business presence with Prudential Insurance occupying two large structures, evidence of cultural vitality in the Huntington Hartford Theater and the corporate offices of the Pantages Theater, and some typical 1950s milieu in the Flying Saucer Café.

Nirenstein's Real Estate Atlas
of the Far Western States
Atlas of the South Pacific States, Volume XIII
1954
Nathan Nirenstein
Nirenstein's National Realty Map Company
Springfield, Massachussets
Los Angeles Public Library

L. A. COUNTY
EXEMPT

Hancock Park

BUSINESS SECTION
CITY OF LOS ANGELES
MIRACLE MILE
0   40   80   120

NIRENSTEINS NATIONAL
REALTY MAP CO.
SPRINGFIELD, MASS.

Parking
PRUDENTIAL INSURANCE CO.

L-830   B-2,284

9-S

Ohrbach's Dept. Store

BOULEVARD

L-121 Parking   *L-67*

Parking   *L-73 Parking*   *L-130 Parking*

BOULEVARD

BOULEVARD

LA BREA

Sunset

The very peak of the land boom of the 1880s took place in the two years 1887 and 1888, when many of the cities or suburbs that encircle Los Angeles sprang from the real estate fever that swept the southland. Places that once were sleepy rancho grazing lands suddenly were given romantic names or the surnames of their developers. Long Beach, Hollywood, Burbank, Glendale, Inglewood, La Cañada, and even Sunset are just a few handles that land dealers created with lots of imagination and sometimes a stretch of the truth. The 1880s saw the population of Los Angeles increase five fold, and the promotional map, which had to stand out in the crowd and sometimes included lush illustration and unbridled salesmanship, had its heyday. Artistry was essential in this fight for attention, as mile upon mile of land was subject to bidding by newcomers arriving to sample the riches of the golden state. Many of these lots were purchased sight unseen—as a matter of fact, many were advertised sight unseen by the sellers. Sunset and the surrounding lots shown on this map went on sale the morning of August 15, 1887, in room 16 of the Los Angeles National Bank. Sunset was purported to be a place that commanded a view of the ocean, Catalina Island, and San Pedro. This new development had the added benefit of being on the line of the Santa Monica steam motor foothill railroad, which traveled the twelve miles to the big city of Los Angeles and its fifty thousand residents.

While this map is simpler than many in the era, it does present an eye-catching suggestion of a sun-soaked place where one could settle into bucolic bliss or join the up-and-coming town of Sunset, with neatly planned streets that would be ideal for raising families or trading up in real estate. The Sunset Boulevard seen here is actually today's Wilshire, but the rest of the map has another story to tell. Rancho San Jose de Buenos Ayres was originally granted to Don Jose Maximo Alanis but then passed to Dr. Wilson Jones and William T. B. Sanford, then to Benjamin "Don Benito" Wilson, and eventually was sold to John Wolfskill and the estate of William Wolfskill in 1884. There was a dispute over the southern holdings of the ranch, with the very same Land and Water Company mentioned as authors who claimed they had "right of way" through the rancho and used that land for the eight hundred lots comprising the town of Sunset. In February 1891 Wolfskill won a judgment again, and the Land and Water Company and Los Angeles and Pacific Railroad returned the lands the railroad had confiscated from him. Later owners of the property eventually took a 384-acre piece to create the University of California at Los Angeles.

Map of the Subdivision of Rancho San Jose de Buenos Ayres and the Town of Sunset Owned by the Los Angeles and Santa Monica Land and Water Co., Situated in Los Angeles Co., Cal.
1887
Surveyed by Theo G. Kocher and Co.
Los Angeles Lithography Company
Colored lithograph
Los Angeles Public Library

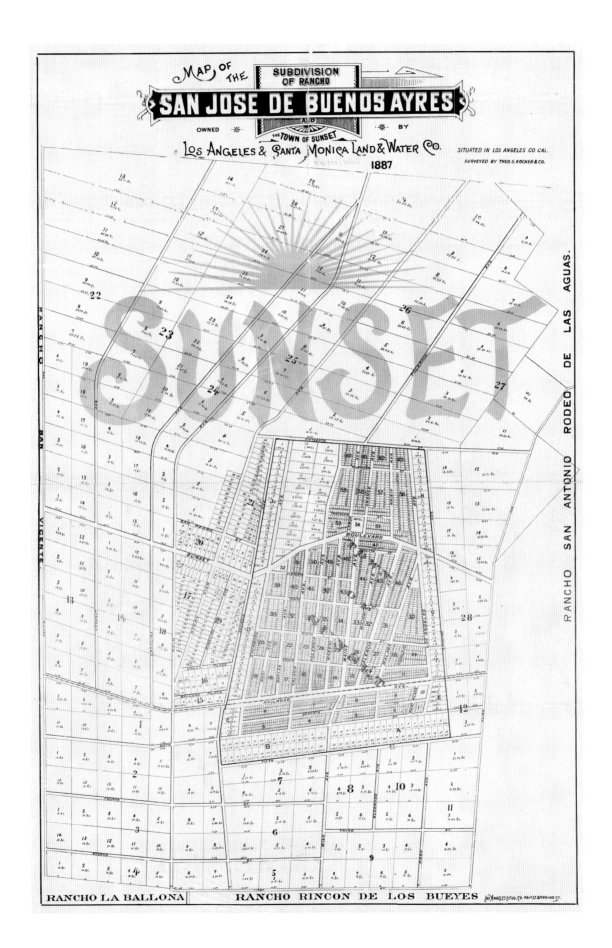

MAP OF THE **SUBDIVISION OF RANCHO**

SAN JOSE DE BUENOS AYRES

OWNED AND THE TOWN OF SUNSET BY

Los Angeles & Santa Monica Land & Water Co.

1887

SITUATED IN LOS ANGELES CO. CAL.

SURVEYED BY THEO. G. KOCHER & CO.

RANCHO LA BALLONA | RANCHO RINCON DE LOS BUEYES

Angeleno Heights

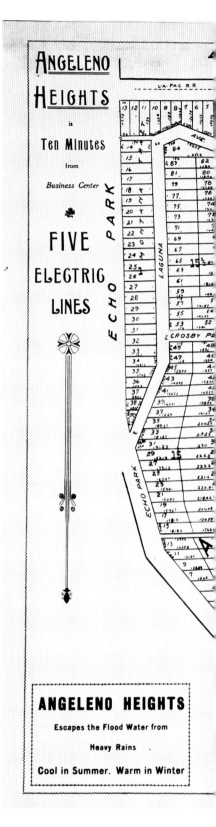

Angeleno Heights—with its magnificent Victorian homes, classic Craftsman-style dwellings, and dramatic vantage point overlooking downtown Los Angeles—is unique in all of the southland and certainly the most impressive historical scene in city limits. Right from the beginning the area had lofty intentions and a prime location. This rather straightforward and dignified tract map announcing the sale of lots in Angelino Heights, restated in all four corners, is a sort of comeback story. In 1886 the area was subdivided and advertised as a suburb by W. W. Stilson and E. E. Hall, who purchased the land from pioneer Prudent Beaudry. Suburb, once a derogatory term, was beginning to signify escape from the hoi polloi with the accompanying noise and dirt of the city. Nowhere could be more natural to provide an oasis of calm and beauty than the lofty hill where Angelino Heights was planned. The place was described by a *Los Angeles Times* columnist called "the Saunterer" in glowing prose: "nature must have been in her most beneficent mood when she fashioned these hills and gave them to Los Angeles for her suburban homes." The original intent was to create a genteel, respectable enclave drawing on the money flowing into the city from newcomers hailing from "Iowa, Kansas, Illinois, Arkansas, Nevada, and New York." Although part of Stilson's selling point was the trolley that ran up Temple Street to the hill, many new residents obviously had their own transportation, evidenced by the elaborate carriage houses that accompany many of the homes. The Spring Street area of commerce was just one and a half miles distant and less than sixteen minutes by streetcar or horse and carriage. Most of the early residents became socialites, and the three tennis courts in Angelino Heights were typical of the upper-crust lifestyle the area symbolized. Lots sold for $500, and the average cost of building these large mansions ran from seven to ten thousand dollars.

Angelino Heights was to rival the "old money" area of Bunker Hill, and large Victorian homes were constructed on the hill. Unfortunately, a banking crisis in 1888 caused much of the construction to cease and the area stopped growing, but some fifty-one masterpieces in the Queen Anne or Eastlake Victorian styles stood majestically on Carroll, Kensington, Douglas, Kellam, and Edgeware avenues. At the time of W. W. Stilson's death in 1888, his widow, Mary, tried to continue the development, petitioning the city to grade and pave streets. Mrs. Stilson had famed architect Arthur Benton build side-by-side homes for her son, Fielding, and herself on Kensington.

When young Fielding Stilson took over the development in 1909, he made this map and started to reinvent Angelino Heights, continuing to stress the quality of the neighborhood and its choice location but also offering more modest prices, five streetcar lines, and the possibility of those outside the Blue Book moving into the Heights. During this revival more architecturally significant homes were built, but this time in the more modest Mission Revival, Craftsman, California bungalow, brownstone, and even Streamline Moderne styles. While there is some debate about Angelino Heights being the first suburb, it certainly remains one of the city's most fascinating places, with many of the original magnificent homes restored and standing in glory.

1909?
Fielding J. Stilson
Printed handbill
Seaver Center for Western
History

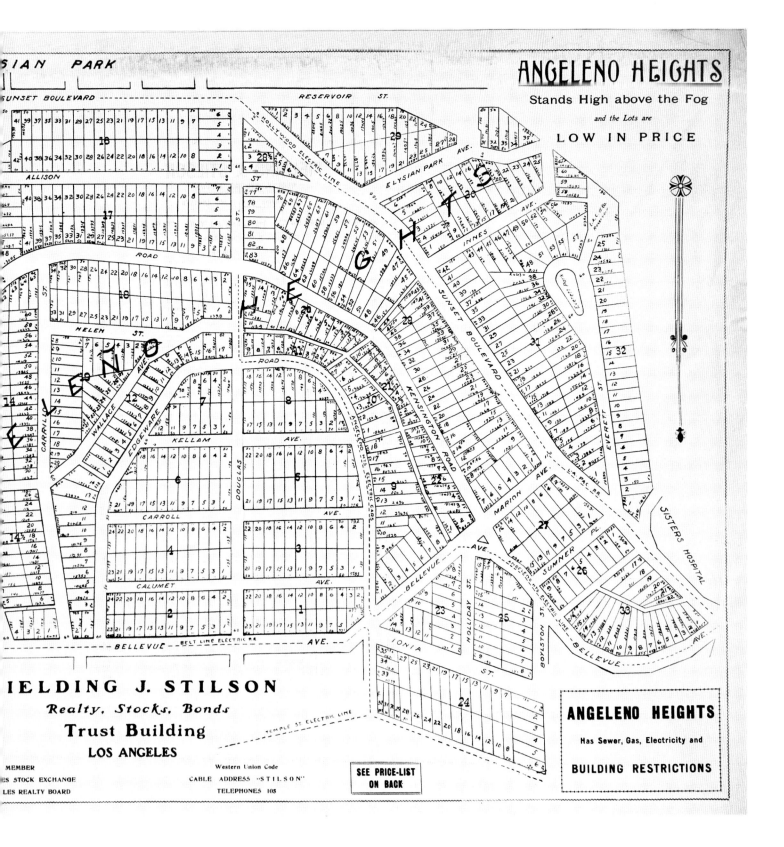

ANGELENO HEIGHTS

Stands High above the Fog

and the Lots are

LOW IN PRICE

IELDING J. STILSON

Realty, Stocks, Bonds

Trust Building

LOS ANGELES

MEMBER

ES STOCK EXCHANGE

LES REALTY BOARD

Western Union Code

CABLE ADDRESS "STILSON"

TELEPHONES 105

SEE PRICE-LIST
ON BACK

ANGELENO HEIGHTS

Has Sewer, Gas, Electricity and

BUILDING RESTRICTIONS

Laughlin Park Tract Number 2099

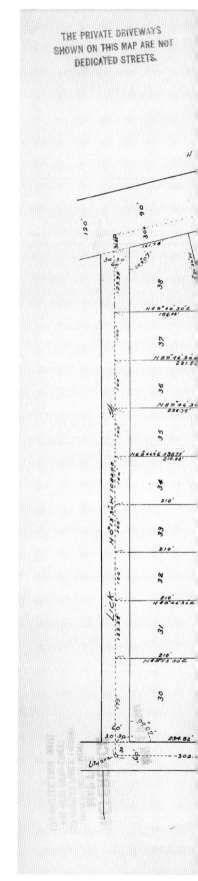

As early as 1909 the movie industry began making its mark on the landscape of Los Angeles with more than a dozen studios appearing all around Hollywood. Unlike the highly popular "maps to the stars' homes," this modest tract map shows the beginnings of a little-known enclave where the established silent film heavyweights were beginning to carve out their own star map. Billed as "the subdivision for people of culture," Laughlin Park became "the place" for movie folk well before Beverly Hills. Developers Homer Laughlin and Wilbur Cummings were behind this deluxe neighborhood developed on part of the old Los Feliz Rancho. The Laughlin Park Tract offered just forty villas on these hills overlooking Hollywood and in some cases with views to the Pacific Ocean. The idea seemed to have taken a while to germinate, since the famed James Lick, the Bill Gates of his day, had conducted mapping and considered subdivision of the area as far back as the 1870s. Lick eventually sold his part to Laughlin as his attention turned toward philanthropy. Homer Laughlin, a very successful financier, first thought he might create his own lushly landscaped Southern California Eden that featured 50,000 trees, shrubs, and native plants. However, when his wife died he lost interest and shortly before his own death he turned the property over to the Laughlin Park Company, which was run by his son, Homer Laughlin Jr. The project was surveyed and platted by surveyor/engineer Fremont Ackerman, who later did the same for the grounds of the UCLA campus. Nathan F. Barratt was the landscape architect responsible for the re-creation of Eden. One of the first residents was Cecil B. DeMille, who bought his fifteen-room mansion for $27,000 in 1916. DeMille proceeded to build homes for several members of his family nearby and never considered moving to Bel Air or Beverly Hills when they became fashionable for the Hollywood "picture icons." The year this map was published DeMille began what would become Paramount Pictures.

Unlike many grand ideas, Laughlin Park was fully realized, and many of the "villas" were situated on large lots with famous architects designing the houses in a typically eclectic Southern California mix of styles ranging from Spanish Colonial to Streamline Moderne. Roland Coate, Carleton Winslow, Lloyd Wright, Cooper Corbett, Julia Morgan, Gordon B. Kaufman, and William J. Dodd were just a few of the architects who designed beautiful homes while producing stunning landscaping to fit into the neighborhood's rustic appeal. Early advertisements promised "a replica of Italy's finest landscape gardens" and indeed they were famous enough to become a regular stop for tourists riding on the Red Car, anxious to see the wealthy residents who could afford $150,000 for these mansions. Everything else about "the Park" was exclusive— the private streets, the lush gardens, and even the sewers all behind five gates that kept the hoi polloi at bay. While Mr. DeMille was the big name, Laughlin Park was also home to Charlie Chaplin, W. C. Fields, Maurice Chevalier, Antonio Moreno, Carole Lombard, singing star Deanna Durbin, Cary Grant, Basil Rathbone, and many more.

Hollywood, Los Angeles
1913
Fremont Ackerman
Laughlin Park Company
Ink on paper
Los Angeles Public Library

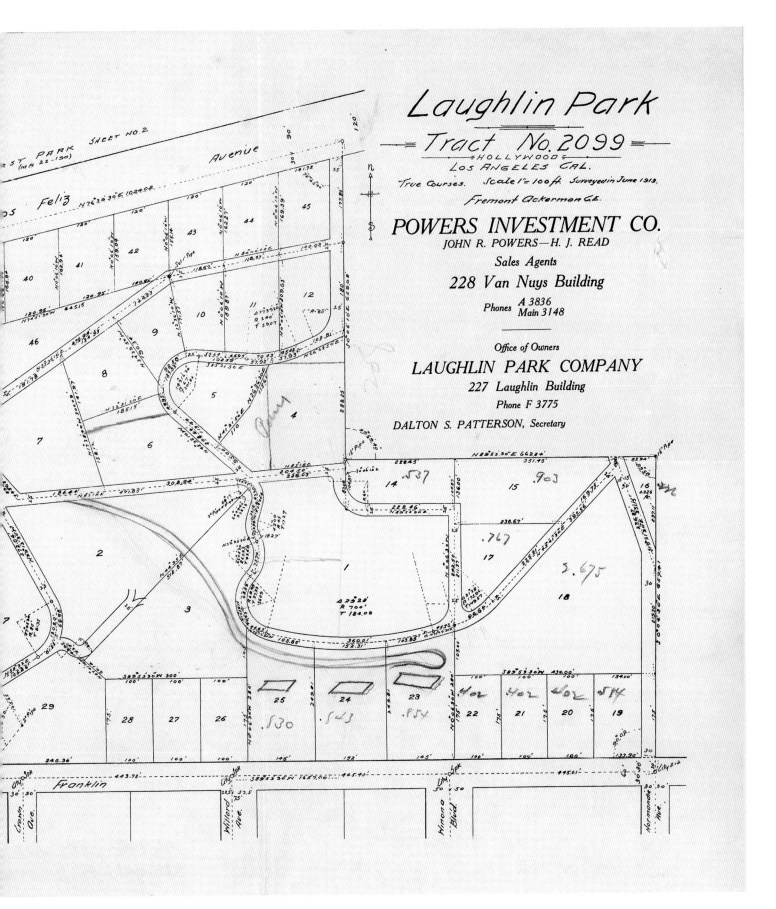

Laughlin Park
Tract No. 2099
HOLLYWOOD
LOS ANGELES CAL.

True Courses. Scale 1″=100ft Surveyed in June 1913.

Fremont Ackerman C.E.

POWERS INVESTMENT CO.
JOHN R. POWERS—H. J. READ
Sales Agents
228 Van Nuys Building

Phones A 3836
Main 3148

Office of Owners

LAUGHLIN PARK COMPANY
227 Laughlin Building
Phone F 3775

DALTON S. PATTERSON, Secretary

Valley Historic

One of the first maps of the San Fernando Valley, this enticing land-sale advertisement displays both a record of the original subdivisions and an idyllic panorama of the twelve-thousand-acre piece of land that once constituted the southern portion of the lands of the San Fernando Mission. The real estate boom that gripped Los Angeles at this time spread to adjacent territories, and the flat expanse of fields and occasional orchards just fifteen miles from the pueblo seemed ideal for settlement despite the lack of a plentiful water source. Yet wheat was being grown and milled there successfully when this map appeared in a campaign by the new owners, who hoped to lure buyers out from the big city and points east. The vast area that eventually would be home to a quintessential Southern California suburbia in the twentieth century was beginning its journey from waving wheat fields to the automobile culture and tract homes.

The land had passed through a succession of owners and uses, beginning with the establishment of the Mission San Fernando by Father Fermin Lasuen in 1797 in what was called Valley Encino after the live oak trees that proliferated on this open plain. With secularization of the missions calling for the division of that land, it was first leased to Andres Pico and Juan Manso by the Mexican government then sold to Eulogio de Celis for $14,000—thirteen square leagues in all. After statehood Celis filed claim with the U.S. Land Commission, and in 1873 it was finally recognized, two years after Andres Pico gave the land to the former governor Pio Pico, who sold it to the San Fernando Farm and Homestead Association headed up by Isaac Lankershim and Isaac Newton Van Nuys. At first they used the land for cattle grazing and some agriculture, but when droughts devastated the livestock it was decided to plant wheat. A large-scale wheat empire was created in the southern half of the valley, then milling operations began, yielding over 500,000 bushels of wheat in one year. By 1876 the Southern Pacific Railroad had connected northern to southern California, and the San Fernando tunnel had been completed, linking the valley with West Los Angeles. Everything was in place for the development of the suddenly accessible and desirable expanse of land, and this map shows twelve thousand acres offered by the Lankershim Ranch Land and Water Company, which had purchased the eastern portion of the property from the Los Angeles Farm and Milling Company (once the San Fernando Farm Homestead Association). The subdivision seen here sold in ten- to forty-acre lots at $5 to $150 each.

Map Showing Subdivision of Lands Belonging to the Lankershim Ranch Land and Water Co.: Being the East 1,200 Acres of the South Half of Rancho Ex Mission of San Fernando, Los Angeles County, California
1887
E. G. Jones, Surveyor
Lankershim Ranch Land and Water Company
Colored lithograph
Schmidt Label and Lithographic Co., San Francisco
Department of Special Collections UCLA

Map Showing Subdivision of Lands Belonging to the

LANKERSHIM RANCH
LAND and WATER Co

BEING THE EAST 12000 ACRES OF THE SOUTH HALF OF THE
RANCH EX MISSION-SAN FERNANDO
LOS ANGELES COUNTY, CALIFORNIA
SURVEYED NOV. 1887 BY E.G. JONES.

◆OFFICE◆
44 NORTH SPRING ST,
LOS ANGELES, CAL.

L. T. GARNSEY, Pres't.   J. E. PLATER, Treas.   F. C. GARBUTT, Sec'y.

DIRECTORS.

L. T. GARNSEY,   A. P. HOFFMAN,
D. McFARLAND,   JAS. R. BOAL,
S. W. LUITWIELER,   F. C. GARBUTT,
S. B. HUNT.

LANKERSHIM

ANGELES RIVER

Map Showing the Locations of the Old *Zanja Madre*, Ditches, Vineyards, and Old Town, etc.

T he availability of water has always been a problem for the city of Los Angeles, and the delivery of this liquid gold to citizens is one of the great conundrums in city history. The problem was originally solved by ditches carved off the Los Angeles River, but as the city grew, the need for better conveyance and storage became urgent. The first of these maps shows the early, rather intricate system of ditches dug off the river to irrigate the land and nourish the people who first settled in Los Angeles. The second shows the larger system of planned reservoirs that would allow large-scale storage and help create waterpower for industry.

At its founding, the pueblo of Los Angeles was placed strategically close to a river, and the much-maligned Los Angeles River provided a watershed of some 834 square miles, with much of the flow underground. The entire basin is a natural underground reservoir, but that water had to be brought to the surface to be usable. Just seven weeks after the founding of the pueblo, the settlers had fashioned a crude *zanja* system with open ditches flowing out from the river to provide water for crops, livestock, and domestic use. However, the delivery of the water was cumbersome, expensive, and fraught with calamity brought on by floods and the destruction of waterwheels, dams, and the crude pipes used for transport. By the mid-1850s the *zanjero* or water master was probably the most powerful person in government since he controlled the flow of this precious commodity. Even in 1850 the price could be as dear as fifty cents a bucket.

The first maps of the zanja system were done by county surveyor Captain William Moore as early as 1857, and his studies seem to have been incorporated into this multifaceted map by city surveyor Michael Kelleher eighteen years later. Kelleher was sworn into the city surveyor's office on May 13, 1875, accepting the charge of surveying parts of the city and delivering maps and property belonging to the City Council. Within two years the great drought of 1877 would wreak havoc in the area, but this map shows a relatively healthy system. Moore's and later Kelleher's maps show the *Zanja Madre* or Mother Ditch following a course along the bluff near the intake spot of the river, boosted by a waterwheel near the Gonzalez house and continuing with auxiliary offshoots skirting the plaza past the Sepulveda adobe and reaching beyond Main and Los Angeles streets. In a rather strange mixture of prevailing languages the river is marked *Rio Porciuncula* near the bottom of this map, but the word "ditch" is used almost exclusively to describe the auxiliary offshoots from the source. Kelleher's map not only shows the *zanjas* but also identifies the very people who depended on this source for water. The many vineyards—which were Los Angeles's first real agricultural successes—needed irrigation, and each and every name and place on the map depended on the *Zanja Madre*. Neatly numbered, the 111 landholders are listed with familiar names, like Olvera, Figueroa, Sepulveda, Stearns, Mascarel, Downey, Pico, and Lugo. Also appearing are the many properties owned by the Los Angeles City Water Company.

No. 148
1875
M. Kelleher
Manuscript
Huntington Library Rare Books

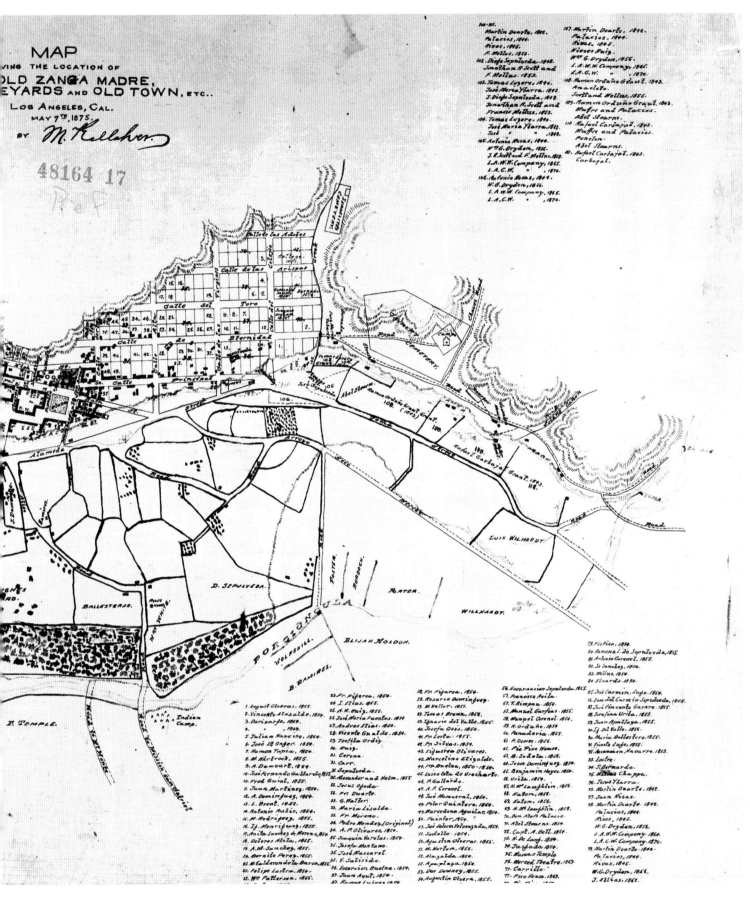

Map of the Reservoir Lands in the City and County of Los Angeles

As early as 1861 there were attempts to regulate and organize the water supply, but finally it was a company called the Los Angeles City Water Company (or the Aqueduct Company of Los Angeles) led by Prudent Beaudry that managed to finally convince the city to allow it to provide water to Los Angeles. In 1868 yet another group, headed by George Hansen, created the Los Angeles Canal and Reservoir Company, which looked to irrigate land to the west and north-west of the established city. Using Beaudry's idea to build a dam in the remote outlying areas to the northwest, the company eventually cut a deal to provide the city with zanjas serving this developing area and to build a large reservoir. Captain William Moore, a close friend of Hansen's and a highly regarded city surveyor in three different stints in the 1850s, '60s and '70s, created this map to show the lands around the proposed reservoir, which looks enormous on this map. Moore was a larger-than-life figure who grew impatient with the infrequent ship's passages from San Francisco and walked to Los Angeles in 1854 to begin his career there.

The course of the water brought from the river northwest of the plaza passed along what is now Glendale Boulevard. The building of a twenty-foot-high dam across a canyon in Echo Park created Echo Park Lake shown at the center of the map. The lots surrounding the bold-print reservoir once de-scribed as "several thousand acres of hill land" would provide payment for the services of the Los Angeles Canal and Reservoir Co. and eventually comprise the current-day neighborhood of Echo Park. An outlet ditch from the dam toward Pearl Street (later Figueroa) contained a seventy-eight-foot drop from dam to ditch that was later used to generate power for a woolen mill—the first industrial facility in the city. Echo Park Lake was Reservoir Number Four but the only one then planned that came to fruition. The water passed right through what is today the Silver Lake Reservoir, continuing to Echo Park.

Many a fortune was won and lost in the attempts to provide water to the citizens until the city bought out the private companies and created the Los Angeles Bureau of Water Works, appointing William Mulholland, once a ditch tender or "Deputy Zanjero" for the Los Angeles City Water Company, as superintendent. Mulholland began a series of projects that changed the face of Los Angeles, including the completion of the Los Angeles Aqueduct in 1913.

1870
Captain William Moore
Lithograph on linen
Seaver Center for Western History

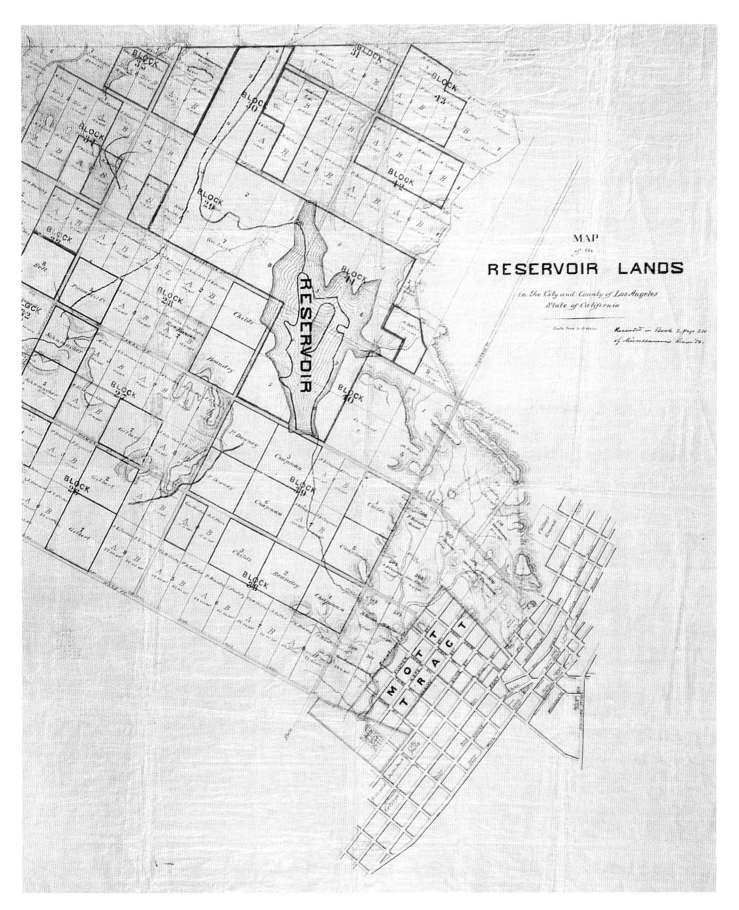

MAP
of the
RESERVOIR LANDS
in the City and County of Los Angeles
State of California

Topographic Map of the Los Angeles Aqueduct
and Adjacent Territory

From the day the first settlers set up their dwellings in Los Angeles, water was the crucial element for survival. At first, the Porciuncula River and the *zanja* system had been sufficient, but as the twentieth century approached it became apparent that supply could not meet demand. Population began doubling every few years, and the city faced a crisis of resources that would halt growth unless something miraculous could occur in the form of massive amounts of freshwater pouring into the city. This map, created by the Water Department of the City of Los Angeles, Board of Commisioners, represents an engineering miracle that delivered Los Angeles from drought—and that may be an understatement. It was estimated that the city would surpass one million residents by 1920, and it was also determined that the old water system could not possibly support more than 300,000 in a good year. The grand plan of the Los Angeles Aqueduct, seen here at the beginning of construction, would solve the problem of water in the city, but it took incredibly audacious and controversial actions to accomplish the feat and several truly extraordinary men to get the job done on time and under budget.

There was some luck but a lot of moxie involved on an innocent camping trip of Mayor Fred Eaton, when he fortuitously spied the huge amounts of freshwater in the Owens Valley far to the north, where it received melted snow from the eastern Sierra Nevada Mountains. Back in Los Angeles, the visionary head of the Los Angeles Water Department, William Mulholland, had been organizing his agency into a model of efficiency and progressive methods, but his calculations told him he had to find water elsewhere to supply a city that was using twenty-six million gallons a day. In July 1904, the consumption ominously exceeded inflow for the first time. Yet to Mulholland, who knew more about water than any man in the west, the Owens Valley seemed unrealistic.

Eaton had seen his opportunity for great things and pressed forward, joining former city engineer Joseph Barlow Lippincott and buying key properties along the route of the natural flow of those northern streams, which coincidentally could take the water entirely by the force of gravity all the way to the mountains north of Los Angeles. When Eaton, Lippincott, and Mulholland finally got together and looked hard at the possibilities, it was decided without any doubts that the Owens Valley was the only viable source of water crucial to the growth of the city of Los Angeles. That is what Mulholland told the Board of Water Commissioners, and despite much controversy from locals in the Owens Valley and accusations of impropriety among city officials posing as representatives of the Federal Reclamation Project, the aqueduct was beginning to take shape.

The *LA Times* blared "Titanic Project to Give City a River" on July 29, 1905, well before the city officially evaluated and accepted the challenge, naming William Mulholland chief engineer and asking the United States Senate for permission for right of way across federal lands to construct the aqueduct. Opposing forces asked President Theodore Roosevelt to intervene, but he wrote that the aqueduct would be "a hundred thousand fold more important to the state and more valuable to the people as a whole if used by the city than if used by the people of Owens Valley." The measure was passed on June 30, 1906, and the voters of Los Angeles approved a twenty-three-million-dollar bond in 1907. This map shows the incredible engineering endeavor of this world-record-breaking feat. There are a lot of numbers but they tell the story better than paragraphs: 233 miles between the beginning and end; 142 tunnels, spanning a total of 52 miles; 3,900 laborers working in heat up to 130 degrees and subfreezing conditions, with 43 dying during the construction; 215 miles of road; 230 miles of pipeline; 218 miles of power transmission line; 377 miles of telegraph and telephone wire; 57 camps for the men; and 3 large reservoirs along the way.

When the aqueduct was dedicated on November 5, 1913, 30,000 celebrants awaited at the Cascades, near the Newhall Pass in the Santa Clarita Valley. They were brought out from Los Angeles by the Southern Pacific Railway for one dollar, given bottles of genuine Owens Lake water, and waived little ten-cent pennants while a band played "Yankee Doodle Dandy." On the bandstand the city fathers sat sweating in the sun while the chief engineer unfurled the flag and president of the Board of Public Works, Lieutenant General Adna R. Chaffee, opened the gate's valves fed by Tunnel 104 of the Aqueduct system. As the first gallons of Owens Valley water gushed down into Los Angeles, Mulholland, a man of great intelligence but few words, turned the proceedings over to Mayor Henry Rose and millions of gallons of water over to the city with the eloquent "there it is Mr. Mayor, take it."

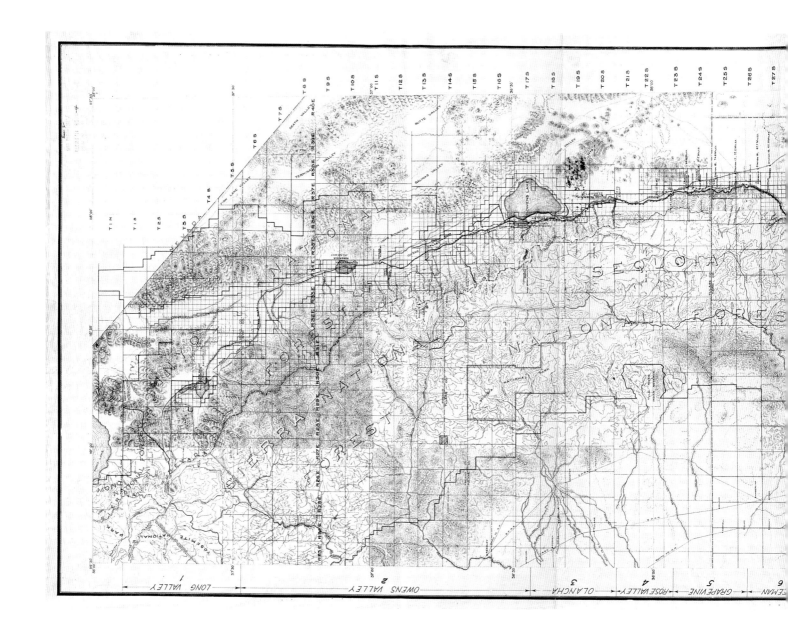

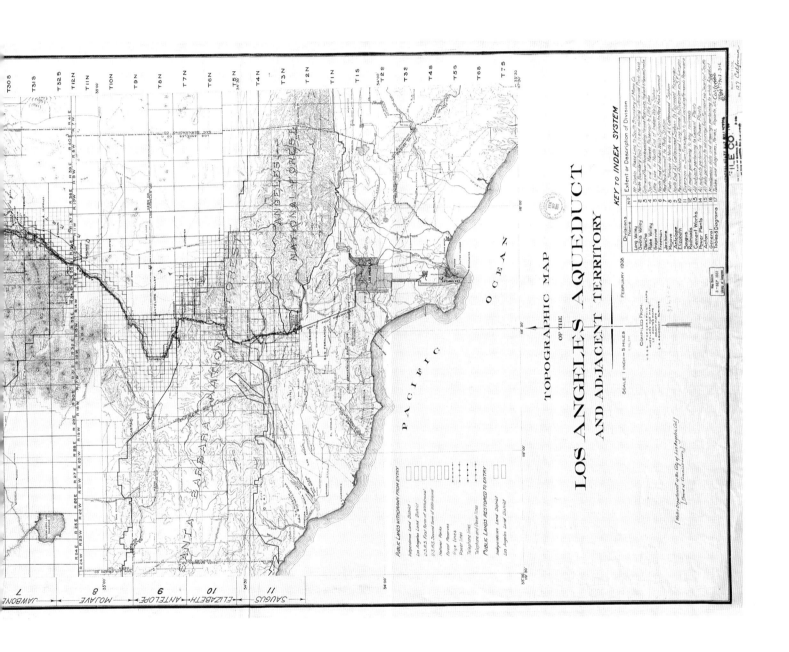

TOPOGRAPHIC MAP
OF THE
LOS ANGELES AQUEDUCT
AND ADJACENT TERRITORY

SCALE 1 INCH = 5 MILES   FEBRUARY 1908

COMPILED FROM

U.S.G.S. TOPOGRAPHIC MAPS
U.S.G.S. SECTIONAL MAPS
LS. COUNTY MAPS
L.A. AQUEDUCT SURVEYS

KEY TO INDEX SYSTEM

Divisions	Extent or Description of Division
Nᵒ Name	
1	Mt. Diablo Base Line to South Boundary of Mono Co.
Long Valley	2 North Boundary Inyo Co. to and including Wagwand River Basin
Owens Valley	3
Olancha	4
Rose Valley	5
Grapevine	6
Freeman	7
Jawbone	8
Mojave	9
Antelope	10
Elizabeth	11
Saugus	12
Fairmoaks	13
Cement Works	14
Power Plants	15
Arden	16
General	17 Tables & Diagrams

PUBLIC LANDS WITHDRAWN FROM ENTRY

Inagependence Land District
Los Angeles Land District
U.S.R.S. First Form of Withdrawal
U.S.R.S. Second Form of Withdrawal
National Parks
Forest Reserves
Pipe Lines
Power Lines
Telephone Lines
Telephone and Power Lines

PUBLIC LANDS RESTORED TO ENTRY

Independence Land District
Los Angeles Land District

Mapping Los Angeles' Missing River
by Joe Linton

"Every map is a fiction. Every map offers choices."
— D.J. Waldie, *Holy Land*

Early on, the Los Angeles River was hard to miss. In 1769, in the earliest extant written account of the Los Angeles area, the Spanish explorer Father Juan Crespi describes the confluence of the L.A. River and the Arroyo Seco as a "lush and pleasant place in every respect." He was, of course, ten thousand years late—the Tongva Native Americans were already well aware of the river, and probably had already mapped it beautifully and reverently.

Mapping and surveying of local waterways and adjacent topology was critical for the construction of the city's initial large-scale public work: the digging of the *Zanja Madre*, completed in 1781. *Zanja Madre* is Spanish for "mother ditch." The network of *zanjas* would soon become an extensive canal system linking the young pueblo with river. Nearly all the *zanjas* utilized topographic contours, hence the system was almost entirely gravity fed. The exceptions to this were a couple of current-driven water wheels which lifted water up to higher contoured *zanjas*. A chunk of the mid-1800s *Zanja Madre*, by then a covered brick culvert, is visible today along the Metro Gold Line tracks at Los Angeles State Historic Park.

The river is a prominent reference point in early maps of *El Pueblo de la Reina de los Angeles* (already shortened from an even longer Spanish title, but soon to be known merely as "L. A.") including Jose Arguello's 1793 mapping of the early plaza and agricultural fields. The river remains central in H. J. Stevenson's 1884 city map (p. 49) ... but then the river starts getting lost.

There are clues to the disappearing river evident in the June 1919 *Map of the Los Angeles River from Los Angeles City Limits to the Pacific Ocean* (p. 100), by the Office of Engineer Maintenance of Way, Los Angeles and Salt Lake Railroad. This exquisite, large-scale map shows the curvy natural lines of the mighty Los Angeles superimposed with the stark, straight lines of the concrete levee walls that would soon encase it.

Due to frequent flooding exacerbated by encroaching development, the region's leaders called in the federal government to "improve" the river. Massive floods in 1917, 1934, and 1938 killed hundreds of people and wiped out homes, businesses, and bridges. The river that nourished the early pueblo became more of a liability than an asset. From the mid-1930s to the early 1960s, at a cost of more than five billion in today's dollars, the once lush and pleasant river was straightened, deepened, and reinforced—then largely forgotten.

The river shrank in prominence in mid-twentieth-century maps. Even when shown, the word river disappears, replaced by the anonymous "Los Angeles County Flood Control Channel," as the river is titled on a 1938 map of Los Angeles' harbor and vicinity. Gradually the freeway system became the navigational touchstone for mapping L. A. The river, nearly entirely encased in concrete, became unmapped ... invisible, hidden ... and no longer perceived as a river.

In the late twentieth century, environmental movements emerged that reconnected great cities with the great rivers running through their cores. Indeed, historic rivers on which the cities were founded. In the 1980s, poets, dreamers, and artists begin to rediscover, reclaim, and restore the Los Angeles River. Elaborate hand-drawn historical maps and surveys guide our way. They show us how to restore and reconnect. We begin drawing new maps.

By hand, I drew a few of these new maps: kids' river scavenger hunt maps, diagrams showing where future bikeways could go, guides for walking, bicycling, and viewing historic bridges. My fellow creek freaks, especially Jessica Hall, use computerized mapping tools to superimpose historic watercourses onto the contemporary landscape, revealing remnant layers of the urban palimpsest. These guide us to forgotten stretches of barely surviving creeks and springs. We begin to tell these histories and to describe a future in which the Los Angeles River is renewed. The renewed river reconnects with the life of the city to which it had given birth.

We look forward to the new landscapes and the new maps that will emerge.

Map of the Los Angeles River from Los Angeles City Limits to the Pacific Ocean

No aspect of the landscape of Los Angeles has been so demeaned and underappreciated as the Los Angeles River. Orientations on maps from the Ord Survey to today are defined by the old river, which was the life's blood of local Native Americans from long before the *Pobladores* came north to found the pueblo. The earliest settlers in the region carved *zanjas* off the river to supply their needs. The flow of this watercourse nourished the people, animals, and crops quite adequately in the early days of the city. The Porciuncula, or later the Los Angeles River, was about fifty miles long and remained relatively unimpeded for more than 130 years.

Up until the connection of the aqueduct in 1913, the Los Angeles River was the chief source of drinking water and irrigation for agriculture. The overpumping of groundwater dried stretches of its bed, which became dumping grounds for every kind of refuse created by the rapidly growing city. By the early twentieth century, this overused and abused river was wrung out and became almost an afterthought as a source of water for the city.

While the Los Angeles River is on most maps, this is one of the few that ignores much of its surroundings and just focuses on the course of the waterway. The map shows southeast Los Angeles County, where floods were common but water was needed for farming. The creation of this Office of Engineer map may have taken some time, from the end of World War I to its publishing in 1919, since it accompanied studies and proposals to find a storm drain system. This tracing of its flow was not a celebration of the positive gifts that the river gave but a fearful plan to tame the floodwaters that had plagued the entire area throughout history. In the early twentieth century, during dry seasons, this part of the river looked more like a broad, sandy, dry wash. The summer dryness was deceptive, because in winter the banks would be breeched by floods caused by storms that roared across the basin and brought torrents down from the mountains toward the flatlands shown here. There were few levees in the city, and the population was lulled into complacency by frequent droughts or just normal rainfall producing less than fifteen inches a year and making the river look tame to the many new arrivals who populated the outlying areas.

This map was drawn by the newly created Los Angeles County Engineer's Office. Its small staff of three engineers, led by James Reagan, attempted to determine an improved course for the unreliable river. They focused on the confluence of the Los Angeles and Hondo rivers, where a dike and diversion canal were planned with moneys provided by congress. A major aim of the flood control plan was to divert the river from the harbor, which was now of greater economic importance due to the opening of the Panama Canal in August 1914. Flood control had been almost nonfunctional in the city during the disastrous flood of 1914, when rain fell at an inch an hour, portions of southeast county were devastated, and three million cubic feet of silt were dumped into Long Beach and Los Angeles harbors. The silt hampered navigation and commerce, so several forces drove the local governments to find a way to tame the floods and keep the harbors clean.

The effort was filled with controversy, and Reagan struggled against adversaries that eventually included Mayor Frederick Woodman, the *Los Angeles Times*, the Chamber of Commerce, and farmers who wanted the river's water for their crops. Still, the first Los Angeles County flood control bond issue passed by fifty-one votes, green-lighting Reagan's plan to divert the river south at Dominguez into a reinforced channel that would empty into the ocean between Long Beach Harbor and nearby downtown Long Beach.

The county's population boomed, with two million people coming into the area between 1900 and 1930. Partially completed flood control measures proved inadequate in 1938, when another huge flood killed 115 people. The flood control plans morphed into a massive project by the Army Corps of Engineers, which turned most of the river into a concrete flood channel.

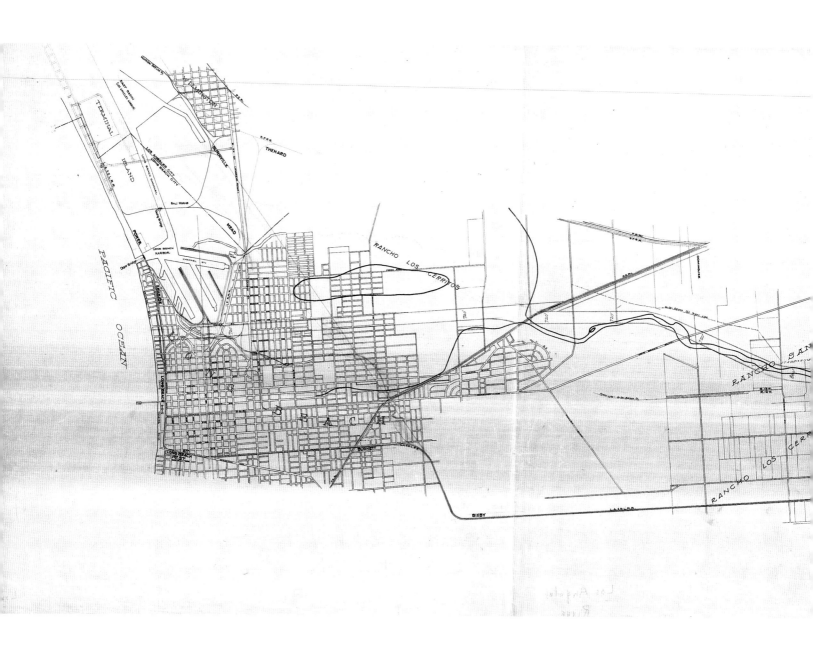

1919
Office of Engineer M of W, LA & SLRR (Maintenance of Way, Los
Angeles, and Salt Lake Railroad)
James Reagan, Los Angeles County Engineer
Lithograph on oilskin
72″ x 21″
Los Angeles Public Library

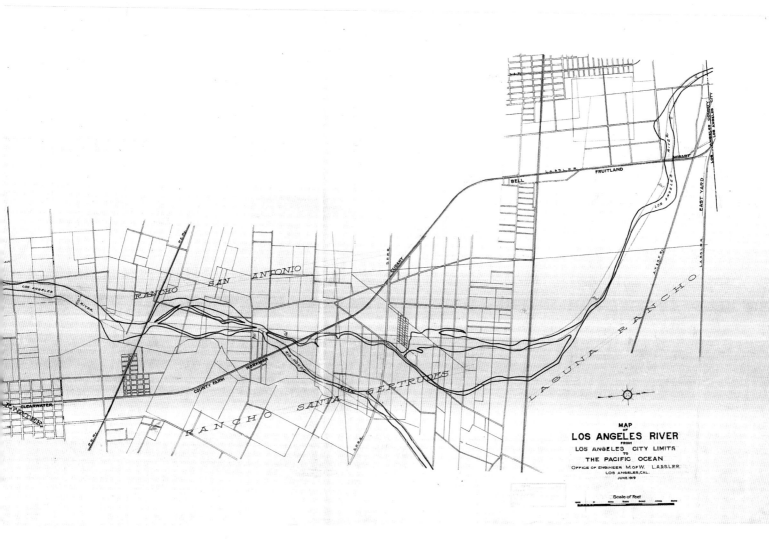

MAP
OF
LOS ANGELES RIVER
FROM
LOS ANGELES CITY LIMITS
TO
THE PACIFIC OCEAN
OFFICE OF ENGINEER M.OF W. L.A.&S.L.R.R.
LOS ANGELES,CAL.
JUNE 1919

Scale of Feet

Map of the Proposed Sewer System for the City of Los Angeles

As the population swelled and real estate boomed, there were long-standing issues that the city had to address. Such big-city amenities as street lighting, road paving, and sewage systems were becoming unavoidable necessities as thousands of people flocked to the southland. European cities like London and Paris had seen epidemics brought on by poor handling of urban wastewater, and the science of building efficient sewers was being developed around the globe. The first sewer committee in Los Angeles was formed in 1869, and Robert LeCouvrier prepared a lengthy paper outlining possible solutions for the of Los Angeles Common Council in 1870. There was no real sewage system in the early days of the city—much of the city's waste went into the *zanja* system, which was showing signs of pollution so severe laws were passed to prohibit such dumping. Once again the Southern Pacific and Santa Fe railroads' arrival between 1876 and 1885, with the accompanying rapid increase in population, accelerated the demand for a real infrastructure in the city. The quest for an adequate sewage system proved to be one of the most controversial and complicated in municipal history.

In 1886 alone, one hundred new homes were being built each month, and public works projects abounded, including eighty-seven miles of paved road and eighty miles of streetcar tracks, along with street lighting and one public building after another. Luckily, the city had the right man at the right time in city engineer Fred Eaton, who had extensive experience in water management working for the Los Angeles Water Company, first as a fifteen-year-old apprentice and then as a general superintendent. In March 1887 Mayor William Workman asked Eaton for a recommendation for a city sewer system, which he brought back within weeks. Then the City Council asked Eaton to consult with noted sanitarian Col. George E. Waring, and by May they had agreed on an interior sewerage system with an outfall to the sea. There would be three interceptor systems to handle a population of 200,000 people, include the east side of the city and featuring a twelve-mile outfall extending to the ocean south of Ballona Creek. The same area that is now filled with rather tony development on land that was once served by sewage. Again the Council asked Eaton to consult an expert, and he turned to Dr. Rudolph Hering, the well-regarded sanitarian who had solved a Chicago sewage problem. Hering prepared a twenty-three-page report that accompanied this map as it was presented to the Council on September 12, 1887. To do the job right, without polluting the ocean at the end of the outfall, Eaton and Hering calculated the cost at a whopping one million dollars. Workman promptly vetoed the plan the next month and set forth a battle that waged for years, featuring several rejections by the voters and hundreds of letters to the editors of local papers, mostly concerning the outfall and the twelve miles of sewage passing through the city.

1887
Fred Eaton
Endorsed by Rudolph Hering
Los Angeles Lithographic Co.
Hand-colored lithograph
Huntington Library

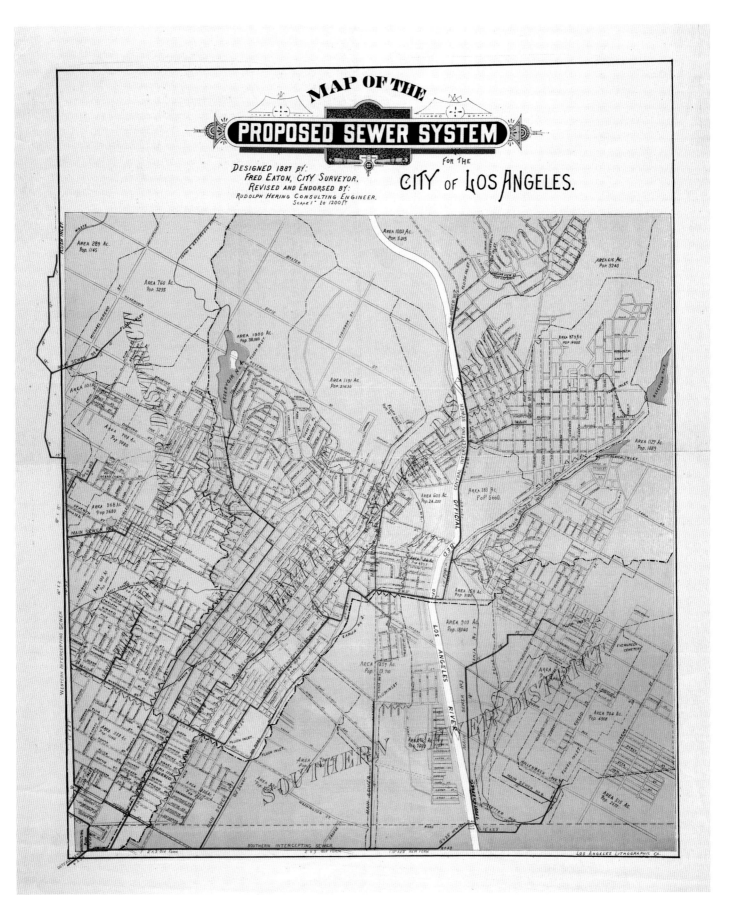

MAP OF THE
PROPOSED SEWER SYSTEM
FOR THE
CITY OF LOS ANGELES.

Designed 1887 by:
Fred Eaton, City Surveyor,
Revised and Endorsed by:
Rudolph Hering Consulting Engineer.
Scale 1" to 1200 ft

USGS Topo

The great national mapping project of the United States Geological Survey reached Los Angeles in 1893 after starting and stopping across the country for fourteen years. Existing under various names and agencies since midcentury, the USGS had been charged in 1879 by president Rutherford B. Hayes to perform the "classification of public lands," surveying 1.2 billion acres of land. In the beginning, the surveying and mapping was intended to support agriculture, but later, as the country changed from an agrarian to an industrial economy, the need for roads, canals, the location of mineral deposits, and water sources became most important. The creation of such surveys dates back to the Land Ordinance of 1785, with its rectangular survey system that divided the landscape into townships and ranges. Thanks to the gold rush, California had one of the few state geologic surveys and a map done in 1891 by the State Mining Bureau that inspired in part the larger effort of a national survey.

While there were some countywide maps of Los Angeles from the nineteenth century, none matches the detail and broad scope of the USGS quadrangle. Created by an eight-man team under the supervision of Director Charles D. Walcott, and then reprinted during the term of George Otis Smith, this map is a sort of bridge between two worlds. Surveyed originally in 1893–94, the city had an inkling of the future with the discovery of oil, the establishment of the Los Angeles Railway, and several land booms that had begun the outward sprawl that continued for another century. The scale translates to approximately one inch to the mile, and about 50,000 people inhabited the expanse shown here. Sold for five cents a sheet at the downtown offices of Stoll and Thayer, the Los Angeles quadrangle was announced for sale in the newspaper on April 28, 1897. The map still maintains the old rancho names, seen in bold print, yet divides the land into townships and shows the rail tracks coming in from the sparsely populated San Fernando Valley through vanished stops like Redcastle, Gaston, Threemile House, and Bennington. Steam and street rail lines crisscross the landscape, heading toward the harbor at San Pedro, west to Santa Monica, east to San Bernardino, and even up the Mount Lowe street rail above Pasadena. The area is wide open, with small population clusters in downtown Los Angeles, East Los Angeles, and Pasadena, or along any of the rail lines. There is a sort of distilled history of the city in the places on this map with both Mission San Gabriel and San Fernando lands, along with the water-poor city's Echo Park Reservoir, the new development of Hollywood, the Soldiers Home in Westwood with its eight hundred residents, and vast suburban spaces like the San Gabriel and San Fernando valleys. Many of the place-names have changed or just became neighborhoods as the city spread and gobbled up individual communities, placing them under the L.A. umbrella. Tropico became part of Glendale, Garvanza joined Highland Park, Shorb became part of Alhambra, Colegrove took up with Hollywood, Vernondale dropped the idyllic "dale" and became industrial Vernon, Ivanhoe is now part of Silver Lake, and Roscoe became sunnier-sounding Sun Valley.

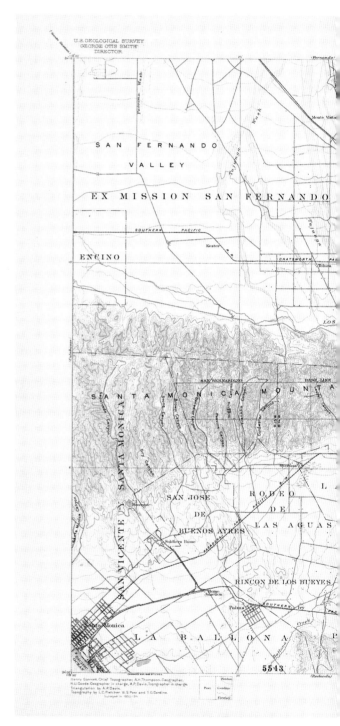

Los Angeles Quadrangle
September 1900 edition
Surveyed 1893–94
Reprinted August 1908
1:62,500 scale
Printed map
31" x 19"
Los Angeles Public Library

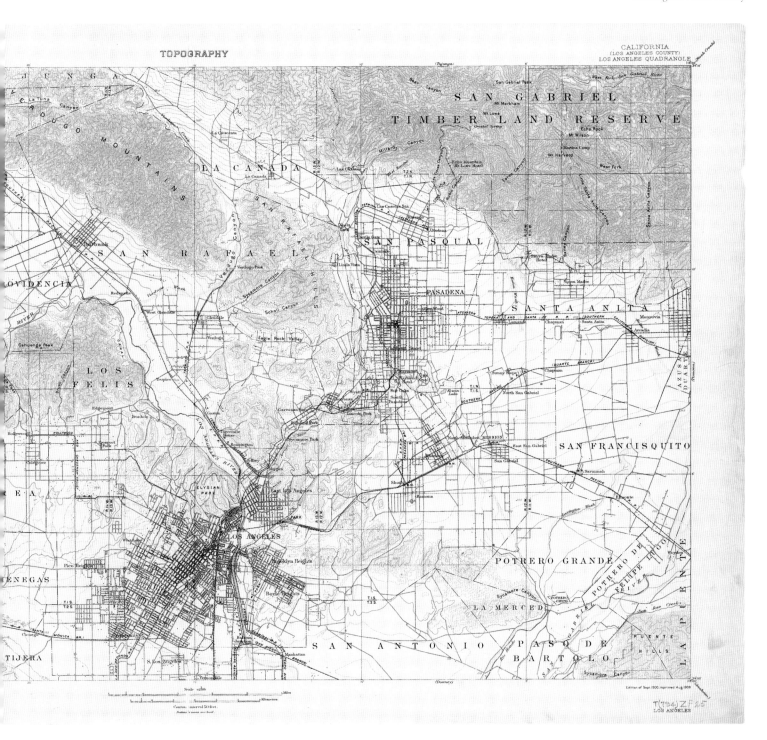

Official Transportation Map of Pacific Electric Railway System Centering in Los Angeles, Cal.

I n these days so far removed from turn-of-the-century mass transit, it is hard to underestimate the critical role of the Pacific Electric Railway's beloved "Big Red Cars" in the growth of the city of Los Angeles and the spread of suburbs across the landscape. Those streetcars traveled from downtown to the San Fernando Valley; to beach cities as far south as Balboa; to far-flung San Bernardino, Orange, and Riverside counties; to points east as far away as Redlands; and north to the romantic and glorious Mount Lowe high above Pasadena. Once the greatest mass transportation system in the world, the Red Cars at their peak stretched over eleven hundred miles of track and had nine hundred cars in service, including six thousand trains a day from the Los Angeles terminal alone.

Trolleys or streetcars began in the city as early as spring 1874 but were generally limited to small areas in downtown Los Angeles. At first horses or mules pulled them, but by the late 1880s electricity took the place of the dray animals—with limited success initially. However, when a powerful railroad family, the Huntingtons, got involved in 1898, things began to change rapidly. Henry, the nephew of Collis P. Huntington of the Southern Pacific Railroad, eventually absorbed several separate street rail operations and placed them under the Pacific Electric Railway name. Many were narrow gauge, but those slated to be the initial segments of interurban lines were standard gauged, meaning the rails were spaced four feet, eight and a half inches apart. Eventually, remaining local trolley lines were incorporated into the three foot, six-inch narrow gauge of the Los Angeles Railway. Huntington saw opportunity in developing areas where the streetcars would eventually travel and purchased much of the desirable land near where the Pacific Electric would place tracks. Other interested parties like Harrison Gray Otis of the *Los Angeles Times* helped by publicizing the opportunities and charms of these far-flung communities with names like Monrovia, Redondo, or Glendale. With the "Big Red Cars" connecting all parts of the county and beyond, the sticks suddenly became the suburbs.

The price of travel was kept relatively low, and in 1928 one could ride anywhere in the city "a day for a dollar"—journeys that offered fifty separate communities to visit. Angelenos could get on a Red Car and ride to Venice beach or Hollywood or just go a dozen stops to Chutes Park for baseball games or a visit to the water slide and zoo. Hikers could take the cars to the foot of the San Gabriels and stroll into the wilderness. The Balloon Route seen here progressed from downtown through Hollywood, out to Santa Monica, Venice, and Redondo, passing Culver City on its way back downtown to 6th and Main. On trips out to places like Long Beach or San Bernardino the cars could travel at speeds approaching sixty miles per hour, announcing their approach with the blast of the trademark air horn. Describing the system *Sunset Magazine* said, "Los Angeles is the center and heart of the most highly developed interurban electric system in the whole world."

Eventually the automobile began to make inroads, and traffic downtown, where all the Red Cars seemed to meet, became intense enough to call for other solutions. In 1927 buses were added to the system, but the

(text continues on following page)

1911
Laura L. Whitlock
Colored lithograph
Los Angeles Public Library
Rare Books Department

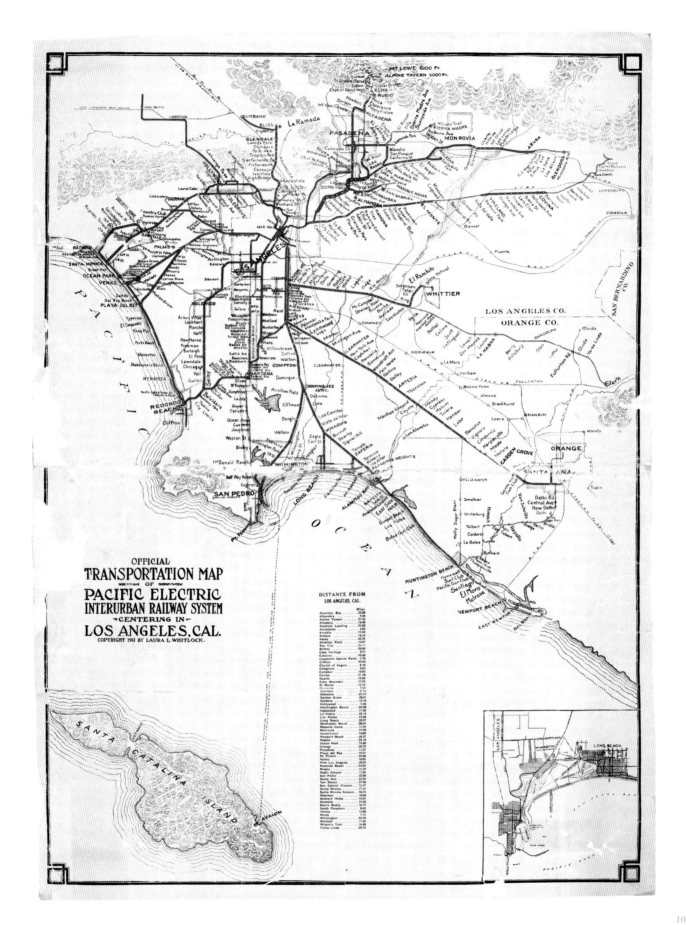

Go Places with the Los Angeles Transit Lines

(text continued from previous page)

rails continued to hum. Despite an all-time high of 109 million passengers in 1945, the Red Car's days were numbered, and when the company was sold to National City Lines, their fate was sealed. Much has been written and said about concerted efforts by several industries to eradicate electric-powered mass transit and their desire to change the city to one of automobiles and gasoline-powered buses. What is certain is that the streetcars, the Big Red Cars (which struggled to April 1961), and the final five Yellow Car lines of the Los Angeles Railway were all gone by March 1963.

The maps shown here represent two versions of the streetcar era in Los Angeles. The first clearly shows the sprawl of Pacific Electric across two of the four counties in the Southern California area, with lines stretching toward Orange County, while offering exhaustive stops radiating out from the downtown headquarters of P. E., stretching from the Alpine Tavern atop Mt. Lowe to Pt. Fermin in San Pedro, where one could hop on a ferry for a short sail to Catalina Island. This wall map was probably available for travelers to consult before embarking on journeys to towns that were only names heard on the radio or places where infrequently seen relatives might live. According to this big picture view, one could jump on a trolley downtown in the late morning and be in exotic Newport Beach for lunch, or ride out to historic Pasadena in just forty-five minutes. One can look at this map and understand just how the population exploded outward toward the suburbs, with the electric cars acting as the vanguard of this new Los Angeles. In 1924 Pacific Electric reached its maximum extension of rail lines. This map is further distinguished as the product of Laura J. (sometimes listed as L.) Whitlock, official map-maker of Los Angeles county, California, and the country's only female map publisher at that time. Six plates of Miss Whitlock's meticulously researched and drawn Official Map of Los Angeles were destroyed in the *Los Angeles Times* bombing of October 1911, leaving her with only the tracings and rights to original surveys done by the city and railways. In the meantime, 20,000 pirated copies were printed and sold around the city, which caused Whitlock to file suit for infringement of copyright. After a grueling eight-day trial, she managed to win her suit and set an important precedent for map copyright. This map, a by-product of that larger work, is one of the very best and most detailed of all streetcar line maps, including hundreds of place-names that have vanished in the ensuing decades. The map also shows in the inordinate amount of "gun clubs" that abounded across the southland for some reason. Here also is an unusual table of distances in metric form from the depot at 6th and Main in downtown Los Angeles. The second, a fold-out map that could be tucked into a gentleman's coat pocket or a lady's purse, is smaller in scale but greater in detail on individual lines. By this time the streetcar's days were numbered, but the system was still efficient and widespread, with much of the basic P.E. outline surviving until 1950. Although this tidy map shows the peak of ridership in the urban area during World War II, it looks toward the era of gasoline-powered buses and automobiles that was looming. Now the routes of the internal combustion coaches joined the lines of the old red and yellow cars, but the rails would be paved over and all would be swept away by the freeways that overtook this once-excellent public transportation system. Still, the designations of lines on this map such as the J-Car and the V-Car and places like "the loop" in Huntington Park at Palm and Seville certainly evoke many warm memories for Los Angelenos.

Official Route Map,
Los Angeles Transit Lines
1945
Los Angeles Transit
Printed map
Los Angeles Public Library

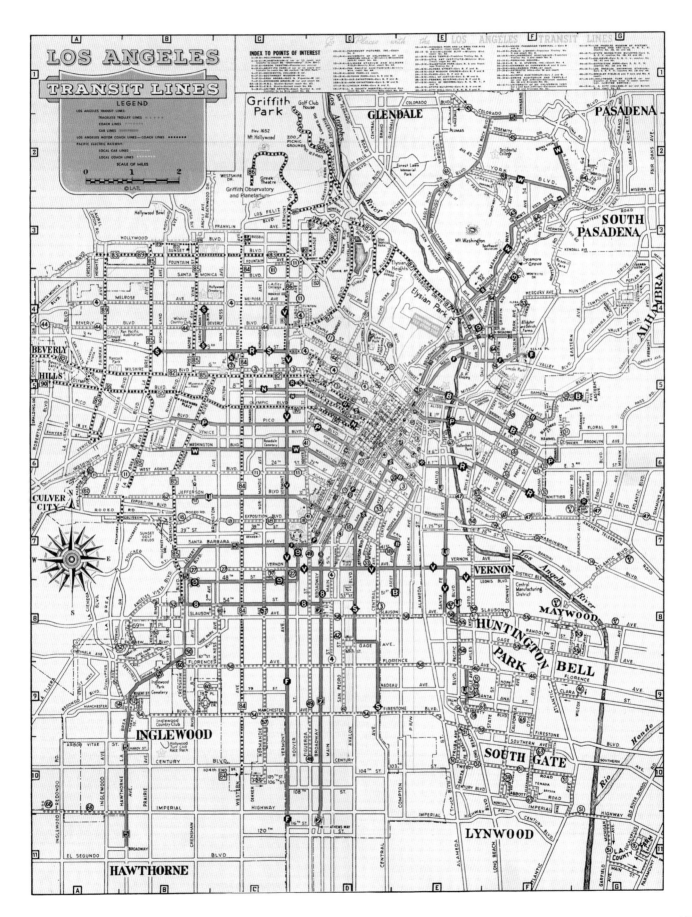

Map of Los Angeles County

The story of the development of the Los Angeles Harbor and the maps that show the transformation from the marshy salt flats first seen there in the sixteenth century to the most productive port in the country could fill a book on its own. We can only hint at the complex progression and add a few names of those giants who went a long way toward supplying the city and creating international commerce that allowed Los Angeles to grow faster than any other metropolitan area in America. Two maps seen here demonstrate the growth and several transformations of the harbor, but they are merely two of many. The first is a simple city wall map created for advertising purposes by the Woodward Hotel in 1912. It shows the entire county of Los Angeles but, more important, it delineates the city limits, including the curious shoestring addition that was annexed just six years before. This was a city readying itself for two major developments that would transform it into an industrial powerhouse. At the time of this map, commercial fishing, shipbuilding, canneries, and lumber shipping for construction across the southland consumed the port.

Seeing the crucial need to control the harbor—with the completion of the Panama Canal on August 15, 1914, promising to increase trade dramatically—the city needed to annex San Pedro and Wilmington, which could not finance the improvements necessary for the huge boost in demand. However, the city charter prohibited this, since the land for annexation had to be contiguous to the existing boundaries. The city petitioned the state to provide legislation, and eventually the Consolidation Act was passed, leading to an election to approve the annexation of this "shoestring." There was some resistance from existing landowners in those areas, but after a couple of tries the city managed to complete the deal in 1909. Voters in both Wilmington and San Pedro overwhelmingly approved entering into the "protection" of the big city. Los Angeles sweetened the deal by providing a ten-million-dollar bond for improvements, along with schools, a library, police, a fish market, and freshwater.

As seen on this map by James P. Chadwick, the strip was close to a half-mile across, stretching from the southernmost boundary of the city of Los Angeles while extending down to Gardena through mostly farms and open land, where it abruptly moved to the right in a westerly direction for a mile and then continued south to the limits of the cities on the coastline. With this creative cartography, the city provided a path and a greater Los Angeles with the harbor intact. The city gained 18.64 square miles of territory in the shoestring and almost ten from Wilmington, plus nearly five from San Pedro.

The harbor began as mud flats and marshes that were used first by the San Gabriel mission monks who brought ox carts back and forth the long forty miles to trade with ships that anchored a mile off the coast and sent long boats to shore. The Spanish government had forbidden trade with foreigners, but such laws were mostly ignored and the area thrived, trading tallow and fur with European vessels that supplied household goods, textiles, and precious sugar. By the time Mexico lifted restrictions in the 1820s, the bay of San Pedro and surroundings was a going concern. When Phineas Banning founded New San Pedro in 1857, he began a center of transportation and commerce that included the area's first rail lines along with fifteen stagecoaches and fifty wagons that traveled constantly from what later became Wilmington. From this small community Banning traded with five western states. Over the latter parts of the nineteenth century the need for a deep-water facility became more and more pressing, and despite competition from Santa Monica to create such a port, a Board of Army Engineers appointed by congress chose San Pedro and Wilmington as the one to develop. The Los Angeles Board of Harbor Commissioners was created and improvements began, including an 8,500-foot rock breakwater, and around 1911 the main channel was widened to eight hundred feet and dredged to thirty feet to accommodate the vessels of that era. In 1912 the Southern Pacific Railroad completed the first major wharf, which enabled loading and unloading right at the docks. By the 1920s the Los Angeles Harbor had become the second largest in the United States and in 1928 handled 26.5 tons of cargo, a record that stood for decades.

1912
James P. Chadwick
Hotel Woodward
Colored lithograph
Los Angeles Public Library

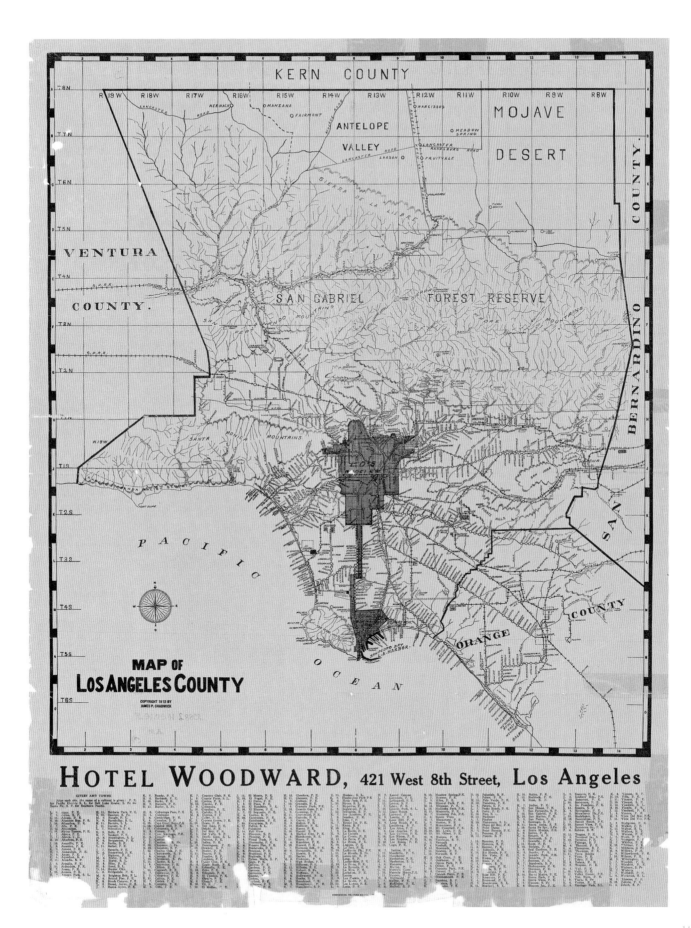

MAP OF
Los Angeles County

COPYRIGHT 1912 BY
JAMES P. CHADWICK

HOTEL WOODWARD, 421 West 8th Street, Los Angeles

Los Angeles Harbor and Vicinity

This map created by the Board of Harbor Commissioners shows the harbor in 1947 after the war effort that transformed the place into a shipbuilding center. The 1937 breakwater extension of 18,500 feet made possible the industry that employed 90,000 people and produced yet another population boom in the area. Los Angeles alone produced 17 percent of goods for the war effort, including twenty-six destroyers from one company. In the center is Terminal Island, once a mudflat where martial law was declared after the attack on Pearl Harbor, and the U.S. Fleet Air Base, where only sixteen planes stood guard at the onset. At Reservation Point, on the southwest corner of Terminal Island, sits the low-security Federal Penitentiary, where Al Capone once resided and refurbished furniture. The outer harbor, the deep-water harbor once dreamed of by pioneers, is fleshed out with six hundred acres of anchorage space. We see the multifaceted docks, which include commercial fisheries, shipbuilding, railroad freight operations, oil production and transport, lumber carriers, passenger ship berths, and even a seaplane anchorage. The map includes depths of water, sometimes as deep as forty feet, and the surrounding land features, including the many oil fields of Union Oil, Richfield, General Petroleum, and Shell. Point Fermin, with the famous lighthouse that was turned into a lookout tower during the war, is at the southwest point, and Fort Macarthur, with its gun batteries for protection of the harbor, sits at the strategic spot near the west channel. Mormon Island, once an attempted religious colony from the 1850s, is now connected to the mainland. Rattlesnake Island, which was renamed Terminal Island, and Dead Man's Island, which was dredged away in an improvement undertaken in 1928, have vanished and are just names from the past.

1947
City of Los Angeles Board
of Harbor Commissioners
Printed map
30″ x 24″
Los Angeles Public Library

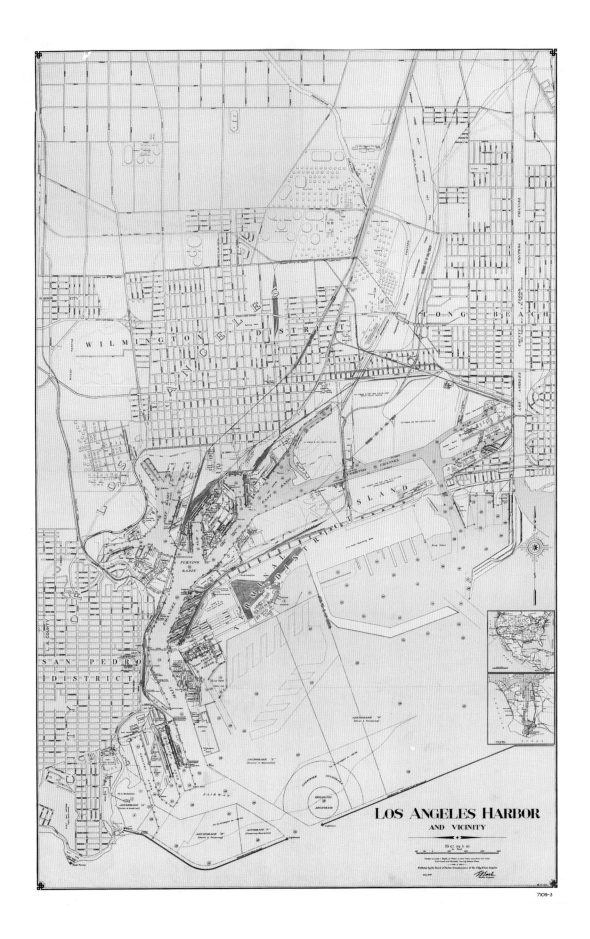

LOS ANGELES HARBOR
AND VICINITY

Scale
in Feet

Published by the Board of Harbor Commissioners of the City of Los Angeles

July 1947

Road Map of Eden: The Auto Club Charts Southern California's Growth

by Morgan P. Yates

The year was 1900, and the road system in Los Angeles consisted largely of unpaved tracks laid out by the dictates of cart paths, wagon roads, and railroad lines that embodied the transportation modes of the past century. Outside the city, dirt paths known only to locals crisscrossed the surrounding orchards and ranches. No signs marked the way. Roads filled with dust in dry weather and turned treacherously muddy when it rained. Developers built roads to serve their new residential areas with no regard for street alignments in neighboring subdivisions. City officials exercised little or no planning oversight. Horse-drawn vehicles and later cable and electric streetcar systems spread their independent transit lines over the landscape. Long before the automobile, traffic chaos and confusion reigned in Los Angeles.[1]

And yet, few objected to this state of affairs. By 1900 Southern California was still shaking off the mantle of frontier life. With its Mediterranean climate and abundant land, the sparsely populated south had attracted health seekers, retirees, and wealthy refugees from harsh Midwestern winters. People generally lived near where they worked and didn't need to travel far. When further destinations beckoned, carriage lines, railroads, or streetcars sufficed. But an agent of change was chugging its way onto the scene in the form of a carriage with its own motive power. Thus began the Age of the Automobile, which for better and worse changed the nature of mobility and the landscape in California and throughout the world. Intertwined with this story in Southern California is the history of the region's predominant motoring club and one of its signature member services: road mapping.

Images from pp. 114-119 are Courtesy of the Automobile Club of Southern California.

Ten affluent Los Angeles businessmen formed the Automobile Club of Southern California in December 1900. It was not the country's first auto club but within twenty years it would become the largest.[2] The club likely would not have survived as an institution had it not shed its original social-club trappings to embrace member and public service. This reorganization occurred in 1906, when the Auto Club adopted an agenda of service and advocacy, drastically reduced its entrance fee, and halved membership dues to $1 a month. The effect on revenues placed added emphasis on membership growth in order to fund the club's ambitious programs. "Join and Boost" became the club's motto.

Three related issues formed the core of the club's service ethic: good roads, suitable signage to mark the way, and informative maps to guide members on their travels. In 1905 Los Angeles County installed its first road markers—concrete mileposts indicating the distance from Los Angeles to outlying communities—but on the whole they proved inadequate. The following year the club took up the cause and created a Signposting Committee, which selected routes between Los Angeles and coastal cities from Santa Monica to Long Beach for its initial efforts. While some main routes were obvious, there was no clear road system to reflect the auto's potential for widespread mobility. Club officials chose additional routes to Santa Barbara and citrus belt hubs like Riverside to place signs, serving as de facto regional planners.

Gathering road information and disseminating it to members in map form grew out of the Auto Club's signposting efforts. The inaugural Tour Book appeared in 1909. It filled up 388 pages with nearly one hundred maps, extensive narrative route descriptions, listings of recommended garages and lodging, examples of Auto Club road signs, and a summary of motoring ordinances. The guide was free to members and sold for $2.50 to the general public. The club updated the guide in 1911, proclaiming, in the booster prose of the day, "that the information contained in this Tour Book is of the dependable and proven variety ... the Motorist may safely surrender himself to the charm of touring through this beautiful Sunny Southern California, where Nature has been so generous in her blessings for the pleasure of man."[3]

Expensive to produce, the tour guide also became quickly outdated. Consequently, the Auto Club's newly formed Touring Information Bureau adopted two new products more adaptable to the changing scene: the strip map, published in 1911, and the folding "area" map a year later.

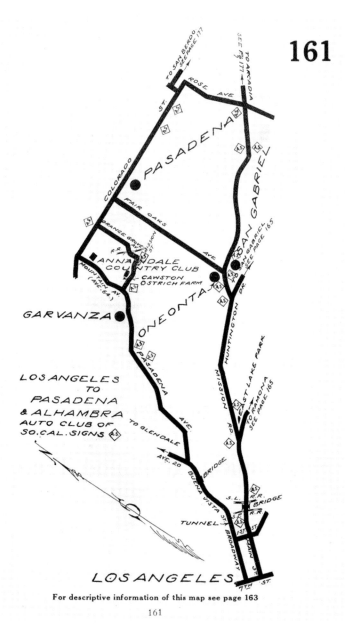

For descriptive information of this map see page 163

Each strip map charted a segment along a linear route, and its distinctive shape had as much to do with the way it was created as how it was used. A 1924 article in the club's member magazine, *Touring Topics*, described the process to readers. The two-person survey crew would sit side by side monitoring specialized instruments (compass, grade meter, altimeter, precisely calibrated odometers) with "one watching the right hand side of the road and the other the left, charting down cross-roads, turns, hills and every other important item .... When you consider the things that have to be accomplished while the car is rolling along at 30 miles an hour it seems almost incredible."[4] Notes from the survey were compiled and provided to the club's drafting department, which produced hand-inked master maps that were rechecked by the road-charting crews before going to the printing department.

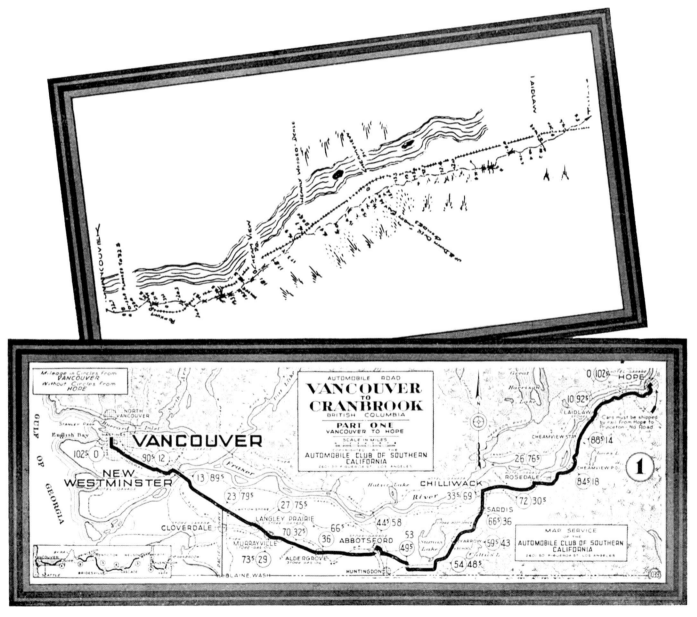

The handy maps measured 3.75″ by 10.5″ and were printed on heavy card stock, which made them durable and easy to use in the open vehicles of the day. Depicting routes in linear segments meant the club had to produce huge numbers of strip maps to address the expanding road network and increased demand by members. More than seven million were issued in 1923 alone, with two hundred new map titles added. Routes to scenic destinations and between major cities were particularly popular. The early maps utilized rudimentary topographical depictions of terrain and symbols for lodging, garages, and sources for gas, oil, and water. Steep grades and road surfaces were also sometimes noted. These details illustrate the conditions auto travelers faced in an era when such things could not be taken for granted.

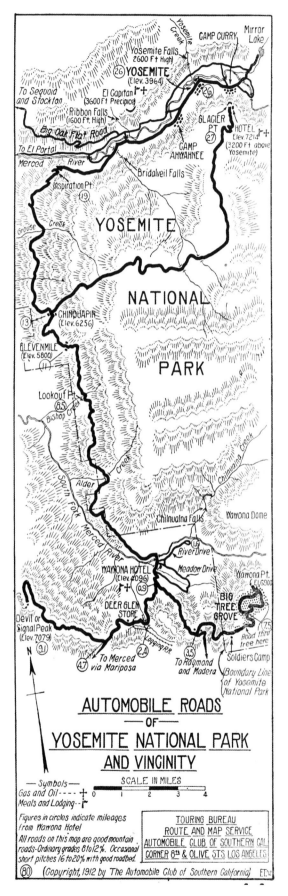

The Auto Club's early area or folded maps provided more general travel information and focused initially on the thirteen Southern California counties making up the club's service region. Area maps also concentrated on the Los Angeles area where the majority of club members lived. Over time club cartographers recognized the superiority of the folded map as a cartographic tool for an increasingly complex road system. During the 1920s, as car-oriented infrastructure spread over the landscape, the need diminished for marking locations of basic automotive necessities. Advances in power and durability greatly increased automotive range, and Auto Club maps evolved to keep pace while becoming more comprehensive and sophisticated. Strip maps appeared less often in members' glove boxes as the club phased them out in the early 1930s. They did live on in bound form in the club's many tour guides well into the 1950s.

The 1920s marked an era of mass migration to Southern California, which underwent a turbulent expansion and assumed the sprawling metropolitan character it retains today. Los Angeles became the first American city to experience the bulk of its growth following the advent of mass-produced automobiles. The regional oil industry boomed again and for a while supplanted agriculture as the state's top economic sector. Other industries blossomed, including moviemaking, aviation, and a host of manufacturing endeavors; the rise of the twin ports of Los Angeles and Long Beach further catalyzed regional economic expansion. During the 1920s Los Angeles snapped up surrounding communities in a flurry of annexation. With room to grow, Los Angeles residents spread out from downtown and came to rely increasingly on the automobile.

A monumental influx of people flowed into Los Angeles during the 1920s—people who were largely ignorant of their new surroundings. And with an intimate knowledge of the region's landscape borne of countless charting trips, the Auto Club's mapping department helped make the region comprehensible to the throng of newcomers. Compared to the beautiful artwork of gas company maps, which featured a compelling visual imagery of automobiling, the Auto Club's maps were rather plain. But they possessed quality where it counted, with the latest road and highway information regularly updated by the club's itinerant survey crews.

These maps succeeded in attracting many new members for the Auto Club. Commercial firms offered to print and sell the maps but the organization chose instead to make them available exclusively to members for free—a powerful enticement for people to join. Today the maps continue to be a signature benefit for club members.

ENDNOTES:

1. Matthew W. Roth, "Concrete Utopia: The Development of Roads and Freeways in Los Angeles, 1910–1950" (Ph.D. diss., University of Southern California, 2007), 34–47.

2. "President Baker's Annual Report," *Touring Topics*, March 1917, 11.

3. *The Automobile Club of Southern California Tour Book: A Careful Compilation of Maps and Touring Information* (Los Angeles: ACSC, 1911), 7.

4. William M. Henry, "The Evolution of the Strip Map," *Touring Topics*, September 1924, 15. The magazine changed its name to *Westways* in 1934 and marked its centennial of continuous publication in 2009.

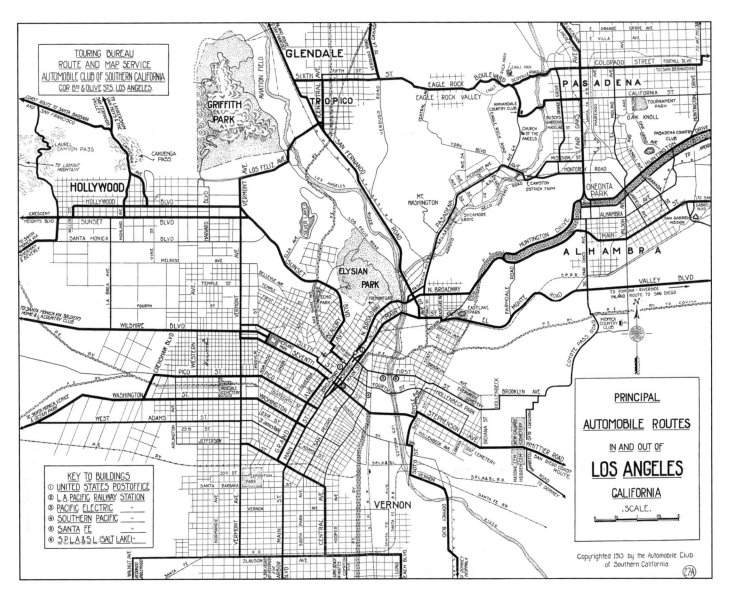

Road Map of Los Angeles and Vicinity

I t is more than ironic that this most instructive map, showing the basic geography of Los Angeles, was done by the Automobile Club years before freeways defined the city. While 1937 was the lull before the storm in Los Angeles politics and geography, the first freeway, the Arroyo Seco Parkway, was a full year away from starting construction and would not be completely finished until January 30, 1941. The sprawling metropolitan area would be altered by a devastating flood in 1938 that would change the infrastructure and landscape radically. The river seen here, meandering through the county from the San Fernando Valley all the way to Long Beach, would be turned to concrete by the Army Corps of Engineers in response to the flood damage before the close of the following year. The automobile had begun to make inroads on the fine streetcar system, and the major arteries are easily discernable here. East-west, we see Mission Road, Whittier Boulevard, Garvey, Huntington, Foothill, Ventura Boulevard, Firestone/Manchester, Wilshire, Atlantic, and San Fernando, along with the swath of the famed Route 66 passing from San Bernardino to Santa Monica. North-south shows Alameda, Long Beach Boulevard, Vermont, Western, Crenshaw, Lakewood/Rosemead, and the picturesque Pacific Coast Highway winding gracefully along the ocean front. Sepulveda stands alone covering a whopping seventy-six miles in this very vicinity.

On one hand the map evokes a time when local travel was done on surface streets or via streetcar, but on the other hand it shows the landscape of the metropolitan area perfectly. The cartographer renders the mountains, many valleys, and small canyons that characterize the surprisingly hilly coastal plains that stretch down to the irregular coastline. The mapmaker's art demonstrates graphically what makes Los Angeles so geographically unique in its place among major American cities.

While Southern California has been described as idyllic in the most glowing of terms, it also presents a few challenges to those who put down roots there. The reasons for the sometimes precarious nature of inhabitance in the area have a lot to do with its position flush against the dramatically rising trifecta of mountain ranges: the coastal, the peninsular, and the transverse, which have been called "the most complicated mountain range in America." The San Gabriel Mountains that form a kind of eastern boundary of Los Angeles offered tourists a wilderness within minutes of the urban center but were also part of the local challenges, with wildfires, floods, and mudslides that sometimes terrified the city lying at their feet. It is one of the steepest mountain fronts in the country, pushed upward by the infamous San Andreas Fault, which looms up from Lower California and snakes around the city on its way toward San Francisco. Earthquakes shake the city and at least ten major ones have rearranged the manmade environment from 1857 to the last devastating shake in 1994.

On the west and to the south is the Pacific Ocean, the once pure and delightfully temperate waters that are forever picturesque but sometimes too polluted for swimming due to sewage backing into bays. Still, the endless summer in the beach towns of Los Angeles county offers ocean swimming, yachting, surfing, and, with 329 days of sunshine a year, some of the most intriguing people watching on the planet.

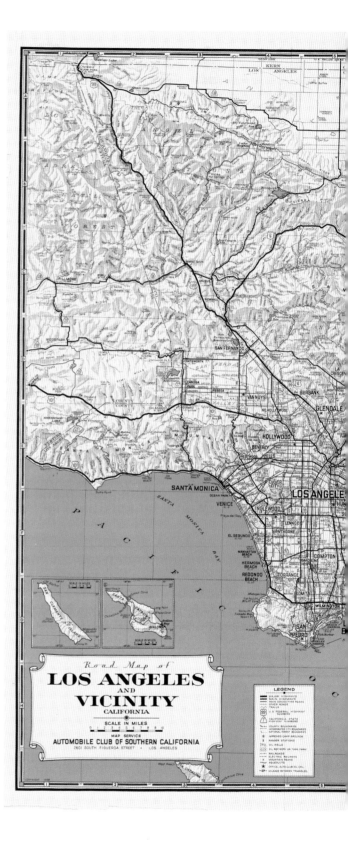

1937
Automobile Club of Southern California
Foldout map
Automobile Club of Southern California

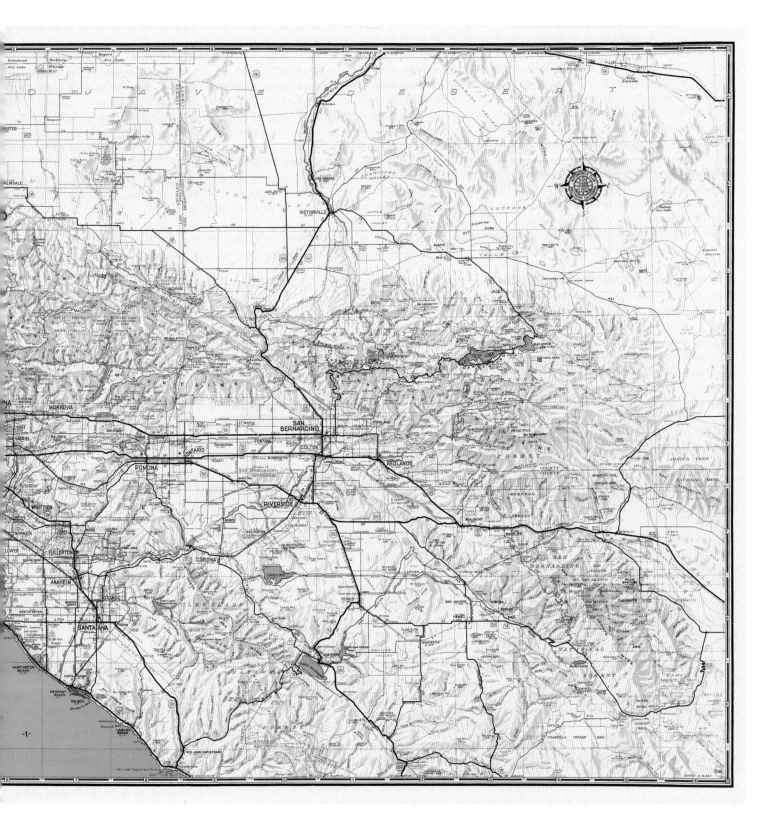

Rueger's Automobile and Miner's Road Map of
Southern California

Henry Rueger was an ambitious and energetic real estate cartographer in Los Angeles who created plat atlases filled with special features showing lots, lot numbers, block numbers, and subdivisions. These eighty-page reference atlases contained townships and ranges plus the names of all property owners with parcels over five acres in size. A list of subscribers was sought, and lithographic reproductions were created for this group, mostly realtors and developers in the county. Yet even Mr. Rueger could not have guessed at the irony of this sideline map made up with all the data collected in making the atlases. This Automobile and Miner's map is a blueprint for the future of the big metropolis that would grow in a rapid sprawl no one could have predicted when Rueger studied the land. President Theodore Roosevelt visited the Fiesta de las Flores that same year, speaking in front of 50,000 rowdy people at the 6th Street Park about Southern Californians' belief in "the future, irrigation, and the Navy." He was alluding to the opening of the Panama Canal that would thrust Los Angeles into the middle of an unprecedented commercial demand and put in motion a great industrial revolution in the city. While irrigation would feed the agriculture of the county, and the Navy might protect American interests on the West Coast, the future was very much about petroleum and industry. The railroads were in place, the aqueduct was on its way, oil was gushing from wells, and Angelinos were lifting their heads up and looking outward, along the roads traced in on this expansive map. Superimpose Rueger's map over one of today, and you will see one freeway route after another in place.

It is indeed ironic that the map contains paved and unpaved roads along with the scattered wells popping up all over the landscape. These same wells would eventually provide the fuel to power the internal combustion-engine automobiles that would offer a freedom unknown up to that time. Interspersed with the mine locations are the earliest routes to spread this auto culture ever outward, offering the ability to spread out from the center of downtown and transport goods from all over Southern California. The scale seems somewhat condensed, with communities bunched along street rail tracks giving San Bernardino and Orange County the appearance of suburbs, but scope seems to have been more important than perfect accuracy. Even though the speed limit was a crawling eight miles per hour and there were just fifteen automobile-related businesses in the city, Rueger guessed the need for a portable map to serve future "auto vagabonds" and entrepreneurs who would turn the city into a full-fledged metropolis.

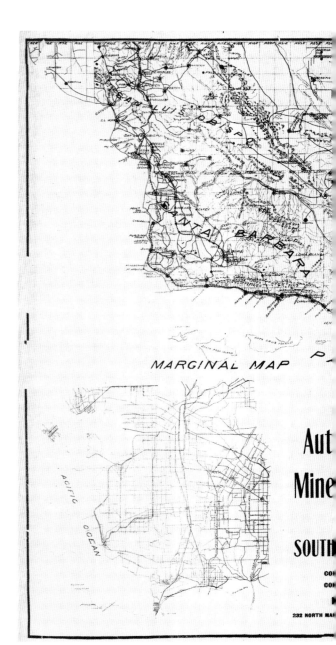

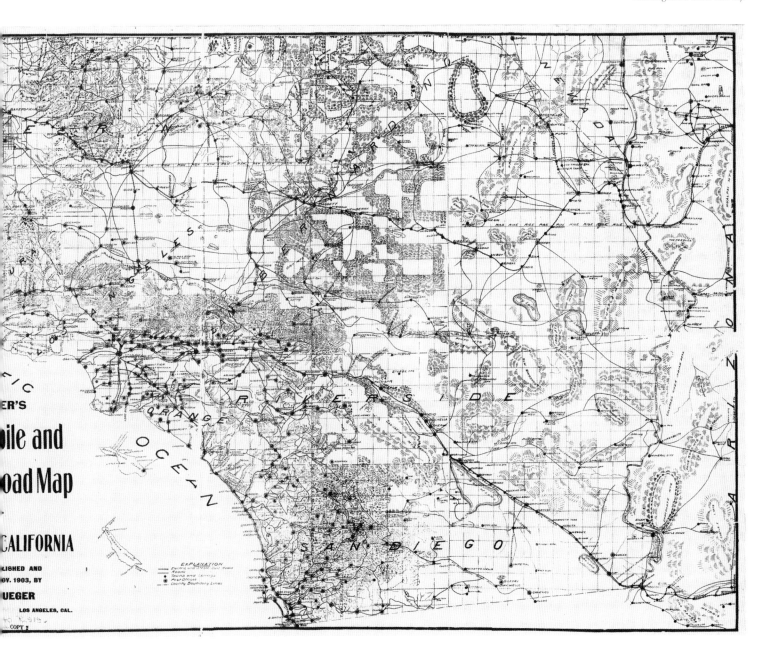

The Panoramic Automobile Road Map and Tourist Guide Book of Southern California

As the automotive age took hold in Southern California a comprehensive street guide became essential, and little gems like this road map and tourist guide filled the bill and then some for neophyte motorists. By the turn of the century the Automobile Club of Southern California began preparing the area for the coming advance in automotive technology by sending out cartographers to survey and map the many roads that covered the southland. The products of such research are these early road guides that offered travelers a rather folksy, step-by-step navigation through the mostly unimproved roads in the basin. Along with actual geography the guides provided a virtual almanac of reference on traveling in Los Angeles, including 180 whimsical looks at stretches of road between southland destinations, drawn with humor and accuracy by graphic artist Willard Cundiff. Moreover, this guide is purported to be the first to use aerial study, with the artist making sketches from a glider, here identified as "the Blonde Angel," flying over the southern part of the state from San Diego up to Santa Barbara.

The first map shows the downtown business district, which was already suffering traffic jams that mixed cars with street rail to disastrous effect. Ironically, the old offices of the Auto Club and the Pacific Electric station are across the map from each other. The battle between cars and streetcars went on for decades, with gasoline winning out over electricity for many complicated reasons.

The second look shows the folksy but accurate navigation of a road trip to La Crescenta from Glendale, heading north on Glendale Boulevard, which would now be the Glendale Freeway. Drivers were made aware of a fork where a "little house" marked the spot: if they veered left they ended up on La Crescenta; if they went right they would head to Pasadena over roads comprised of smooth stretches as well as rough, slightly sandy portions.

The third look takes us east over 7th street, crossing the bridge over the river through Boyle Heights and following Stephenson Avenue (now Whittier Boulevard), all the way out to the Quaker-founded community of Whittier. If you wished to take a turn to Downey you would merely wait until you saw the two barns and make a right.

The Panoramic Automobile Road Map and Tourist Guide Book of Southern California had much more than directions though, and paging through it you could get information on fishing or piscatory, trolley trips, the California Alligator Farm, Cawston's Ostrich Farm, the Bimini Baths, all public parks, places of worship, local fruits by season, the six newspaper offices, restaurants, auto makers, hotels, trips to Mt. Lowe, "the scenic wonderland of the Southland," and what to do if a defective coil was detected.

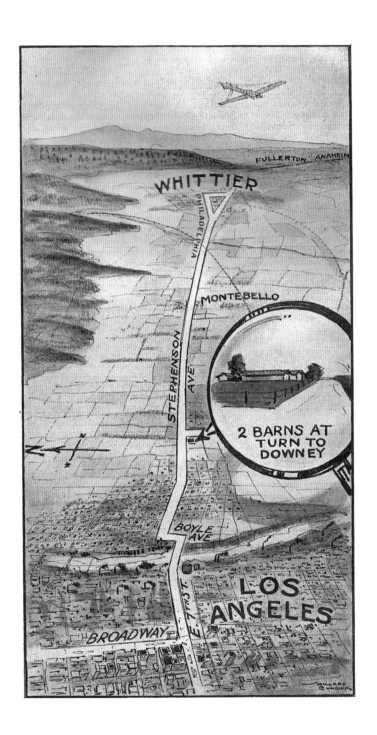

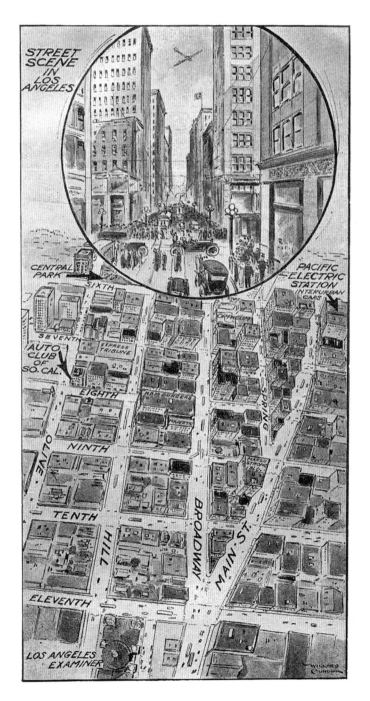

1914–15
Willard Cundiff
Cadmus Press
Los Angeles Public Library

Views of Oil Fields around Los Angeles

Oil was the talk of the town again when this three-view map was created by husband and wife cartographers Clarence Samuel and Edna Marie Farncrook, reflecting the recent spate of discoveries that had pumped new life into the petroleum industry in Los Angeles. Not only does this tidy pictorial portray the many oil fields that sprouted up throughout the late nineteenth and early twentieth centuries but it shows land for sale in areas like Clearwater, where lesser-known companies like Artesia Oil, Cal-Petro, Truman Oil, and the Bellflower Oil syndicate were sinking wells next to the likes of Standard Oil. The black-gold fever that had gripped the city and brought thousands of people and plenty of cash to Southern California at the end of the nineteenth century was burning hot once again.

This was the second real oil boom in the city, the first begun by Edward L. Doheny, who drilled the first well in 1892 with a sharpened end of a eucalyptus tree in a small area near downtown that eventually became known as the Central Area of the Los Angeles City Oil Field. Yet, as the twentieth century rolled on, many of the wells that dotted the city became depleted and the end seemed in sight for the huge, money-making industry. Oil prices collapsed in 1901 (due in part to electricity), after a rush to capitalize on the resource had turned the city into thousands of backyard oil producers. On this map Los Angeles almost seems a sad afterthought, sort of disappearing into the background despite the Salt Lake Field near the famed La Brea tarpits that was the leading oil field in Southern California in 1905.

However, engineers managed to find three more untapped areas as the 1920s began an automotive age and gasoline was desired more than ever. Huntington Beach in 1920, Santa Fe Springs in 1921, and Signal Hill near Long Beach in 1921 were found to have large deposits that set forth an absolute frenzy of real estate haggling. In particular, Signal Hill had just been subdivided for home sales when oil was found in dramatic fashion, and derricks popped up immediately on almost every available lot. When Shell Oil engineers finally got their first strike on the hill, a gusher flowed some 114 feet high and sent investors running for real estate offices. The map meticulously draws in the oil derricks, but even this rosy picture does not capture the staggering numbers, including 108 on one small area in Long Beach, aptly named "porcupine or pincushion hill." Signal Hill, whose name comes from the local Tongva Indians' use of the place to make signal fires, became one of the world's richest fields, producing 14,000 barrels a day. Thanks to this find, California became the nation's number-one oil producer and the source of one quarter of the world's petroleum.

The Farncrooks were active graphic artists throughout the 1920s but when Edna drowned in a tragic accident at Lake Arrowhead and the great crash turned the city upside down, Clarence stopped producing art and became an engineer serving the city of Vernon.

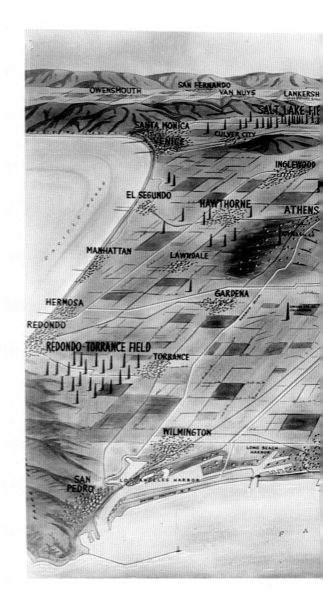

1922
C. S. & E. M. Forncrook
4.7" x 9.4"
Library of Congress

Map of Hollywood

Although the word Hollywood has many more meanings than just the topynomic moniker, it was once just a collection of hay fields, orchards, sheep-grazing land, and vegetable plots in the boondocks. Around 1886 Horace Henderson Wilcox (sometimes called Harvey, other times Horace) and his wife, Daeida, were out for a Sunday drive through the Cahuenga Valley when they stopped their carriage, took a look around, and liked what they saw. Wilcox hatched a plan to develop a perfect suburb and set about buying up the land, subdividing some 640 acres, and creating the city of Hollywood, which ironically was to be founded on the Christian principles of sobriety and Protestant piety. This map, distributed by Wilcox from his Spring Street realty office, paints a rosy picture of that dream, with the Pacific Ocean seemingly just a stone's throw from the perfect grid layout spreading out from the main intersection of Prospect and Weyse (later Vine Street). The campaign that launched this map promised choice land with ocean views, two railroads, a grand hotel, Sunset Boulevard one hundred feet wide and six miles long, concrete walks, and fine water for the "future home of the wealthy." This piece of paradise was just $350 an acre. Much was made of the area as possessing wonderful soil and resting in a frostless belt that added to the fecundity of the land. Wilcox had high hopes and planned to offer free land to churches that might want to put down roots there, but the land boom that raged at the time of this map fizzled by 1888. However, by the time Wilcox died in March 1891, Hollywood was established and the streets he lined with pepper trees became a destination for those venturing out from Los Angeles just six miles to the east.

Some of what Wilcox promised in the map came true, such as the fine homes that lined Prospect (which became Hollywood Boulevard) and the dream of a grand hotel (seen in the map insert), but the ocean view might have been a stretch. Hollywood was incorporated in 1903 after getting a fine trolley that ran along Sunset Boulevard, and the famed Hollywood Hotel was completed along with a high school that same year. The villa and gardens of famous artist Paul DeLongpre near the corner of Cahuenga and Prospect became one of the first tourist attractions in the city, and as early as 1907 the baby steps of the movie industry were being taken. By 1910 the need for water outweighed the citizens' zeal for autonomy, and the area was annexed by the city of Los Angeles.

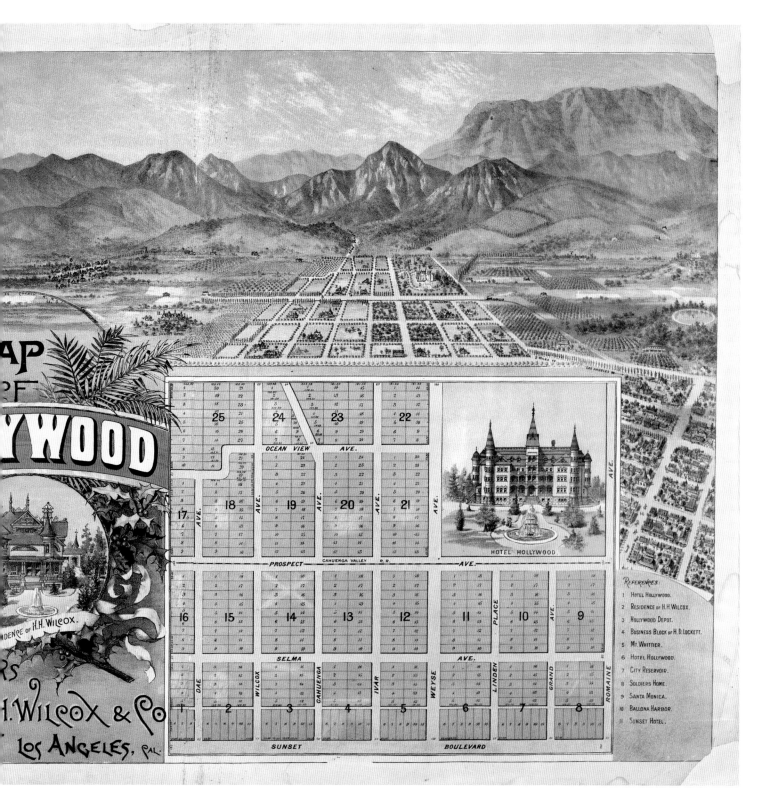

1887
H. H. Wilcox and Company
Los Angeles Litho
Harvey Henderson Wilcox
Colored lithograph
Huntington Library

Hollywood 1915

The established and highly respectable citizens of the Hollywood area may have been horrified by the sudden invasion of "theatricals" to their former teetotaling, quasireligious community in the years between 1911 and 1918. The area seen on this map was in a period of rapid transition. Hollywood had been annexed by the city of Los Angeles in 1909 but had little connection to the flesh peddlers downtown. Legend has it that the movie people were not even allowed to deposit money in the local banks, but before the locals had time to react, the place was sprouting studios on every corner.

Originally, the fledgling movie industry was established on the East Coast, with Thomas Edison holding the power of patents that drove the newcomers west. Los Angeles had its first movie studio, the Selig Polyscope Company, in place at nearby Edendale, and the Nestor Company followed suit in Hollywood around October 1911. Early "studios" might have been just raised wooden planks with curtain enclosures and no roofs or walls, but by 1915 this map shows fifteen movie companies in Hollywood, including the famous Lasky Studios barn where Cecil B. DeMille directed the first feature film, *The Squaw Man*, in February 1914. A large part of the draw for the moviemakers was the open land of this suburb of Los Angeles that was still quite bucolic with farmhouses, orchards, and the famed pepper trees planted by Horace Wilcox lining Hollywood Boulevard.

Sidney B. Reeve, a veteran Los Angeles civil engineer working out of the Title Insurance building downtown, created this fire insurance survey independent of the big underwriting mapmakers, highlighting the growing number of studios in red ink. Despite the publishing date of 1915, this sheet shows some studios that would not exist for several years. It is most probably the case in fire insurance maps that the date listed is only the creation point, and changes were made up to 1918, when places like the listed Chaplin and William Fox studios were built at the end of World War I. Some of the companies seen on this map evolved into the "big five," including the William Fox Studio (Twentieth Century-Fox), Metro Pictures (MGM), Famous Players/Lasky Studios (Paramount), and Warner Bros., which would take its place on Sunset Boulevard in 1919. The Hollywood Cemetery seen near the middle of the map became part of the mystique, offering "a resting place of Hollywood immortals," including early film pioneers Cecil B. DeMille and Jesse Lasky, along with such movie stars as Rudolph Valentino, Douglas Fairbanks, Paul Muni, and Tyrone Power. By the mid-1920s the area was producing eight hundred films a year, and when talkies were introduced in 1927 Hollywood commenced a golden age that continued for three decades.

Map of the Central Locations of Studios of Motion Picture Corporations, Hollywood (Los Angeles) California 1915
S. B. Reeve
Colored lithograph
Seaver Center for Western History

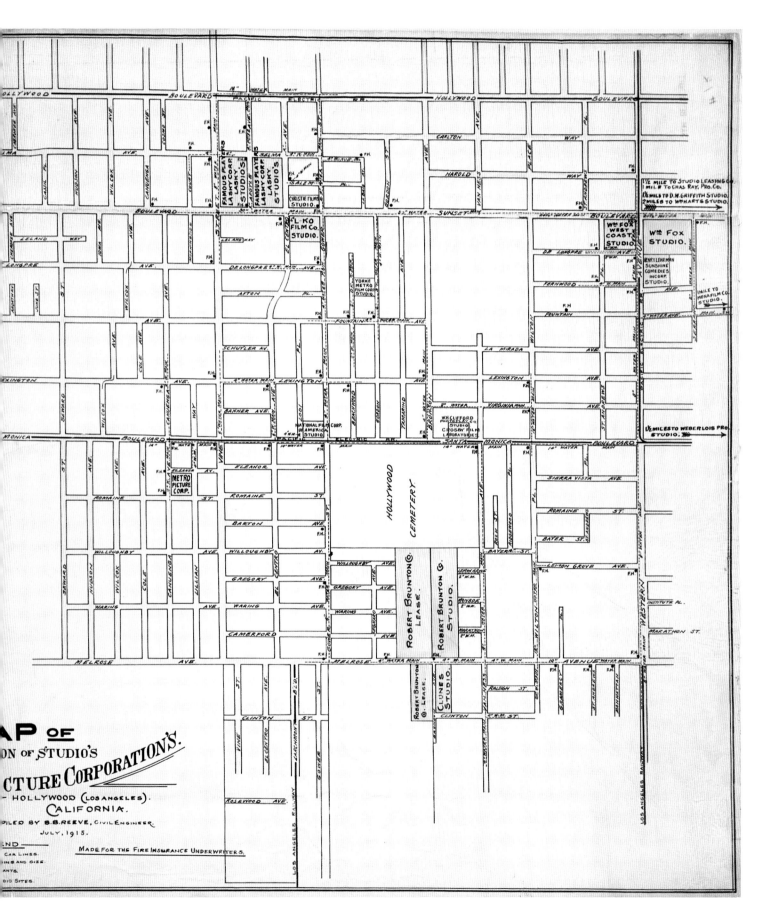

MAP OF
ON OF STUDIO'S
CTURE CORPORATION'S.
— HOLLYWOOD (LOS ANGELES).
CALIFORNIA.
PILED BY S.B.REEVE, CIVIL ENGINEER.
JULY, 1915.
MADE FOR THE FIRE INSURANCE UNDERWRITERS.

END
CAR LINES.
INE AND SIZE.
ANTS.
DIO SITES.

Hollywood 1925

The second map, created by the Security Trust Savings Bank in 1925, shows Hollywood as a boomtown filled with glamour and easy money, the envy of all of America. True movie studios started a little farther east in an area now known as Edendale, but by the time of this map the film industry was well established, and studios proliferated. The first was Nestor at Sunset and Hoover in 1911, quickly followed by Fox Film at Western and Sunset, Samuel Goldwyn at 7210 Santa Monica Blvd., Harold Lloyd Corporation at 1040 Las Palmas, Pickford-Fairbanks (later called United Artists) at 1041 N. Formosa, and Warner Bros. at 5842 Sunset. There were also ornate movie palaces to exhibit the films, like Grauman's Egyptian, Grauman's Chinese, finished in 1927, and Warner Bros. in 1928. They competed for glamorous premieres with the motion picture theater district in downtown Los Angeles, where the idea of movie stars and Hollywood took root. In truth, the area was probably more like what Fred Allen said: "Hollywood is where people from Iowa mistake each other for stars." However, there was more to the city than tinsel, as evidenced by the incomparable Hollywood Bowl (completed) in 1922, Immaculate Heart College, twenty-three churches, and the charming hillside communities near Lake Hollywood (here marked as "reservoir" and "Hollywoodland," where the landmark Hollywood sign now shines down on the city).

Contrary to what much of the country thinks, Hollywood is a neighborhood, not a city separate from Los Angeles. Yet it is the only one with exact boundaries that have continued since the annexation in 1910, as seen on this little map done by the Security Trust Savings Bank as part of seductive brochure entitled "Hollywood the Beautiful." The bank, founded in 1889 by Joseph R. Satori, had an early presence in Hollywood, including five establishments marked by the red stars, and became the second largest bank on the west coast after consolidating with other financial institutions and becoming Security First National Bank. The Security First National Bank maintained an important collection of historical documents pertaining to local history—including maps, chamber of commerce ephemera, and photographs—until the 1980s, when it was dispersed to archives in Southern California.

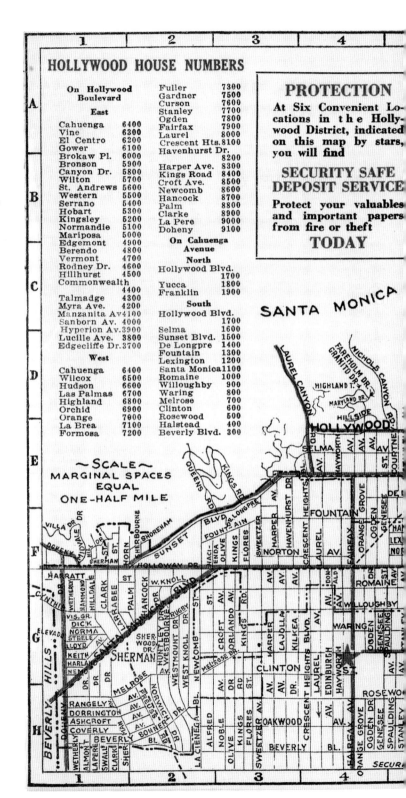

1925
Security Trust and Savings Bank
Printed map from book
12" x 8"
Los Angeles Public Library

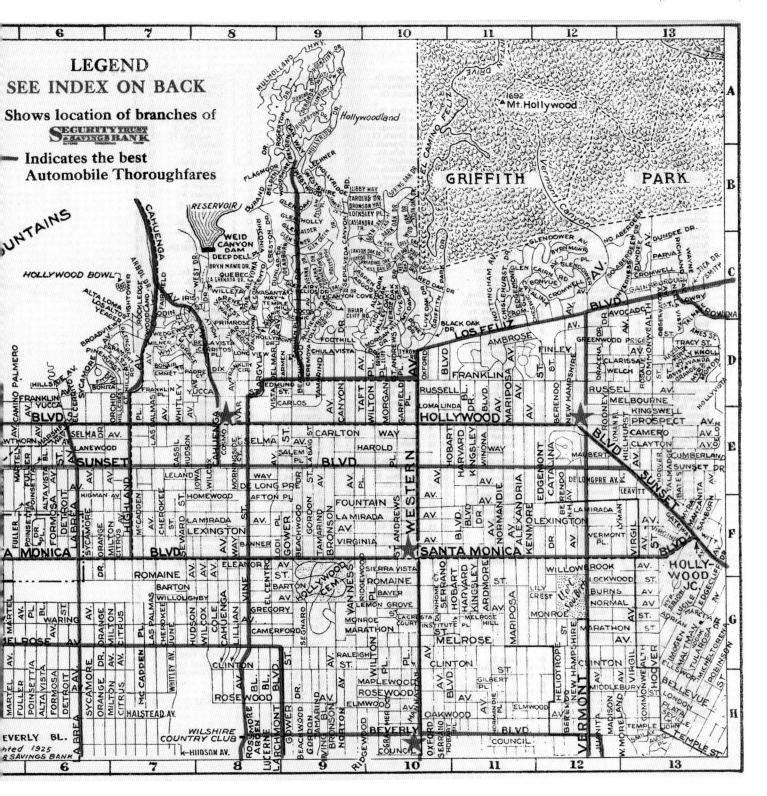

Hollywood Film Capital of the World

The war was over, money was flowing, and the country was feeling frisky in the glow of victory and sudden prosperity. Tourism in Southern California was once again a big deal, with an industry trying to figure out a way to lure the rest of the country to visit. Maps, especially lighthearted pictorials, were all part of this campaign. This whimsical look at Tinseltown is a tourist map sold in souvenir shops after World War II that paints the typically glamorous picture of Los Angeles as a film capital. Hollywood, as seen here, is the exaggerated center of Los Angeles, and places like downtown, the east side, or anything south of Pico Boulevard are afterthoughts in the fun-filled metropolis. This tourist's Hollywood actually encompasses much of the landscape extending beyond the original boundaries but accurately depicts the movie studios that operated in the peak years. RKO, the old Twentieth Century-Fox (Hollywood), Paramount, Samuel Goldwyn Studios, Warner Bros., and Columbia are right in Hollywood. Metro Goldwyn -Mayer, Twentieth Century-Fox, and the Hal Roach studios seem a stone's throw away in Culver City, while Republic and Universal appear to sit atop mountains in North Hollywood. The "principal thoroughfares" are all surface streets, except for the lone future freeway, here called the Arroyo Seco Parkway heading toward Pasadena. The original owner of this fold-up pictorial map has made notes on places to take out-of-towners, signifying "Indian relics," in Highland Park, "to Catalina" at the harbor, "sights" on Wilshire Boulevard, "night" for the Griffith Park Observatory, and even "home" that seems to have been Pacific Palisades.

The siren song is sounded to vacationers who could tour homes of movie stars, shop at the Farmer's Market, lunch at the Brown Derby, or see new motion picture releases at Warner Bros. or Grauman's Chinese or Egyptian movie palaces. As humble as it might be, this map demonstrates what the rest of the planet saw as Los Angeles when visiting Southern California. In a time before the huge amusement parks and major league sports, Hollywood was the big draw, but just about every outdoor activity under the sun is represented. Polo, speedboat racing, sport fishing, baseball, horseback riding, football, tennis, golf, thoroughbred racing, ice skating, sunbathing, and swimming are offered in the ever-sunny southland. There is some small measure of an intellectual component, however, with four universities shown along with the Shrine Auditorium, the Hollywood Bowl, the Southwest Museum, the Planetarium, and the world-famous Coconut Grove nightclub in the Ambassador Hotel. Strangely, some vestiges of the old L.A. still are shown on the map, including many oil wells, the Cawston Ostrich Farm that had been one of the city's first tourist draws, Catalina Island where marlin apparently ogled starlets, and the Ocean Park pier where folks could still dance to big band music.

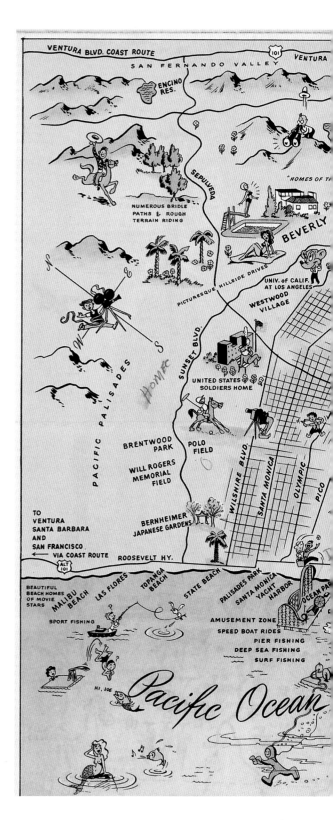

1946(?)
Lowell E. Jones
Hester and Smith Inc.
Colored lithograph
Collection of Jim Heiman

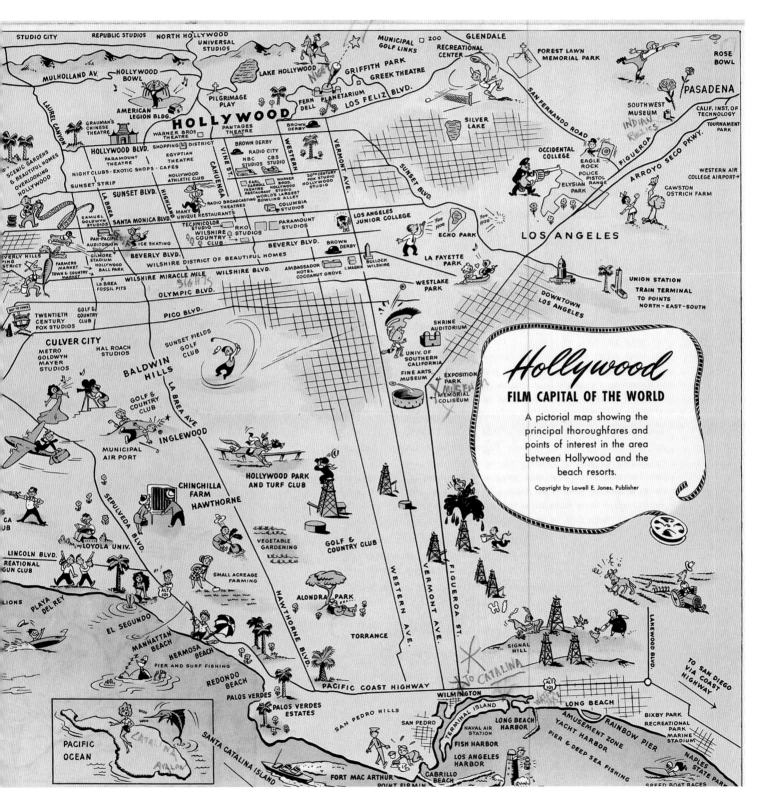

Hollywood
FILM CAPITAL OF THE WORLD

A pictorial map showing the principal thoroughfares and points of interest in the area between Hollywood and the beach resorts.

Copyright by Lowell E. Jones, Publisher

Mapping Tourism in Southern California

by Dydia DeLyser

Designed to lure, tourism maps depict eye-catching points of interest, striving to draw attention and visitors to what might be mistaken for mundane places. Too often understood as boosterist chamber-of-commerce products intended to separate visitors from their cash at attractions not otherwise worth mentioning, in fact, tourism maps need not be derided for exaggerating points of interest: all maps, as necessarily selective, scaled-down representations of the world, must "lie." Could maps depict the world at full scale and with full precision, they'd lose both their narrative, story-telling function and their ability to fit in the glove box.

Understood in this way, these colorful confections of tourist cartography reveal not only points of purported tourist interest but, more important, spatial stories rooted in, and possibly unique to, time and place. Thus rather than disparaging such maps for their flawed portrayals of reality, or reproaching them for portrayals relevant in their day and not ours, the very selectivity evidenced in such maps can illuminate both historical and social cartographies of times now past.

For if maps are designed to inform (as the Ord Survey surely was), they must most often also entertain. This is no different for mid-twentieth-century "Roads to Romance" maps than it is for the creations of Renaissance cartographers, whose depictions of the New World not only (we now know) inaccurately rendered its coastlines (depicting California, for example, as an island), but also deliberately included fanciful creatures—the monsters of land and sea that filled the maps' empty spaces and lured the eyes and imaginations of map readers. But it is in these "flaws" of cartography—the errors, the deliberate distortions, and the purposeful "lies"—that the historical-cultural meanings of such maps can perhaps most directly be revealed.

Just as the sea monsters in sixteenth-century maps were central to the ways that those maps conveyed their cultural meaning, the fanciful places depicted on Southern California's tourist maps—whether grounded in fact like the Hollywood studios, or fiction like the grave of "Ramona"—now also provide intimate insight into a selective geography and a selected way of understanding the region. They reveal not an inclusive, multicultural past in the way we would now choose to understand our present, but rather a past scripted as the present (and the future) by those then in power. In this way, such maps should be understood both for the joyous landscapes and places they depict as for the vexacious landscapes they omit—like Fort Moore Hill, site of the Siege of Los

Angeles in 1846; the "Calle de los Negros," location of the Chinese massacre of 1870; "Ink Alley" on 1st and Broadway, site of the bombing of the Los Angeles *Times* in 1910; Mount Vernon Junior High School, from where young Marion Parker was kidnapped before her brutal murder by Edward "the Fox" Hickman in 1927; the swath of destruction carved from the Santa Clarita Valley to the sea after the St. Francis Dam Disaster in 1928; the points of resistance and arrest during the Los Angeles Dressmakers' Strike in 1933; the businesses forced to close when Japanese Americans were interned at relocation camps in 1942; the places of unrest and protest during the Watts Riots in 1965; or the MacArthur Park Elks Club Lodge, site of the "St. Valentine's Day Massacre" when the LAPD riot squad descended upon a punk-rock concert in 1979. Most places, after all, must be understood in more complex ways: the missions as places of repression *and* devotion, an underdeveloped community as a place of poverty *and* home, a beach as a site of relaxation *and*, sometimes, shark attack.

Seen from the perspective of production, of using maps to draw tourists to the region, such omissions may be easy to understand. Yet the view that all such maps are produced only from the perspective of boosters is equally limiting, for it obscures the origins of many tourist attractions as places willed into being, as places demanded by the tourists themselves, and masks the agency of millions of tourists in creating landscapes of pleasure, leisure, and diversion in Southern California.

The ability to meet, let alone become a movie star, is out of reach for most who buy Maps to Stars' Homes. Yet engaging with those maps—reading them and then passing through their landscapes—allows tourists to personally, physically connect themselves to important narratives of the region, in this case, perhaps, the myth of "being discovered," along with glamorized notions of fame and stardom in Hollywood.

Most of us don't know today if sea monsters really seemed credible to a sixteenth-century audience (although we might imagine that they did). Regardless, depicting such creatures on a map served to dramatize the whole map, along with the very idea of journeying across the landscapes depicted. Contemporary tourism maps are no different. Exaggerated images, fictional places, and lurid color schemes draw the eyes, the mind, and, if the map is successful, the body (and perhaps its wallet) as well. Understood from this perspective, tourist maps of Southern California can offer vivid insights into the social cartographies of pleasure in the region's past.

The Travelure Map of Los Angeles and Vicinity

The cluster of memorable maps produced in the early 1930s seems somehow appropriate as it marks almost the exact halfway point of the journey from the first surveyed plan of 1849 to the present. In the year of the Olympics many of the finest tourist enticement maps ever made appeared with very humble intentions, but their extremely talented cartographer-artists were competing for visitors' attention. The beautiful Travelure Map is unique from the other looks at the city at this time yet maintains the zealous boosterism that typifies the era. The wide-scope look overflows with color and enthusiasm for local charms, like the cornucopias spilling abundance on either side of the title. While the choices for inclusion are wildly eclectic, there are four basic components: history, flora and fauna, celebrities, and attractions.

Historical vignettes are interspersed around the border with the state flower, the golden poppy; the original twenty-one California missions; and events of great importance, such as the end of Spanish rule, admission to the union, the discovery of gold, and the arrival of the Pony Express. Folklore and local color are evident, with mentions of the Chinese Dragon Festival, the Fiesta de las Flores of the 1890s, Ramona's marriage and village, the "King's Highway," the early use of the *carreta* (ox-cart) for hauling freight, and the rather romantic but vague "Spanish romance." The physical climes are given a sheen too, as "oranges and snow," eucalyptus (health trees), "the Desert in Spring," "Home Among the Roses," and "Yucca in Bloom" call out to those journeying to the warmth of Southern California. All of this came with the regular draws like the Hollywood Bowl, Grauman's Chinese Theater, Gay's Lion Farm, Olympic Stadium, Wrigley Field, assorted movie studios, movie star mansions, and the many airports that show the city to be a leader in aeronautics.

One detail that does not make it onto most of the tourist maps of the day is the Angelus Temple, the huge church at the edge of Echo Park that was home to famous "Sister" Aimee Semple McPherson, one of the first radio preachers and a national celebrity throughout the 1920s and '30s. Despite six years of scandals that shook the church to its foundations the place was a regular stop on tourist buses. The temple was founded in 1923 and was regularly packed with the faithful who came to hear the voice of Miss Aimee, who was said to have filled the five-thousand-plus-seat church three times a day, seven days a week.

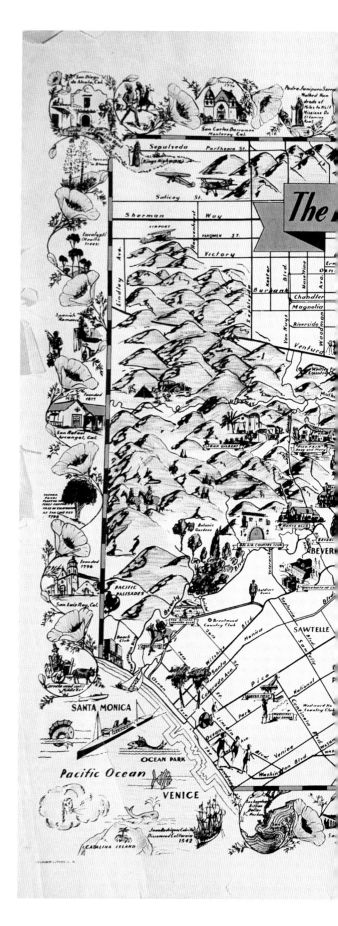

1932
Anita L. Weathers and
Ron G. Hermanson
The Travelure Map Co.
Neuner Litho
Colored lithograph
Seaver Center for Western History

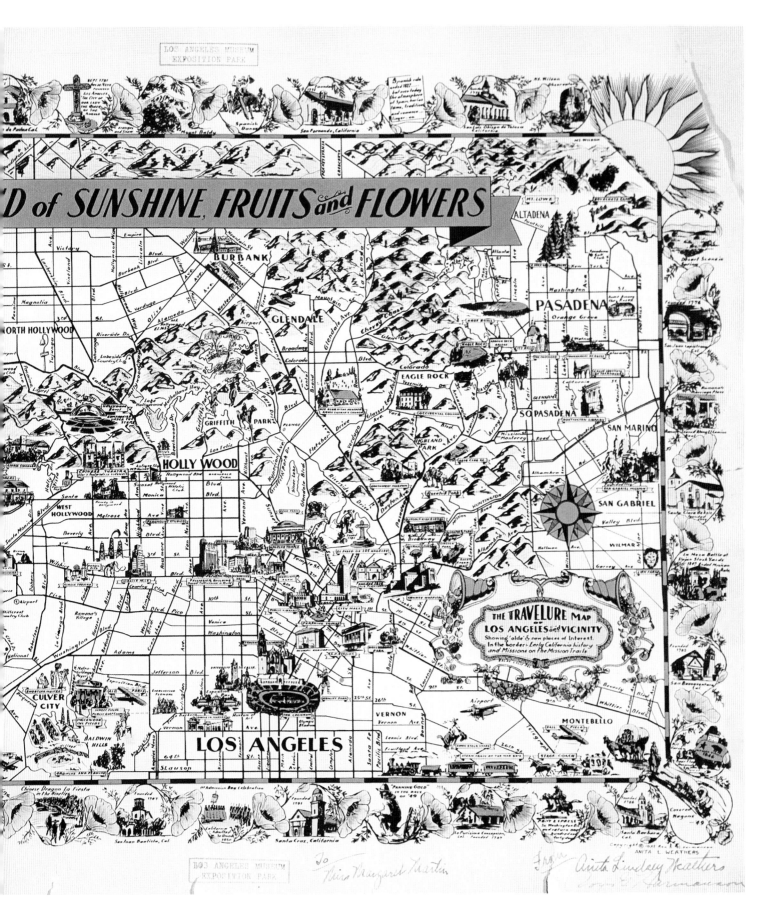

Greater Los Angeles

While the early 1930s represented an economic plunge of unprecedented levels, the city of Los Angeles hardly blinked in attempting to attract cash to the area. An attempt to paint a beautiful and tidy picture of southland charms, the pictorial map rose in popularity with both advertisers and the public. Offering the classic profile of the greater Los Angeles area, this eye-catching, wide-angle look at the metropolitan area of "Greater Los Angeles" demonstrates an amazingly broad view of the city's recreational, industrial, and cultural vibrancy. What makes K. M. Leuschner's map even more valuable is the index that takes the visitor to this seemingly well-ordered city set up like a New York City grid. As an accurate bit of cartography, the map is not even close to reality, but as a work of art it is worthy of depicting "the wonder city of America," spiced by the young artist's playful sense of humor. A graduate of the Berlin Royal Academy of Fine Arts, Karl Moritz Leuschner left Germany in 1906 and settled in Rochester, New York, where he studied and taught art. In 1926 he came to Los Angeles, where he lived for ten years, distinguishing himself as an expert on color and color harmony. He worked for various lithographers as a graphic artist while working on a doctorate at the University of California during that time. Leuschner taught at local night schools and the Otis Art Institute, eventually creating a color chart that is still used today.

Though published in the year of the Olympics in Los Angeles, this map only minimally mentions the Olympic auditorium, the Olympic village, the understated Olympic Stadium (later Memorial Coliseum), and the Olympic rowing course. Instead there is representation of several rubber manufacturers, including U.S. Rubber, Firestone, Goodrich, and the Goodyear plant and blimp hovering over the well-represented Long Beach. All of the oil fields can be found along the southern petroleum belt, from Venice to Torrance to mighty Signal Hill, then Dominguez and out to Santa Fe Springs. The points of interest chosen are eccentric and drawn with some reflection of the mapmaker's tastes. Well-known landmarks like the Rose Bowl, the Greek Theater, downtown, and Hollywood are subtly mentioned, while unusual tourist spots appear, such as "Crystal Pier Nude Sun Baths," "Deodars Miles of Christmas Trees," "Johanna Smith Pleasure Ship" (one of several gambling ships cruising off the coast), the Yagoda Sat-Sanga Hindu-American Temple, and the "Home of Mental Physics" at 9th and Grand. The fairly new UCLA is given a rather royal treatment, while the older USC is dwarfed by the "Crenshaw Fairways" golf driving range and many of the eighteen colleges in the area are represented. Golf seems to have sung a siren song, with such courses and country clubs listed as Montebello, Midwick, Santa Monica, Portrero, Fox Hills, Bellevue, Royal Palms, Westwood Hills, Wilshire, Bel-Air, Riviera, Griffith Park, and Annandale all the way out in Pasadena.

Leauschner does list nightclubs on Central Avenue, like "Topsey's" or "Sebastian's New Cotton Club" along with airfields, amusement piers, cemeteries, ballparks, movie star homes, gardens, movie studios, refineries, and, in one grand nod to history, both missions.

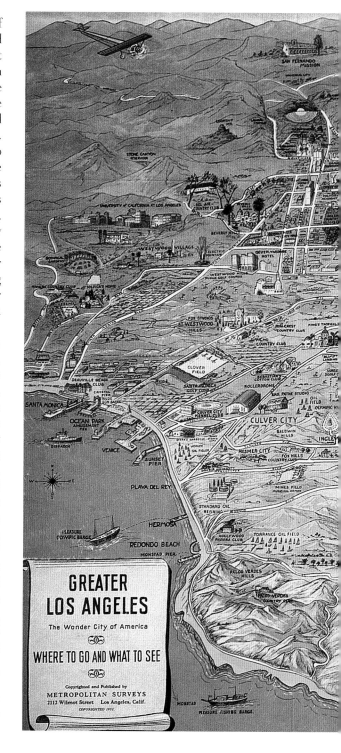

The Wonder City of America: Where to Go and What to See
1932
K. M. Leuschner
Western Litho Company, Metropolitan Surveys
Colored lithograph
21.3" x 33.1"
Seaver Center for Western History

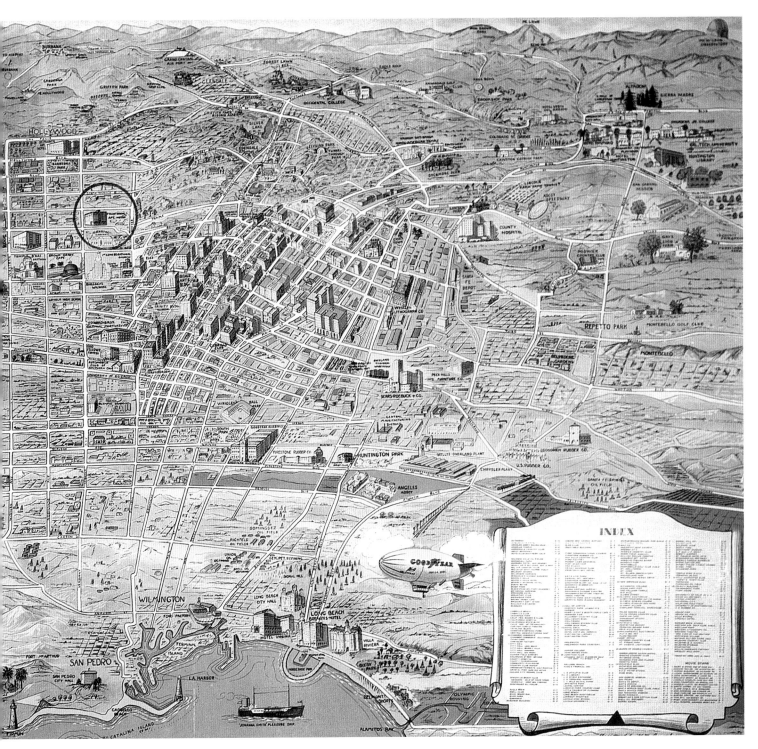

Official Sightseeing Map of Los Angeles City and County

This map attempts to be all things to all tourists, combining the lure of the Los Angeles tourist guide with a classy map to the stars' homes. Distributed widely at places where automobiles might stop, the foldout guide was produced by the ubiquitous All Year Club of Southern California, which had joined with the Auto Club and Highways Commission in literally putting the city on the map since the early 1920s. Founded by a powerhouse collection of local business leaders on June 1, 1921, the club came out of the chute spending a million dollars on a three-year ad campaign to bring folks out to "the wonders of the summer climate" in the southland. An august group that included *LA Times* owner Harry Chandler, Henry O'Melveny, Edward Dickson, and Doctor Frank Barham initiated the formation that was then supported by hoteliers, realtors, railroad companies, and various businessmen that became the All Year Club. It saturated the East Coast and Midwest with glossy magazine-brochure descriptions of the glorious climate and glamour of the region that slowly changed into "an all-year resort." Just a fifteen-hour plane ride from New York City would deliver a winter visitor to golf, hiking in the San Gabriel Mountains, thoroughbred racing at beautiful Santa Anita, and a nightlife in Hollywood that was legendary.

The map tells the story without wasting too many words and shows a vacation paradise beyond just the sunshine. There is a focus on two of the city's parks: Griffith, with horse trails, three golf courses, the Zoo, gardens, and the Greek Theater; and, across town, Exposition Park, with the famed Memorial Coliseum, the Natural History Museum, and the University of Southern California. There is a curious mix of old and new, including the Old Plaza and Church, Olvera Street, and two of the original missions, along with the new technologies, particularly motion picture and radio broadcasting studios and a blimp landing field at 3rd and La Brea. The All Year Club always sought a balance and was careful to point out the existence of the arts in this sunny Eden, as demonstrated by the Planetarium, the Philharmonic Auditorium, the Huntington Library, the Southwest Museum, and the marvelous Hollywood Bowl, where one might enjoy "symphonies under the stars" for as little as fifty cents. The Los Angeles metropolitan area is made to sound so appealing, but in this rosy scene there is still a caveat on the reverse side of the brochure, warning those fleeing the Dust Bowl and the Depression not to come unless they had money in their pockets when they arrived. As Woody Guthrie's song said "California is a garden of Eden/ a paradise to live in or see/ But believe it or not, you won't find it so hot/ If you ain't got the do re mi."

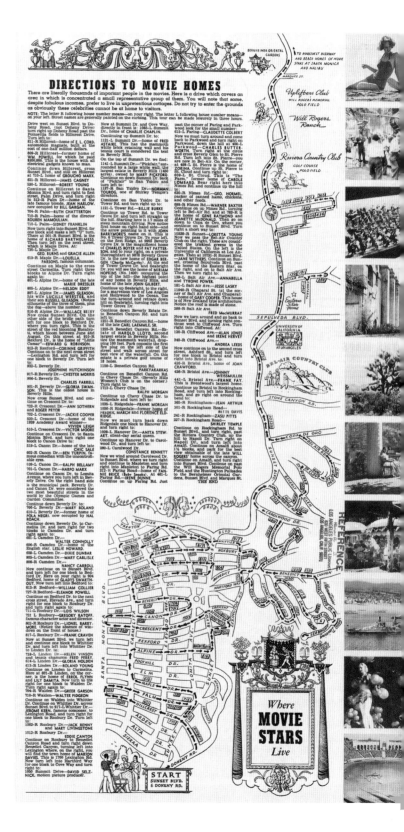

Sightseeing Map of
LOS ANGELES AND HOLLYWOOD

This map shows that portion of the City of Los Angeles in which the chief sightseeing points are concentrated. For points of tourist interest in other sections of the City and County, consult the two maps on the reserve side.

SCALE IN MILES

WHAT THERE IS TO SEE

Below are given the salient features of the main sightseeing points which are not explained on the map itself. For further detailed information on these or other points of tourist interest consult: Official Tourist Information Bureau of The All-Year Club.

AUTOMOBILE CLUB OF SOUTHERN CALIFORNIA—free touring information and maps to tourists, 35 other offices in principal Southern California cities.
BROADCASTING STUDIOS—special sightseeing tours daily, 40c.
CASA DE ADOBE—authentic reproduction of ranch house of 1800.
CHAMBER OF COMMERCE EXHIBIT—depicting agricultural and industrial progress of Los Angeles County.
CHINESE QUARTER—fine Chinese foods and merchandise.
CITY HALL, CIVIC CENTER—modern buildings. Take elevator for City Hall tower view.
HOLLYWOOD BOWL—20,000-seat amphitheatre for finest music, 50c-$1.50.
JAPANESE GARDENS—colorful gardens in miniature, admission 25 cents.
JAPANESE QUARTER—centers in First street, interesting shops, theatres, Temple.
LA BREA FOSSIL PITS—asphaltum pools from which skeletons of prehistoric monsters are obtained.
MULHOLLAND DRIVE—magnificent vistas of city and valley.
OLD PLAZA—birthplace of Los Angeles, Old Mission Church.
OLVERA STREET—genuine Mexican street market, Avila Adobe, restaurants, shops.
OSTRICH AND ALLIGATOR FARMS—especially interesting farms.
PARKS—Los Angeles has 87 municipal parks.
PHILHARMONIC AUDITORIUM—concerts, symphonies, dance and music recitals of greatest artists.
PILGRIMAGE PLAY—America's Passion Play.
POLICE PISTOL RANGE—in Elysian Park, public invited, gardens, range.
PUBLIC LIBRARY—art gallery, lecture rooms, reading rooms, splendid architecture.
SOUTHWEST MUSEUM—depicts ancient cultures of the southwest.
STUDIOS—glimpses of sets, actors in make-up can often be seen from streets.

GRIFFITH PARK

PLANETARIUM—OPEN DAYS & EVENINGS EXCEPT MONDAYS

GREEK THEATRE—BEAUTIFUL OUTDOOR SETTING

BRIDLE TRAILS—MT. HOLLYWOOD & OTHER PEAKS

FERN DELL AND BOTANICAL GARDENS

THREE GOLF COURSES OPEN TO THE PUBLIC

TENNIS COURTS

ZOO AND BIRD SANCTUARY

PLAYGROUNDS—SWIMMING POOLS

EXPOSITION PARK

ART GALLERIES
HISTORICAL MUSEUMS
NATURAL HISTORY
ANCIENT FOSSIL REMAINS
ROSE GARDENS
AGRICULTURAL AND INDUSTRIAL EXHIBITS
NATIONAL GUARD ARMORY
BOWLING ON THE GREEN
LOS ANGELES MEMORIAL COLISEUM + FOOTBALL TRACK—PUBLIC EVENTS
SWIMMING POOLS
TENNIS COURTS
CHILDRENS PLAYGROUND

MOVIE STARS' HOMES DRIVE STARTS 1.7 MILES WEST OF HERE

REFERENCE

Historical and Recreational Map of Los Angeles

One of the few marvelous cartes created by artist Jo Mora, this pictorial masterpiece gives an astonishing amount of Los Angeles history on one sheet. An immigrant from Uruguay, Jo Mora was an accomplished sculptor, book illustrator, cartoonist, painter, and mapmaker. Mora's jocular commentary, extensive knowledge of Western history, and graphic art skills made him the foremost practitioner of the form that has grown in popularity since its heyday in the 1920s, '30s, and '40s. In the dedication to author, editor, archaeologist, and one-time city librarian Charles Lummis, Mora insists that the viewer take a lighthearted view of the city and its path to the present, writing "I render my message in the humorous manner as I'd rather find you with a smile of understanding than a frown of research."

However, packed around the edges of the actual landscape is a tour of history and geography that starts at the foundation of the pueblo and ends with a look to the future of 1950. Included are the costumes and names of the original pobladores, neophytes, Franciscan brothers, and Native Americans he calls "gentiles." There is a nod to the Battle of San Pascual, where the Californios battled the U.S. forces in 1846, a mention of the man who killed the legendary outlaw Joaquin Murrieta, a description of the Pony Express, the coming of the railroads, electricity, the discovery of oil, real estate booms, baseball, water filching, earthquakes, the harbor, and even the kinds of fish available in the waters of the nearby Pacific. Mora cleverly conveys the population growth as ladies in period costume blowing up larger and larger balloons, expanding from forty-four souls to one and half million. He also mentions agriculture and the arrival of oranges, limes, silkworms, and Belgian Hares to the city of the angels. Even cataclysms like the Depression and earthquakes seem kind of fun coming from the pen of Señor Mora. The actual map of the city floating in the center of all this history covers the San Fernando Valley to Pasadena, down the coast from Malibu to Seal Beach, and the harbor at San Pedro all the way up to movie studios in Burbank.

1942
Jo Mora
Colored lithograph
Los Angeles Public Library
Reproduced with permission
from the Jo Mora Trust

Historic Roads to Romance

The post-war boom in tourism in the southland coincided happily with the golden age of pictorial mapping, producing some the finest examples of the form, filled with color, imagination, and some fair stretching of the geographic truth. Exceptional among these hybrids of graphic art and cartography was the "Historic Roads to Romance" series produced by the Roads to Romance Association from the 1940s well into the 1960s. "Highway Boosters" from San Diego, Riverside, San Bernardino, and Imperial counties joined Los Angeles in a constellation to mark and market notable locations, thereby educating the public and creating interest in the overall area. David Olmstead of Long Beach came up with the idea and gathered twenty-eight Southern California enthusiasts at the Mission Inn in Riverside in 1941 to develop the concept of establishing historical monuments that might also be represented on tourist maps. World War II halted the effort, but the plan stayed alive. The first placement was on July 28, 1944, at the spot of the Battle of Rio San Gabriel, with guest speaker Leo Carrillo addressing the folks at the San Gabriel Mission. Local tub-thumpers included John Anson Ford, County Supervisor William A. Smith, Olmstead, Senator Ed Fletcher, and Walter Knott of the famous Berry Farm. The Roads to Romance Association staged horse shows and rodeos in Pomona, hosted Spanish luncheons at the missions, subsidized county fairs, and turned to former *Saturday Evening Post* illustrator Claude Putnam to create a series of enticing pictorial maps covering the Mexican border to Santa Monica and all the way to the California state line along the Colorado River to the east. Commodore Putnam, an avid yachtsman, always included the Pacific Ocean in his portrayals of the "tourist paradise" of Southern California.

Despite its commercial intent the map does focus on truly historic places and less on popular attractions. Los Angeles might feature a director in Hollywood, the Rose Bowl, Olvera Street, and the Fair Grounds but there is also the historic Plaza, the Pico House, both local missions, and several adobes, such as the Palomares and San Rafael. There are outdoor opportunities abounding from what appears to be an abundance of lakes, including the impressive-looking Salton Sea, alongside the Anza Trail, the old Butterfield Stage Route, the El Camino Real, and the path of the Mormon Trail snaking through the Cajon Pass. The map includes some unusual choices, including the vineyard city Guasti, the Golden Chariot Mine, and the grave of the fictional character Ramona, she of the Helen Hunt Jackson novel that did much to increase tourist interest in the area.

Putnam's border traces local history, starting with the mastodons found in the La Brea tar pits and following Father Serra, Gaspar de Portola's expedition, Juan Bautista de Anza's inland trek, and Juan Rodriguez Cabrillo coming ashore at San Diego bay.

California's Southern Empire Tourist Paradise
1946
Claude G. Putnam; Research by Karl J. Brown
Roads to Romance Association, Inc.
Colored lithograph
Los Angeles Public Library

Historic
Roads To
Romance
CALIFORNIA'S
SOUTHERN EMPIRE
Tourist Paradise
Cartography by Claude G. Putnam
Research by Karl J. Brown
COPYRIGHT 1946 BY
ROADS TO ROMANCE ASSN., INC.

Olympics Map

There are many reasons why Los Angeles developed into a major American city, including the railroads, the harbor, oil, the aqueduct, the automobile, the movies, the streetcars, and the ideal climate. However, one event more than any other gave the city a place on the international stage, and that was the Summer Olympics of 1932. It was a minor miracle that William May Garland, the U.S. representative to the International Olympics Committee, went to Rome eleven years earlier and managed to bring the event to this rather remote location. Despite the guarantee of good weather in Los Angeles, seven of the original nine Olympics had been held in Europe, and the West Coast of the United States seemed like the end of the earth to cash-strapped countries. Six months before the games were to begin, no country had responded, and even though the main venue, the Memorial Coliseum (then called the Olympic Stadium), was expanded to seat more than 105,000 spectators, few tickets had been sold. Only about half the number of athletes from the 1928 Amsterdam Olympics could travel to Los Angeles . Yet when the time came, the city bloomed and the games were a huge success. There was great ballyhoo on the streets, with colorful flags and banners decorating the metropolitan area, parades, and the spectacular opening ceremony that drew 105,000 delirious fans. The giddy local populace 50,000 strong gathered outside the stadium just to drink in the energy, while Vice President Charles Curtis opened the festivities, the Olympic flame was ignited, and five thousand doves of peace were released. Despite the challenges, thirty-seven nations participated and the level of competition was extremely high, with eighteen world records equaled or broken. The great Mildred "Babe" Didrikson won three medals and swimming superstar Helene Madison took three golds, while the United States won a total of 103 medals. The Olympics gave the city great pride and are said to have garnered a profit of one million dollars for the organizers, led by William May Garland himself as president of the Olympic Committee.

This highly popular foldout map was created by the Union Oil Company, with a mileage assist from the Automobile Club, and handed out to visitors planning to attend the events scattered across the metropolitan area. Artist Mary Hall Atwood was a muralist and pictorial mapmaker who had recently moved to Los Angeles from Paris. Even as early as 1932 the map was suggesting motor trips, and the main highways, major streets, and event locations are drawn with a crisscross finding aid on the corners. It announces the first Olympics that were conducted in just sixteen days, from July 30 to August 14, and matches events with venues like Griffith Park, where the shooting competition took place; to San Pedro, where yachting was undertaken; and Olympic Park (now called Exposition Park), where the marathon, lacrosse, equestrian jumping, and the opening and closing ceremonies took place.

1932
Mary Hall Atwood
Union Oil Company, Los Angeles
Three-color print
22˝ x 17˝
From the collection of Jim Heimann

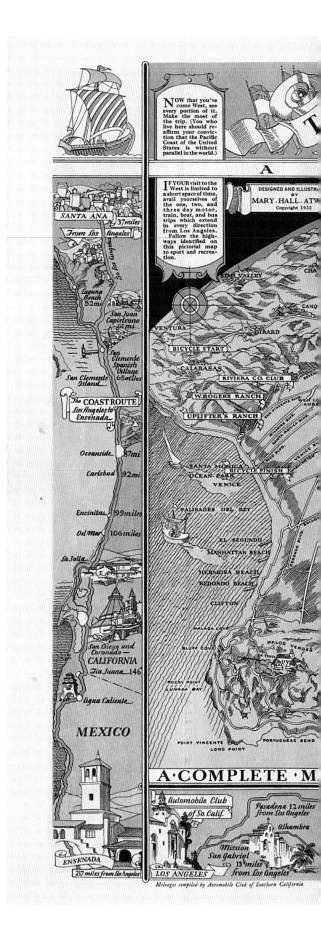

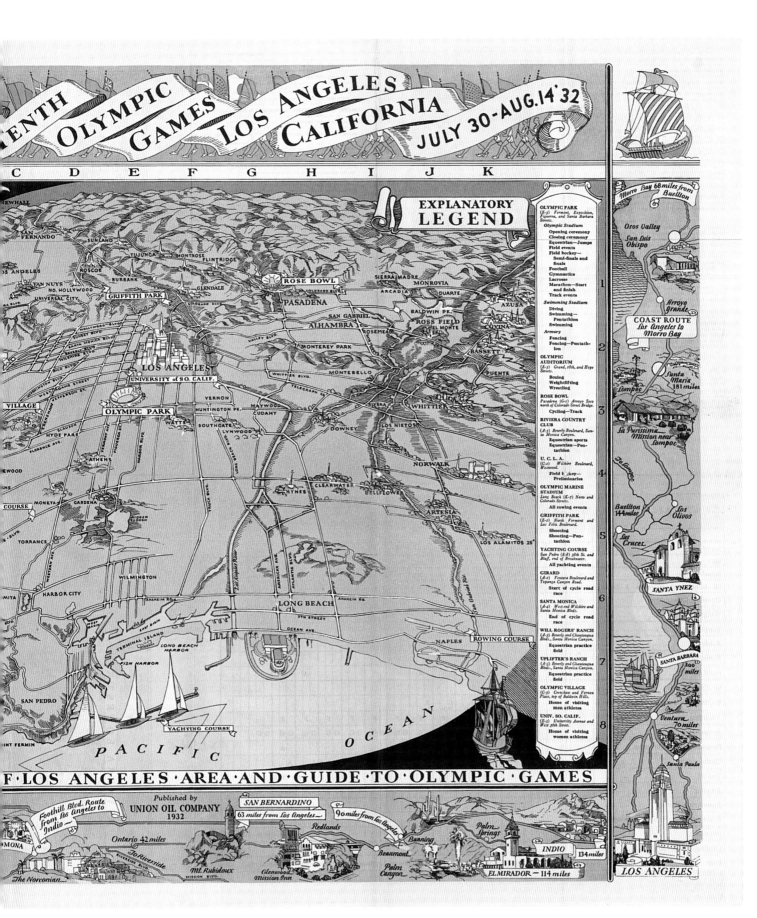

TENTH **OLYMPIC** GAMES · **LOS ANGELES** CALIFORNIA · JULY 30-AUG. 14 '32

EXPLANATORY LEGEND

OLYMPIC PARK
(E-3) Fernand, Exposition, Figueroa, and Santa Barbara Streets.

Olympic Stadium
Opening ceremony
Closing ceremony
Equestrian—Jumps
Field events
Field hockey—
Semi-finals and finals
Football
Gymnastics
Lacrosse
Marathon—Start and finish
Track events

Swimming Stadium
Diving
Swimming—
Pentathlon
Swimming

Armory
Fencing
Fencing—Pentathlon

OLYMPIC AUDITORIUM
(E-3) Grand, 18th, and Hope Streets.
Boxing
Weightlifting
Wrestling

ROSE BOWL
Pasadena (G-1) Arroyo Seco north of Colorado Street Bridge.
Cycling—Track

RIVIERA COUNTRY CLUB
(A-3) Beverly Boulevard, Santa Monica Canyon.
Equestrian sports
Equestrian—Pentathlon

U. C. L. A.
(C-2) Wilshire Boulevard, Westwood.
Field hockey—Preliminaries

OLYMPIC MARINE STADIUM
Long Beach (K-7) Neoto and Colorado Streets.
All rowing events

GRIFFITH PARK
(E-1) North Fernand and Los Felix Boulevard.
Shooting
Shooting—Pentathlon

YACHTING COURSE
San Pedro (E-8) 36th St. and Bluff, end of Breakwater.
All yachting events

GIRARD
(A-1) Ventura Boulevard and Topanga Canyon Road.
Start of cycle road race

SANTA MONICA
(A-4) West end Wilshire and Santa Monica Blvds.
End of cycle road race

WILL ROGERS' RANCH
(A-3) Beverly and Chautauqua Blvds., Santa Monica Canyon.
Equestrian practice field

UPLIFTER'S RANCH
(A-3) Beverly and Chautauqua Blvds., Santa Monica Canyon.
Equestrian practice field

OLYMPIC VILLAGE
(C-3) Crenshaw and Fernon Place, top of Baldwin Hills.
Home of visiting men athletes

UNIV. SO. CALIF.
(E-3) University Avenue and West 36th Street.
Home of visiting women athletes

OF · LOS · ANGELES · AREA · AND · GUIDE · TO · OLYMPIC · GAMES

Published by
UNION OIL COMPANY
1932

Foothill Blvd. Route from Los Angeles to Indio

POMONA — Ontario 42 miles — To Riverside
The Norconian · Mt. Rubidoux · Glenwood Mission Inn

SAN BERNARDINO 63 miles from Los Angeles
Redlands

90 miles from Los Angeles
Beaumont · Banning · Palm Canyon · Palm Springs
EL MIRADOR — 114 miles · **INDIO** 134 miles

Morro Bay 68 miles from Buellton
Osos Valley
San Luis Obispo
Arroyo Grande

COAST ROUTE
Los Angeles to Morro Bay

Santa Maria 181 miles
Lompoc
La Purissima Mission near Lompoc
To Gaviota
Buellton 14 miles
Los Olivos
Las Cruces
SANTA YNEZ
SANTA BARBARA 100 miles
Ventura 70 miles
Santa Paula

LOS ANGELES

Maps of the Stars Homes

by William J. Warren

You're driving down Sunset Boulevard in Beverly Hills and at a number of corners see easel type signboards blaring "STAR MAPS." Do movie stars really live here? Yes, but not nearly as many as did seventy years ago. It all started with a movie idol named Mary Pickford. She lived here during World War I and opened her house to some service men for tea. She convinced some of her neighbors that this was a patriotic thing to do and so needed a map. That's how the map of the stars homes was born.

In 1933 an enterprising candy maker, Wesley G. Lake, saw an out-of-date map that sparked his interest. In his spare time he searched real estate records and found a large concentration of Hollywood luminaries had moved west to Beverly Hills. He designed a map with a border of names and addresses, placed red stars on strategic home locations, numbered the rest, and drew a suggested route line to cover many star's homes in succession by automobile. America was gaga over Hollywood's star system; to be able to see an actual movie star's home became a quest. Soon Lake found his map business a booming success and hired young men to hawk them to the hordes of tourists cruising Sunset Boulevard, the main drag through the glamour capital. Lake, and later his daughter, Vivienne Welton, updated his map quarterly and it became a best seller.

In the early days, movie people were happy to see their names featured. Few turned down this free publicity and would sometimes contact the family when they planned to move. "Be sure the next issue has our new home listed," they would advise. Tour buses sometimes found lesser names out watering their yards when the bus passed on a known schedule. Vivienne combed real estate records religiously and sometimes would knock on doors. "Is this where I can get an autographed picture of Ms. X?" If the answer was, "Oh no, you have to go to the studio for one of those," she knew she had hit pay dirt in her quest for updated information.

Two names changed Hollywood—Sharon Tate and Charles Manson. Manson's followers' brutal murder of Tate and her friends shocked the community. Personalities became anxious to hide their real home addresses. Today, all you can see of most of their homes are locked gates and high surrounding walls. Yet the maps live on in many variations. Mapmakers have always been plagiarists. The updated Lake map is still available, but so are many rip-offs of this seminal map, made by unnamed copiers. Some lurid versions exploit locations of murders or suicides connected with Los Angeles.

Still there is nostalgia connected with seeing a home such as that of Bing Crosby, virtually unchanged from 50 years ago. A little digging will turn up the beautiful Encino rancho where Clark Gable rode in the San Fernando Valley. Unfortunately, his home site is now a multistoried garage for a bank.

Another change has been the addition to maps of other "Stars," sports and television personalities, and even an occasional politician. Landmarks like Pickfair, the home Douglas Fairbanks built when he married Mary Pickford, are still located. Of course, Pickfair today bears no resemblance to the original hunting lodge, having undergone more facelifts than the dozens of stars who visited over the years. The gate still says "Pickfair." Who could ask for more?

So today's maps list many "last homes" of names we can still recognize from the Golden Age of Hollywood, along with the names of rock stars many of us have never heard of. Bring your kids with you on your self-guided tour through La-La Land; they'll be able to identify them for you. And who knows, you might actually see one of those folks behind dark glasses strolling down Rodeo Road…

Places of Interest in Los Angeles and Vicinity

CASA MANANA ___ Culver City
JONATHAN CLUB ___ 545 S. Figueroa St.
AMBASSADOR HOTEL ___ 3400 Wilshire Blvd.
BILTMORE HOTEL ___ 515 S. Olive St.
BURNHEIMER GARDENS..16980 Sunset Blvd., Pacific Palisades

Studios

CHARLES CHAPLIN ___ 1416 N. La Brea Ave.
WALT DISNEY ___ 2400 W. Alameda Ave., Burbank
SAMUEL GOLDWYN, Inc. ___ 1041 N. Formosa
METRO-GOLDWYN-MAYER ___ Culver City
R-K-O—PATHE ___ Culver City
HAL ROACH ___ 8822 Washington Blvd.
UNITED ARTISTS ___ 1041 N. Formosa
TWENTIETH CENTURY-FOX ___ 10260 Orion Ave.
UNIVERSAL CITY CORP. ___ Universal City
WARNER BROS.-FIRST NATIONAL ___ Olive Ave., Burbank
REPUBLIC PICTURES ___ 4024 N. Radford

★ ★ ★

The listings herein are frequently revised and effort is always being made to secure accuracy, but the publisher does not assume any responsibility for errors or changes of address.

SOUVENIR MAP

and Guide to Starland Estates and Mansions... A Fascinating Trip Through Movieland

SPRING ISSUE—1947

The majority of noted picture people are located on this map. The guide is enlarged showing Beverly Hills and vicinity to enable you to easily locate your star.

THE ADDRESSES APPEARING ON THIS MAP ARE PRIVATE HOMES. PLEASE DO NOT INTRUDE.

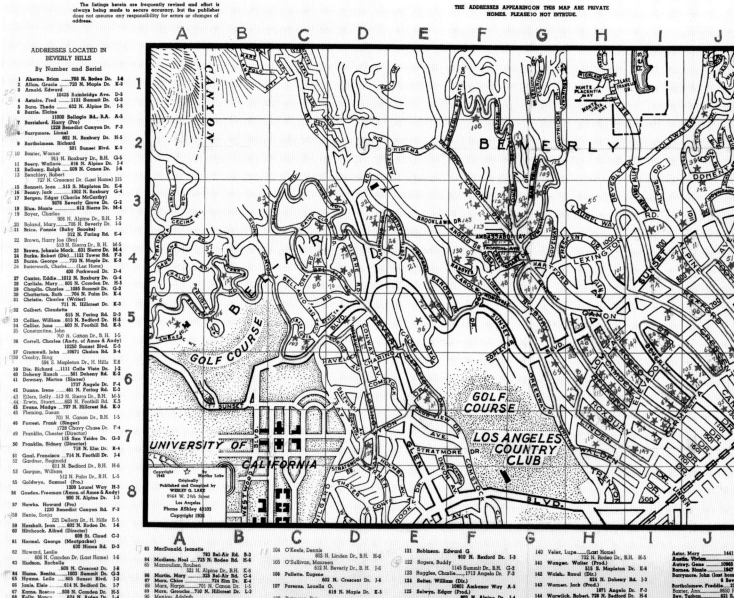

ADDRESSES LOCATED IN BEVERLY HILLS
By Number and Serial

1 Aherne, Brian ___703 N. Rodeo Dr. I-4
2 Allan, Gracie ___720 N. Maple Dr. K-3
3 Arnold, Edward ___10425 Bainbridge Ave. D-5
4 Astaire, Fred ___1121 Summit Dr. G-3
5 Bara, Theda ___632 N. Alpine Dr. J-5
6 Barrie, Elaine ___11000 Bellagio Rd., B.A. A-5
7 Barrisford, Harry (Pro) ___1228 Benedict Canyon Dr. F-3
8 Barrymore, Lionel ___902 N. Roxbury Dr. H-5
9 Bartholmess, Richard ___501 Sunset Blvd. K-3
10 Baxter, Warner ___911 N. Roxbury Dr., B.H. G-5
11 Beery, Wallace ___816 N. Alpine Dr. J-4
12 Bellamy, Ralph ___609 N. Canon Dr. J-6
13 Benchley, Robert ___727 N. Crescent Dr. (Last Home) J15
15 Bennett, Joan ___515 S. Mapleton Dr. E-6
16 Benny, Jack ___1002 N. Roxbury G-4
17 Bergen, Edgar (Charlie McCarthy) ___9876 Beverly Grove Dr. G-2
18 Blue, Monte ___612 Sierra Dr. M-4
19 Boyer, Charles ___906 N. Alpine Dr., B.H. I-3
20 Boland, Mary ___706 N. Beverly Dr. I-5
21 Brice, Fannie (Baby Snooks) ___312 N. Faring Rd. E-4
22 Brown, Harry Joe (Bro) ___513 N. Sierra Dr., B. H. M-5
23 Brown, Johnnie Mack ___631 Sierra Dr. M-4
24 Burke, Robert (Dir)___1121 Tower Rd. F-3
25 Burns, George ___720 N. Maple Dr. K-3
26 Butterworth, Charles (Last Home) ___400 Parkwood Dr. D-4
27 Cantor, Eddie ___1012 N. Roxbury Dr. G-4
28 Carlisle, Mary ___805 N. Camden Dr. H-5
29 Chaplin, Charles ___1085 Summit Dr. G-3
30 Chatterton, Ruth ___704 N. Palm Dr. K-4
31 Christie, Charles (Writer) ___711 N. Hillcrest Dr. I-4
32 Colbert, Claudette ___615 N. Faring Rd. D-3
33 Collier, William ___813 N. Bedford Dr. H-5
34 Collier, June ___603 N. Foothill Rd. K-5
35 Constantine, John ___707 N. Canon Dr., B. H. I-5
36 Correll, Charles (Andy, of Amos & Andy) ___10250 Sunset Blvd. D-5
37 Cromwell, John ___10671 Chalon Rd. B-4
38 Crosby, Bing ___594 S. Mapleton Dr., H. Hills E-6
39 Dix, Richard ___1111 Calle Vista Dr. J-2
40 Doheny Ranch ___501 Doheny Rd. K-2
41 Downey, Morton (Singer) ___1737 Angelo Dr. F-4
42 Dunne, Irene ___461 N. Faring Rd. E-3
43 Ellers, Sally ___513 N. Sierra Dr., B.H. M-5
44 Erwin, Stuart ___603 N. Foothill Rd. K-4
45 Evans, Madge ___707 N. Hillcrest Rd. K-3
46 Fleming, Susan ___701 N. Canon Dr., B. H. I-5
48 Forrest, Frank (Singer) ___1728 Chevy Chase Dr. F-4
49 Franklin, Chester (Director) ___115 San Ysidro Dr. G-3
50 Franklin, Sidney (Director) ___718 N. Elm Dr. K-4
51 Gaal, Francisca ___714 N. Foothill Dr. K-4
52 Gardner, Reginald ___611 N. Bedford Dr., B.H. H-6
53 Gargan, William ___512 N. Palm Dr., B.H. L-5
55 Goldwyn, Samuel (Pro.) ___1200 Laurel Way H-4
56 Gosden, Freeman (Amos of Amos & Andy) ___900 N. Alpine Dr. I-4
57 Hawks, Howard (Pro) ___1230 Benedict Canyon Rd. F-3
58 Henie, Sonja ___225 Delfern Dr., H. Hills E-5
59 Hersholt, Jean ___602 N. Rodeo Dr. I-5
60 Hitchcock, Alfred (Director) ___609 St. Cloud C-3
61 Hormel, George (Meatpacker) ___630 Nimes Rd. D-3
62 Howard, Leslie ___606 N. Camden Dr. (Last Home) I-6
63 Hudson, Rochelle ___609 N. Crescent Dr. I-6
64 Hume, Benita ___1003 Summit Dr. G-3
65 Hyams, Leila ___805 Sunset Blvd. I-3
66 Janis, Elsie ___614 N. Bedford Dr. I-6
67 Karns, Roscoe ___808 N. Camden Dr. H-5
68 Kelly, Nancy ___623 N. Bedford Dr. I-6
69 Kelly, Patsy ___819 N. Roxbury Dr. G-5
70 Kent, Barbara ___285 Bel-Air Rd. D-4
71 Kibbee, Guy ___605 N. Crescent Dr. I-6
72 Kruger, Otto ___210 Woodruff Ave. D-5
73 Laemmle, Carl, Jr. (Pro.) ___1051 Benedict Canyon Rd. F-3
74 Lauck, Chester (Lum of Lum & Abner) ___815 N. Rexford Dr. I-4
75 Leeds, Andrea ___303 St. Pierre Rd., B.A. D-4
76 Livingstone, Mary ___1002 Roxbury G-4
77 Lloyd, Harold ___1225 Benedict Canyon Dr. F-3
78 Logan, Ella (Singer) ___606 N. Rodeo Dr. I-5
79 Lorre, Peter ___722 N. Linden Dr. H-7
80 Lubitsch, Ernest (Director) ___268 Bel-Air Rd. D-4
82 Lyons, Arthur ___503 Sunset Blvd. K-3

83 MacDonald, Jeanette ___783 Bel-Air Rd. B-3
84 Madison, Noel ___725 N. Rodeo Dr. H-6
85 Mamoulian, Rouben ___521 N. Beverly Dr. K-6
86 Martin, Mary ___325 Bel-Air Rd. C-4
87 Marx, Chico ___724 Elm Dr. I-6
88 Marx, Harpo ___701 N. Canon Dr. I-5
89 Marx, Groucho ___710 N. Hillcrest Dr. I-3
90 Menjou, Adolph ___722 N. Bedford Dr., B. H. H-6
91 Merkel, Una ___603 N. Rexford Dr. I-5
92 Milestone, Lewis (Director) ___1103 San Ysidro Dr. G-3
93 Milland, Ray ___726 Elm Dr. I-4
94 Miranda, Carmen ___616 N. Bedford Dr. I-7
95 Montgomery, Robert ___522 N. Beverly Dr., B.H. I-6
96 Moore, Constance, 717 N. Rexford Dr. I-5
97 Morgan, Frank ___1025 Ridgedale Dr. F-4
98 Morgan, Ralph ___265 Strada Corta Road C-5
99 Mobray, Alan ___1019 Chevy Chase Dr. F-4
100 Murphy, George, 614 N. Oakhurst Dr. M-4
101 Myers, Carmel, 904 N. Crescent Dr. H-4
102 Nixon, Marion, 10801 Ambasac Way A-5
103 Nugent, Elliot (Director) ___625 Strada Corta Rd. C-5

104 O'Keefe, Dennis ___802 N. Linden Dr., B.H. H-5
105 O'Sullivan, Maureen ___612 N. Beverly Dr., B. H. I-6
106 Pallette, Eugene ___502 N. Crescent Dr. J-6
107 Parsons, Louella O. ___619 N. Maple Dr. K-5
108 Patterson, Pat ___906 N. Alpine Dr., B.H. I-3
109 Pickford, Mary ___1145 Summit Dr. G-2
110 Pidgeon, Walter ___710 N. Walden Dr. H-7
111 Powell, Eleanor ___728 N. Bedford Dr. H-6
112 Powell, William ___1113 Tower Rd. F-3
113 Preston, Robert ___1705 Chevy Chase Dr. F-4
114 Price, Vincent ___1021 Chevy Chase Dr. F-4
115 Raft, George ___1218 Cold Water Canyon Rd. J-1
116 Rathbone, Basil, 10728 Bellagio Rd. B-5
117 Ratoff, Gregory ___510 N. Hillcrest Rd., B.H. L-5
118 Ritz, Al ___622 N. Roxbury Dr. I-7
119 Roach, Hal ___610 N. Beverly Dr. I-6
120 Robson, May (Last Home) ___510 N. Bedford Dr. J-7

121 Robinson, Edward G ___910 N. Rexford Dr. I-3
122 Rogers, Buddy ___1145 Summit Dr., B.H. G-2
123 Ruggles, Charlie ___1713 Angelo Dr. F-3
124 Seiter, William (Dir.) ___10801 Ambasac Way A-5
125 Selwyn, Edgar (Prod.) ___803 N. Alpine Dr., B.H. I-4
126 Selznick, David O. (Prod.) ___1050 Summit Dr. G-3
127 Stahl, John (Prod.), 658 Nimes Rd. B-5
128 Stanwyck, Barbara ___807 N. Rodeo Dr., B.H. H-5
129 Stephenson, Henry___659 Siena Way B-4
130 Stewart, Anita ___1028 Hanover Dr. F-4
131 Stuart, Gloria ___814 N. Bedford Dr. H-5
132 Swarthout, Gladys ___904 N. Bedford Dr. H-5
133 Sullivan, Ed. (Columnist) ___621 N. Alta Dr. L-4
134 Taurog, Norman (Dir.) ___243 No. Delfern Dr. E-5
135 Taylor, Kent ___707 No. Rodeo Dr. H-6
136 Taylor, Robert, 807 N. Rodeo Dr., B.H. H-5
137 Torres, Raquel. 471 N. Parkwood Dr. D-5
139 Turpin, Ben ___602 N. Canon Dr. Last Home J-4

140 Velez, Lupe (Last Home) ___732 N. Rodeo Dr., B.H. H-5
141 Wanger, Walter (Prod.) ___515 S. Mapleton Dr. E-6
142 Walsh, Raoul (Dir.) ___824 N. Doheny Rd. J-3
143 Warner, Jack (Prod.) ___1871 Angelo Dr. F-2
144 Warwick, Robert, 728 N. Bedford Dr. H-6
145 Wilcox, Cary ___300 Bel-Air Rd. C-4
146 Wilson, Lois ___711 N. Roxbury Dr. H-7
147 Withers, Jane ___10731 Sunset Blvd. B-5
148 Young, Roland ___614 N. Linden Dr. I-7
150 Zorina, Vera ___1711 Tropical Ave. F-3

ADDITIONAL ADDRESSES
Not Located by Number or Serial

Abel, Walter ___267 Conway Ave. W.W.
Alexander, Ben. 1971 N. Catalina Ave., Hol.
Ameche, Don ___4704 White Oak, N.H.
Angel, Heather ___621 N. Waldron Dr. K-5
Annabella ___139 Saltair Ave. Brt.
Arlen, Richard ___Howden Ranch Devonshire Blvd., Chatsworth
Armitta, Henry (Last Home) ___301 S. Rodeo Dr. J-5
Armstrong, Robert ___Sleepy Hollow, Encino
Arthur, Jean ___13130 Boca de Canyon. Brt.

Astor, Mary ___1441 S...
Austin, Vivian
Autrey, Gene ___10965 Bl...
Barnes, Binnie ___1947 Bl...
Barrymore, John (last home)
Bartholomew, Freddie ___228...
Baxter, Ann ___8650 Pin...
Bey, Turhan ___621 S. H.
Blondell, Joan
Bogart, Humphrey
Boles, John
Boyd, William ___8358
Brent, George ___9885 C...
Brown, Joe E.
Brown, Tom ___51
Bruce, Nigel ___701
Burke, Billy ___219
Cagney, James. 2043 Cold...
Capra, Frank (Director) 221...
Carrillo, Leo ___639 E.
Carrol, Earl ___1114
Colman, Ronald ___190...
Cooper, Gary ___11940 C...
Cooper, Jackie ___1445 W...
Crawford, Joan
Crosby, Larry
Cugat, Xavier ___
Davies, Marion ___141...

Famous Night Clubs and Cafes

BILTMORE BOWL (Biltmore Hotel), 5th & Olive, Los Angeles
BROWN DERBY RESTAURANTS—
    1628 N. Vine St. .... Hollywood
    9537 Wilshire Blvd. .... Beverly Hills
    3377 Wilshire Blvd. .... Los Angeles
CIRO'S, 8433 Sunset Blvd. .... Hollywood
COCOANUT GROVE (Ambassador Hotel), 3400 Wilshire Blvd.
EARL CARROLL'S, 6230 Sunset Blvd. .... Hollywood
MOCAMBO NIGHT CLUB .... 8588 Sunset Blvd.
ROMANOFF'S .... 326 N. Rodeo Dr., B.H.
SEVEN SEAS, 6904 Hollywood Blvd. .... Hollywood
THE PALLADIUM .... 6215 Sunset Blvd.
THE PLAYERS .... 8225 Sunset Blvd.
THE TROPICS, 421 N. Rodeo Dr. .... Beverly Hills
TOM BRENEMAN'S HOLLYWOOD CAFE
    1525 N. Vine St., Hollywood
TROCADERO, 8610 Sunset Blvd. .... Hollywood
SLAPSY MAXIE'S, 5665 Wilshire Blvd. .... Los Angeles

PREMIERE THEATRES

CARTHAY CIRCLE, 6316 W. San Vincente Blvd., Los Angeles
FOUR STAR, 5112 Wilshire Blvd. .... Los Angeles
GRAUMAN'S CHINESE, 6925 Hollywood Blvd. .... Hollywood
PANTAGES, 6233 Hollywood Blvd. .... Hollywood

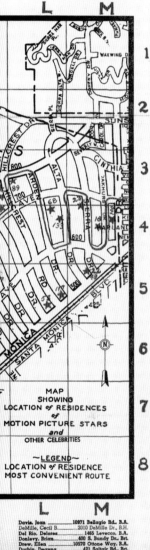

MAP
SHOWING
LOCATION of RESIDENCES
of
MOTION PICTURE STARS
and
OTHER CELEBRITIES

~LEGEND~
LOCATION of RESIDENCE
MOST CONVENIENT ROUTE

ADDITIONAL ADDRESSES
Not Located by Number or Serial
(Continued)

Gurie, Sigried .... 13664 Sunset Blvd., S.M.
Hale, Alan .... 1940 Outpost Circle, Hol.
Hall, Jon .... 12805 Sunset Blvd., Brt.
Harrison, Rex .... 10353 Strathmore Dr., H.H.
Hayworth, Rita .... 11806 Bellagio Rd., B.A.
Hepburn, Katherine
    9966 Beverly Grove Dr., B.H.
Herbert, Hugh .... 12321 Moorpart, N.Hol
Hervey, Irene .... 120 N. Cliffwood Ave., Brt.
Hodiak, John .... 8650 Pine Tree Place, Hol.
Hope, Bob .... 10346 Moorpark, N.H.
Hopkins, Miriam .... 1400 Tower Grove Dr., B.H.
Horton, Edward E. .... 5521 Amstoy St., S.F.V.
Hutton, Betty .... 309 S. Rockingham Ave., Brt.
Jessel, George .... 972 Ocean Front, S.M.
Jones, Buck .... 14050 Magnolia Ave., Burbank
Johnson, Van .... 757 Kingman, S.M.
Karloff, Boris .... 714 N. Foothill Rd., B.H.
Kelly, Gene .... 506 N. Alta Dr., B.H.
Kelly, Patsy .... 8760 Shoreham Dr., Hol.
Kent, Robert .... 506 N. Alpine Dr., B.H.
Kenyon, Doris .... 315 N. Saltair Ave., Brt.
Kern, Jerome
    (Last Home) 917 N. Whittier Dr., B.H.
Kibbee, Guy .... (Last Home)
Kaye, Danny .... 1710 Angelo Dr., B.H.
LaMarr, Hedy .... 2727 Benedict Canyon Dr., B.H.
Lamour, Dorothy .... 9131 Calle Jovela
Langford, Frances .... 12805 Sunset Blvd., Brt.
Lasky, Jessie .... 181 Saltair Ave.
Laurel, Stan .... 20213 Strahers Rd., Canoga Park
Ladd, Alan .... 4961 Cromwell Ave., Hol.
Lee, Dixie .... 594 S. Mapleton Dr., H. Hills
Le Roy, Mervin (Dir) .... 312 St. Cloud Rd., B.H.
Levine, Nat (President Republic Pictures)
    214 N. Beverly Glen, B.A.
Logan, Ella .... 12812 Sunset Blvd., Brt.
Loy, Myrna .... 9301 Cherokee Lane, B.H.
Lupino, Ida .... 1766 Westridge Ave., Brt.Hts.
MacLaglen, Victor .... Fairhaven, La Canada
MacMurray, Fred .... 289 N. Saltair Rd., Brt.
March, Frederic .... 2180 Mandeville Canyon Rd
    Brt.
Marsh, Joan .... 1326 San Ysidro Dr. B.H.
Marshall, Herbert .... 518 N. Roxbury Dr., B.H.
Massey, Illone .... 120 So. Medio Dr., Brt.
Miller, Ann .... 300 Delfern Dr. H.H.
Montez, Maria .... 514 N. Walden Dr., B.H.
Morley, Karen .... 707 N. Foothill Rd., B.H.
Moore, Colleen .... 345 St. Pierre Rd., B.A.
Moore, Victor .... 510 N. Crescent Dr., B.H.
Muir, Esther .... 9171 Hazen Dr., B.H.
Nagel, Conrad .... 1507 Benedict Canyon Rd.
Nolan, Lloyd .... 406 N. Cliffwood Ave., Brt.
O'Brien, Jane .... 12728 Parkyns Ave., Brt.
O'Brien, Pat .... 196 S. Rockingham Ave., Brt.
Pitts, Zasu .... 241 N. Rockingham Rd., Brt.
Power, Tyrone .... 139 Saltair Ave., Brt.
Raymond, Gene .... 783 Bel Air Rd., B.A.
Rogers, Ginger .... 1605 Gilcrest
    Cold Water Canyon
Roger's Ranch, Will .... 14253 Sunset Blvd.
Rogers, Roy .... 12039 Ventura Blvd., S.F.V.
Romero, Caesar .... 371 N. Saltair R., Brt.
Rooney, Mickey .... 4410 Dinsmore Ace., S.F.V.
Russell, Andy .... 5070 Libbett St., Encino
Russell, Rosalind .... 817 N. Beverly Dr., B.H.
Saunders, George .... 9060 Shoreham Dr., Hol.
Shearer, Norma .... 707 Ocean Front, S.M.
Sinatra, Frank .... 8358 Sunset Blvd., Hol.
Skelton, Red .... 265 N. Layton Dr., B.H.
Southern, Ann .... 723 Crescent Dr., B.H.
Smith, Alexis .... 3920 Maryellen St., S.F.V.
Smith, C. Aubrey .... 2821 Coldwater Canyon, B.H.
Starrett, Charles .... 9121 Hazen Dr., B.H
Stewart, James .... 12731 Evanston St., Brt.
Stokowski, Leopold .... 9330 Beverly Crest Dr., B.H.
Stromberg, Hunt .... 144 N. Mapleton Rd., B.H.
Sullivan, Margaret .... 12928 Evanston St., Brt.
Talbot, Lyle .... 261 S. Crescent Dr., B.H.
Talmadge, Norma .... 630 N. Alpine Dr., B.H.
Tamiroff, Akim .... 629 N. Alta Dr., B.H.
Taylor, Elizabeth .... 703 N. Elm Dr., B. H.
Teasdale, Veree .... 722 N. Bedford Dr., B.H.
Temple, Shirley .... 227 N. Rockingham Ave
    Brt. Hts.
Tone, Franchot .... 507 N. Rexford Dr. B.H.
Tracy, Lee .... 101 S. Rockingham Ave., Brt.
Tracy, Spencer .... 5085 White Oak, Encino
Trevor, Claire .... 10940 Bellagio Rd., B.A.
Turner, Lana .... 535 Perugia Way, B.A.
Tyler, Tom .... 2746 Beiden St., Hol.
Vallee, Rudy .... 7430 Pyramid Pl., Hol.
Von Stroheim, Eric .... 307 N. Bristol Ave., Brt.
Walburn, Raymond .... 306 N. Alpine Dr., B.H.
Wallace, Richard .... 11080 Chalon Rd., B.A.
Warner, H. B. .... 526 N. Canon Dr., B.H.
Wayne, John .... 312 N. Highland Ave., Hol.
West, Mae .... 570 N. Rossmore Ave., Hol.
Whalen, Michael .... 1681 Benedict Canyon Rd.
    B.H.
Wilcoxon, Henry .... 1458 Kings Rd., Hol.
Williams, Warren .... 4717 Encino Ave., S.F.V.
Wray, Fay .... 235 Tilden Ave., W.W.
    125 Copa De Oro Rd., B.A.
Wyler, William (Director)
Young, Loretta .... 280 Carolwood Dr., B.H.
Young, Robert .... 607 N. Elm Dr., B.H.

EXPLANATION OF ABBREVIATIONS

B.A.—Bel Air		S.M.—Santa Monica
Hol.—Hollywood		Brt.—Brentwood
L.A.—Los Angeles		N.H.—North Hollywood
B.H.—Beverly Hills		W.W.—Westwood
Glnd.—Glendale		H.Hills—Holmby Hills
W.L.A.—West Los Angeles		
S.F.V.—San Fernando Valley		

Davis, Joan .... 10971 Bellagio Rd., B.A.
DeMille, Cecil B. .... 2010 DeMille Dr., B.H.
Del Rio, Delores .... 1465 Lovecco, B.H.
Donlevy, Brian .... 400 S. Sundy Dr., Brt.
Drew, Ellen .... 10570 Ottone Way, B.A.
Durbin, Deanna .... 421 Saltair Rd., Brt.
Dunn, James .... 9936 Durant Dr., B.H.
Durante, Jimmy .... 511 N. Beverly Dr., B.H.
Eddy, Nelson .... 485 Helvern, Brt.
Edwards, William .... 4101 Dixie Canyon
Fairbanks, Doug. Jr. .... 1515 Amalfi Dr., B.H.
Flynn, Errol .... 7740 Mulholland Dr., Hol.
Forbes, Ralph .... 1464 Linda Crest Dr., B.H.
Foster, Norman .... 1100 Stone Canyon Rd., B.A.
Foster, Preston .... 9101 Hazen Dr., B.H.
Francis, Kay .... 1010 Benedict Canyon Rd., B.H.
Gable, Clark (Gable Ranch) .... Encino, Cal.
Garber, Jan .... 2301 Beaumont Lane, B.H.
Garbo, Greta .... 603 N. Beverly Dr.
Garland, Judy .... 185 Denslow Ave., W.W.
Garson, Greer .... 680 Stone Canyon Rd., B.A.
Gaynor, Janet .... 10424 Valley Spring Lane, N.Hol.
Gilbert, Billy .... 2021 Los Palos Dr., L.A.
Goddard, Paulette .... 1464 Linda Crest Dr., B.H.
Grable, Betty .... 1219 Stone Canyon Rd., B.A.
Grahame, Margot .... 600 N. Walden Dr., B.H.
Grant, Cary .... 1018 Ocean Front, S.M.
Green, Richard .... 2936 Mont Calm Hol.
Greenwood, Charlotte .... 806 N. Rodeo Dr., B.H.

*Souvenir Map and Guide to Starland Estates and
Mansions: A Fascinating Trip Through Movieland*
1947
Martha Lake
Wesley G. Lake, Publisher
Los Angeles
24" x 19"
Collection of William J. Warren

Venice of America

Everything about the place seemed magical, from the streets named Zephyr, Lorelei, and Verona Court, to the features described as the Grand Canal, the Pleasure Pier, Venus Canal, St. Mark's Island, the chariot track, and the Pacific Promenade. This map of "Venice of America" lays out the lofty dream of the remarkable Abbot Kinney selling real estate in a proposed resort like no other in the country: a place of class and charm, where one could enjoy uplifting lectures, attend great theater, and stroll among the best in society while sea breezes cooled a scene, like something out of a Renoir painting. The crisp subdivision with open public spaces separating cozy domiciles from entertainment and commercial areas demonstrates the "City Beautiful" ideal, with the added appeal of the Pacific Ocean for a backyard. One could buy or rent delightful cottages on tidy twenty-five-by-one-hundred-foot lots right on picturesque canals, where gondoliers guided real gondolas down the way while singing Italian arias for blissed-out tourists. No mere swimming pool here but a bathing lake was at the center, and there was to be an aquarium, fine hotels, a first-class theater, a bathhouse, a boathouse, and a wonderful two-and-a-half-mile miniature railroad surrounding the project like a string of South Sea pearls.

Abbot Kinney was a cultured man, well traveled and multilingual. He had a dream of creating this cultural mecca, which he spread before potential investors at his "information bureau" in downtown Los Angeles at the Hotel Angelus. Kinney finally broke from his partners in the Ocean Park Improvement Company in early 1904 and set to work creating this dreamscape. When folks made purchases in the "infant city" the local papers would publish the names like blessed events, and "Doge" Kinney, as he was sometimes called, managed to get rail lines to connect Venice to Los Angeles and nearby Santa Monica. Often called "sand dune town" because it was placed upon a drained marsh, Venice was made to look like its European model, complete with a Piazza San Marcos and Italian Renaissance architectural style.

The actual construction, however, was no dream but featured labor-union busting, months of construction washed away by winter storms, and the budget straining to realize this extravagant plan. Miraculously the pier and auditorium were finished on time, and an astonishing 25,000—possibly 40,000—people showed up for the grand opening on July 4, 1905. Swimming races, lectures on Theodore Roosevelt's presidency, band music, three thousand American flags, a tennis tournament, a lady's tea, electrical displays, and fireworks were part of the celebration. While Venice never really reached Kinney's lofty intent, it did eventually prosper and continue even into the 1940s. It then went through a series of changes but always seemed to remain fascinating.

Despite Kinney's intention to boost the IQ of the area by offering some nine hundred lectures and theatricals along Chatauqua ideals, the public seemed more interested in lowbrow pursuits. The lectures and drama translated to a sixteen-thousand-dollar loss in the first year, but roller coasters, freak shows, vaudeville, and carnival amusements brought the endeavor back into the black in following years.

1905
Los Angeles County,
California
Abbot Kinney Company
Colored lithograph
Los Angeles City Archives

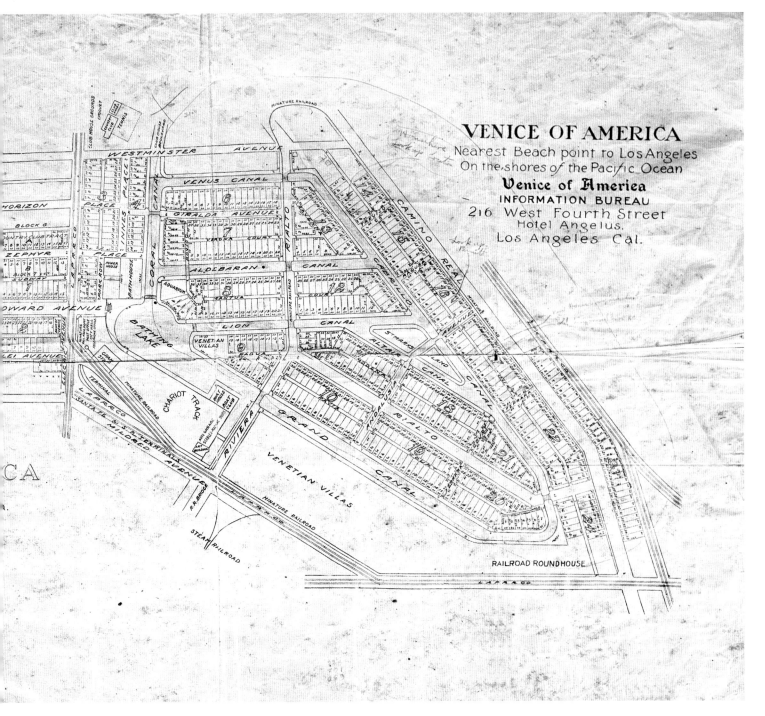

Simons Brick Company—Yard No. 3

You may see the name on the USGS topographic quadrangles of Bell that were published later in the century, but for the most part you will not see Simons Brickyard on street guides of Los Angeles. The exception is this very detailed early wall map of that faraway portion of the city that lists "Simons" on the Atchison, Topeka and Santa Fe freight rail line at the edge of what was then called Newmark, which later became Montebello. It was almost as if the place existed in an alternative universe and in some ways it certainly was invisible to the population at large. The well-meaning industrialist Walter Simons founded the brickyard in 1905. By all accounts he truly loved his workers and thought he was providing them opportunities that were impossible in their native country. Yet Simons Brickyard, despite the Gilded Age paternalism, created a form of segregation that involved thousands of workers brought from Mexican states like Jalisco, Michoacan, and Guanajuato to work in the rural Montebello brickyard and live in one of the few company towns in the state of California. It can be said that the company and those hard-working Mexicans were responsible for much of the physical growth of the city, since Simons bricks formed the structure of businesses, universities, hospitals, homes, and hotels that were products of the real estate booms in the early twentieth century. In their heyday there were eight Simons plants scattered around Southern California.

The work was very hard, sometimes beginning at 3 a.m. and continuing in shifts up to twelve hours a day in the good weather. In the early years the company produced thirty rail cars a day, comprised of 160,000 bricks during a day's work. Some said the system at Simons was hacienda style, with unskilled "peons" doing backbreaking labor as overseers watched under an all-powerful owner who reaped great economic benefits while the workers lived in relative poverty. Labor unions were strictly forbidden, and a moral code was strictly enforced.

As business increased and the brickyard covered some 350 acres of land, entire families were brought from Mexico to labor. Bonuses were offered by management for babies that might eventually join the workforce, which reached three thousand at one point. Beyond the backbreaking labor involved in making these bricks, there were a self-contained community that had a company store where company scrip and tokens were spent on essentials and an appointed town sheriff kept the peace. It had the Mount Carmel Catholic Church, a dancehall, a post office with its own postmark, and small houses where the workers lived without electricity, gas, or indoor plumbing. Liquor was forbidden, and at night the gates of the compound were locked. Yet the resilient residents found ways to make the best of the rigid system and raised families, had fiestas, formed baseball teams (equipped with full uniforms with jerseys emblazoned "Simons" across the chest), staged professional boxing matches, and even produced company bands that were good enough to march in the Rose Parade. The Vail School provided by the company made little concession for the Spanish-speaking pupils, and many of the children had to seek education elsewhere, some by joining the armed services during the world wars. In the early years, when the Simons families did make rare excursions outside the company town to outlying communities, they were treated as second-class citizens and subjected to blatant discrimination. Later, some residents managed to work outside the compound and did assimilate somewhat into Montebello, even sending children to the high school and taking work in the nearby walnut fields. Simons Brickyard saw business decline due to competition, the Depression, and the banning of brick buildings after the 1933 Long Beach earthquake, but continued into the early 1950s when old Mr. Simons died and left thousands of dollars to the last twenty-six loyal employees. Some of the residents of Simons still gather and celebrate their families' experience at the brickyard, even using words like "Camelot" for a time and place that was their own.

Map of the Southern Portion of Los Angeles County
Jacob and Rock Publishers
1908
Colored lithograph on oilskin
Los Angeles Public Library

Following page: map detail.

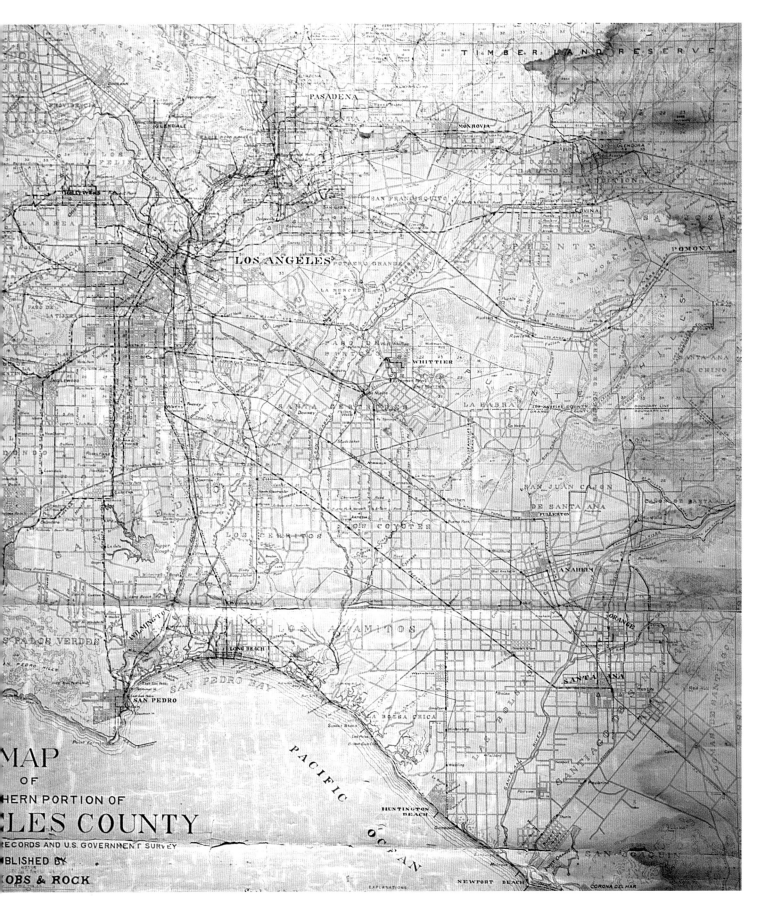

MAP
OF
HERN PORTION OF
ELES COUNTY
RECORDS AND U.S. GOVERNMENT SURVEY
BLISHED BY
OBS & ROCK

Chavez Ravine

The sleepy, bucolic, rolling hills called Chavez Ravine, nestled in the middle of Elysian Park, figure large in Los Angeles history, much larger than the open spaces shown here in the first Baist atlas of the city. This map shows the blank slate of the place before the neighborhoods that sprung up here in the 1920s and '30scalled Palo Verde, La Loma, and Bishop. Once known as "Rock Quarry Hills" or "Stone Quarry Hills," the land seemed like country within the city from the beginning, when the ravine got its name from Julian Chavez, a Spanish-speaking pioneer and member of the very first county board of supervisors in 1852. Chavez acquired the land before statehood and held onto it after the Americans came, getting his grubstake by trapping and trading in the old pueblo. Chavez Ravine and Elysian Park are forever tied together, especially after the city made the hills a park for perpetuity in 1886, setting forward hundreds of little dramas. There were endless discussions about roads into and out of Chavez Ravine, the creation of a "Pest House" or smallpox quarantine hospital, the shenanigans of the Los Angeles Brick Company blasting dynamite charges, the possibility of oil drilling, the founding of the Barlow Tuberculosis Sanitarium, and even the construction of a huge naval armory in the early 1940s.

Yet nothing compared with the intrigue and controversy of the upheaval brought on by the displacement of hundreds of families, mostly poor Mexicans, Filipinos, and African Americans. The ravine presented a close-knit community that thrived without a lot of money or help from the government. Yet the families in Chavez Ravine managed to grow twenty acres of oats and hay on the hillsides as a voluntary part of the war effort, producing fourteen tons of grain from this unexpected source. The three communities were once described by famed photographer Don Normark as a "poor man's Shangri-la," but the city had been eyeing the property from as far back as the turn of the century for one project or another. After World War II there were progressive social idealists who believed they could improve the lives of the people in Chavez Ravine along with thousands more by constructing public housing on the land, and the city began buying land using eminent domain. The idea of the program had a noble source in the Los Angeles Housing Authority's Frank Wilkinson, who believed this was an opportunity to create economic justice and aid social reform by building low-cost residential developments. Wilkinson even had the great Richard Neutra designing the high-density housing, with schools and playgrounds included in the plan. The resistance of the families who had lived contentedly in Chavez Ravine is legendary, but the city promised them first choice in the future, and many sadly took the money and waited while a way of life was obliterated forever. McCarthyism played a major role in destroying the well-meaning plan, but the city went ahead with the evictions of the residents and eventually traded the land to the newly arrived Los Angeles Dodger organization, which eventually built Dodger stadium. The actual construction of the stadium centered where Mount Lookout appears on this map, and the place where generations lived happily in the Ravine was covered with asphalt and made into parking lots.

Baist's Real Estate Atlas of
Surveys of Los Angeles
G. Wm Baist
1910

Mesmer City

W hen this map was created in the mid-1920s it was a flush time in Los Angeles, with oil flowing, movies being made, airplanes roaring over the basin, and real estate investors and industrialists searching the wide-open spaces of the county for available land. This highly exaggerated little sketch shows mighty Mesmer City, with lots being offered by George Bray on a great expanse of untapped resources to the southwest of downtown Los Angeles. Like the great Oz, the place stood behind a curtain of words that no one had actually seen, but it all looked great. The Mesmer City Corporation Limited had been busy developing the area for five years when it trumpeted this opportunity where the subdivision appeared to be twice the size of the local community of Culver City and equal to Baldwin Hills. Mesmer City went on the market in August 1924, proferred by Mr. George Bray and described as part of the "bay district," despite the only occasional whiff of sea breezes from the Pacific a few miles away. Stories connected with the area are filled with bombast, as in Mr. Bray leading a procession of thousands to the local college dedication in his Reo Flying Cloud automobile. Mesmer City roars like a lion on the map but in reality it just purred like a house cat.

The land was originally owned by Joseph Mesner, son of pioneer Louis Mesner, a Frenchman who made his fortune in early bakeries and hotels in the city. Joseph continued his father's success and eventually purchased the tracts where the street and city took his name. While Mesmer City was mentioned in the newspapers and even telephone books, it was in reality just a little piece of the land, less than ten streets long and certainly not comparable to the five square miles of Culver City. However, in the days before postal codes, place-names stuck for practicality's sake, including the rather unique circus town Barnes City, which was founded and annexed by the city within a couple of years, but the name stuck for decades. Eventually the Baker Airport, which became the Culver City Airport the following year, took shape around 1927 and made a border on Mesmer. Loyola University's new campus was built nearby in 1929 but not quite close enough to make Mesmer the place promised on the map, as evidenced by the suit filed by actor John Boles, who expected more. The event that put Mesmer City on the motion-picture map was the use of its land for the filming of the classic *The Good Earth* in 1936, but mention of the place pretty much faded in the 1950s.

1924
George A. Bray Company
Handbill
Los Angeles Public Library

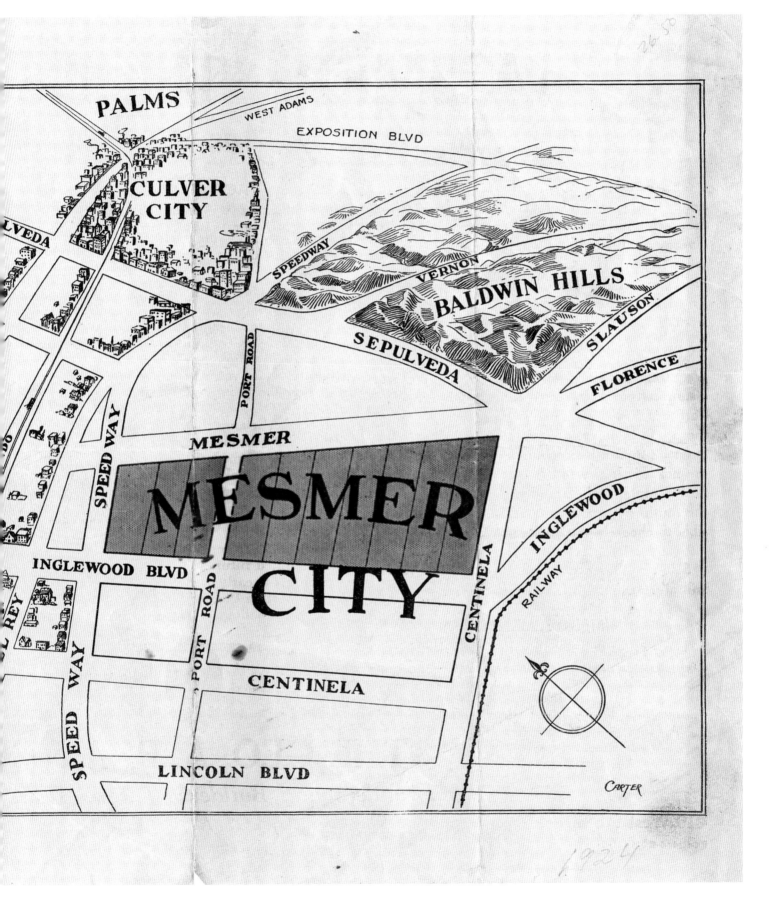

PALMS

WEST ADAMS

EXPOSITION BLVD

CULVER CITY

SPEEDWAY

VERNON

BALDWIN HILLS

SLAUSON

LVEDA

PORT ROAD

SEPULVEDA

FLORENCE

SPEED WAY

MESMER

MESMER CITY

INGLEWOOD

INGLEWOOD BLVD

CENTINELA

RAILWAY

EL REY

PORT ROAD

SPEED WAY

CENTINELA

LINCOLN BLVD

CARTER

Barnes City

Barnes City, named for the flamboyant Al G. Barnes, a.k.a Alpheus George Barnes Stonehouse, was almost as colorful and controversial as the man who created the most identifiable circus in Los Angeles for decades. This map shows the Barnes Square tract in Baldwin Hills, which was the winter quarters for the Al G. Barnes Circus from 1919 on and a city unto itself for 254 performers and a menagerie. Barnes and his troupe traveled on a deluxe private train with forty cars named after southland cities all around the U.S. and Canada, some 35,000 miles annually, then returned here in the off-season. Four thousand animals lived on the land during winter months, including zebras, hippos, apes, wolves, pumas, polar bears, lions, tigers, seals, ostriches, horses, birds of all description, and "Tusko," the eight-thousand-pound elephant that Barnes rode into the circus ring as master of ceremonies during shows.

Mr. Barnes at first sought to have Barnes City incorporated into Los Angeles, but he faced stiff opposition. The forces against Barnes included the La Ballona Improvement Association, citizens of nearby Albright City, the city of Mar Vista, and the Artland Club, with their fifteen acres set aside for artists and sculptors. All fought for their own recognition from city hall, and wild charges flew, including insistence that Barnes City would soon be known by a "simian cognomen," in their words "Monkeyland," thus making a laughing stock out of the entire region. Barnes took center stage in the fight and managed to get a handpicked board of trustees in place to ensure his city would be incorporated. In a supposedly tainted election, the Barnes slate won and his brother was named mayor.

A homeowners group that opposed the "Barnes faction" meanwhile turned back that board of trustees and eventually reversed the incorporation in February 1926, forging ahead for annexation by the City of Los Angeles. On September 14, 1926, after a bitter campaign, a municipal election went two to one in favor of the annexation, but realtor George Bray filed a suit questioning the legality of the election on a technicality the following day. A series of similar suits filled Superior Court and the matters of taxation were debated until October 4, 1930, when it was permanently named as part of Los Angeles. In the winter of 1927, when the Barnes Circus came off the road, it did not return to this Barnes City but relocated to Baldwin Park near El Monte. Barnes subdivided his properties and put them on the market, as seen on this map that removed the circus from Barnes City forever. The land was worth more than the circus, but Barnes was only able to hold that together in the lean times of the Depression for a short time. He sold the circus in 1929 to the American Circus Corporation for a million dollars, but Barnes City faded from memory in the next ten years and eventually became part of Mar Vista.

Barnes Square Tract
1928
George Forncrook
Barnes Realty Corporation
Newspaper handbill
Seaver Center for Western History

THIS TRACT---MY FORMER WINTER QUARTERS

ON WASHINGTON BOULEVARD

BARNES REALTY
CORPORATION
OWNERS AND SUBDIVIDERS
Arthur W. Knowles
— AGENT —
1513 W. 7TH ST. ◼ LOS ANGELES

R PARTICULARS AND VALUABLE INFORMATION

Nautical Map of Catalina Island

T here probably was no one in the history of Los Angeles who knew more about navigation than Captain Frank Jansen, who drew this crisply detailed nautical chart of Catalina Island sometime in the late 1920s. Jansen was a master mariner who spent eighteen years at sea and sailed around the world four times. Off and on he also taught the science of navigation and nautical astronomy in New York City and then crossed the continent to the Pacific Ocean and Los Angeles. He settled somewhat on land as an instructor for the University of Southern California, where he taught hundreds of local mariners in twelve-week classes. Each session featured three navigational cruises per term, with participants sometimes eschewing charts and using only the stars to guide them. Among his pupils were G. Allen Hancock of Hancock Park and German film director F. W. Murnau, whose yacht "Bali" Jansen brought back from Tahiti to San Pedro after his death. A self-described "old sea captain," he lectured tirelessly on navigation all around the city, even within the newer science of aeronautics. Jansen invented a celestial sphere used in ocean navigation in his youth and created charts including this beauty, which ignores the tourist Catalina and focuses instead on depths and anchorages to guide those sailing in the waters.

Although the pop song says Santa Catalina is "twenty-six miles across the sea," it is very much a part of Los Angeles, with people and history that link it to the mainland. In fact Catalina, as the locals call the island, is a mere twenty-two miles south-southwest of the city limits and part of an archipelago in the Channel Islands. Originally settled by the Tongva Indians and called Pimu, the island was "claimed" for Spain in 1542 by Juan Rodriguez Cabrillo and then named Santa Catalina by Sebastian Vizcaino in 1602. Not much happened for the next three centuries besides otter hunting, fishing, and the use of the island as a smuggling base to the big city. Catalina always offered challenges to permanent residency due to the lack of freshwater, but George Shatto purchased the land from the James Lick Trust in the great real estate boom year of 1887. Hoping to build a great resort, he founded the town of Avalon and began steamer service from Los Angeles. Shatto passed on the same hope, after the money ran out, to the new owners, the sons of Phineas Banning. The Bannings did manage to make Avalon into a resort community, paving roads inland, building a dance pavilion, and finishing the grand Hotel Metropole. However, the first of several disastrous fires occurred in 1915 that, along with the economic strains of World War I, drove the Bannings to finally sell shares to the public, including the chewing gum magnate William Wrigley Jr. Wrigley so loved the island he bought out all other shareholders in 1919 and the family maintained ownership for the next fifty-five years.

Catalina was a popular destination for vacationing locals for decades and boasted one of finest venues for swing music in the country at the Casino Theater and Ballroom in Avalon, built in 1929. Visitors enjoyed a fine movie palace called the Avalon Theater that showed feature films nightly, along with other attractions like the glass-bottom boat tours, the aquarium, and the St. Catherine Hotel. Over the years the island was used as a motion picture location in more than five hundred films, forever connecting Catalina to Hollywood.

1928 (?)
Captain Frank Jansen
Colored lithograph
22″ x 24″
Los Angeles Public Library

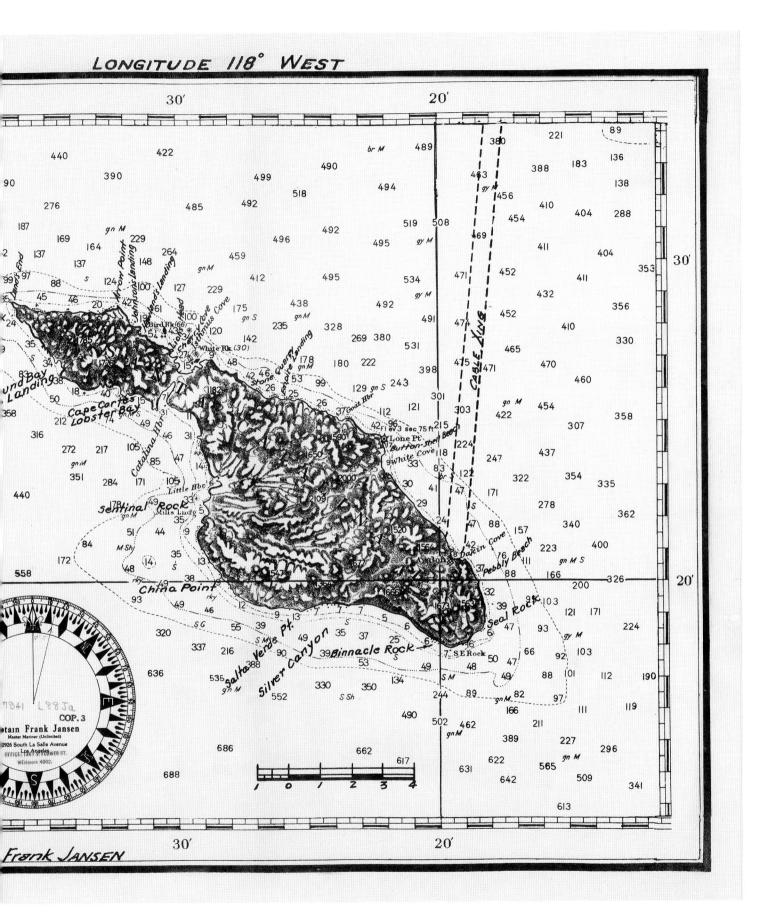

Frank Jansen

Arnold Schoenberg's Los Angeles

While this map was created for a brochure announcing a Los Angeles Philharmonic program called the "Schoenberg Prism" it captures a colorful era in the arts around Southern California involving a group of talented exiles that fled political persecution in Europe and enriched the city with their art, music, and literature.

The focal point here is the great composer Arnold Schoenberg, who seems to have taken to the southland enthusiastically after arriving in 1934 at the age of sixty with his young wife Gertrud and infant daughter Nuria. He was called "iconoclast" and "genius" by local newspapers and quickly found friends and musical contacts across the Los Angeles landscape. His twelve-tone harmonic system was controversial but groundbreaking in classical composition. His first job was lecturing at USC on "the modern idiom" but he soon achieved a professorship at UCLA where the music department and performance hall bear his name to this day.

Many of Schoenberg's fellow expatriates made homes nearby, including Bertold Brecht, Thomas Mann, Lion and Marta Feuchtwanger, and Otto Klemperer, as indicated here. Musicologists state that the arrival of sophisticated European émigrés like Arnold Schoenberg made Los Angeles into the center of the classical music world during the 1930s and 1940s. Many of the finest instrumentalists in the world of classical music came here and played in concert and in studio orchestras, participating in the symphonic film scores that have come to be accepted as great art on their own.

Arnold Schoenberg was one of the first artists to speak out against anti-Semitism and worked tirelessly all over the area trying to help artists escape the terrors of the Nazi regime.

He taught and wrote music while living in Brentwood on the now infamous Rockingham Avenue (location of O. J. Simpson's home) but traveled to many prominent performing venues to conduct, including the Philharmonic and Trinity Auditoriums in downtown Los Angeles and Royce Hall on the UCLA campus.

Schoenberg's compositions were performed all over the map seen here, from the Biltmore Hotel, Los Angeles City College, and Bovard Auditorium at USC, to the Ambassador Hotel and the open-air glory of the Hollywood Bowl. His influence was great as a teacher, performer, and mentor to musical artists ranging from the great film composer Alfred Newman to the avant-garde John Cage as well as many other writers, architects, actors, and performers.

Los Angeles was blessed by this influx of true musical genius and possesses to this day a very sophisticated audience for modern classical music. Not just a creature of the arts, Arnold Schoenberg was also an avid tennis player; note the La Cienega courts where he battled none other than George Gershwin on the clay.

2001
William Kent Advertising and Design
24" x 19"
The Los Angeles Philharmonic
Los Angeles Public Library

ЅOENBERG's LOS ANGELES

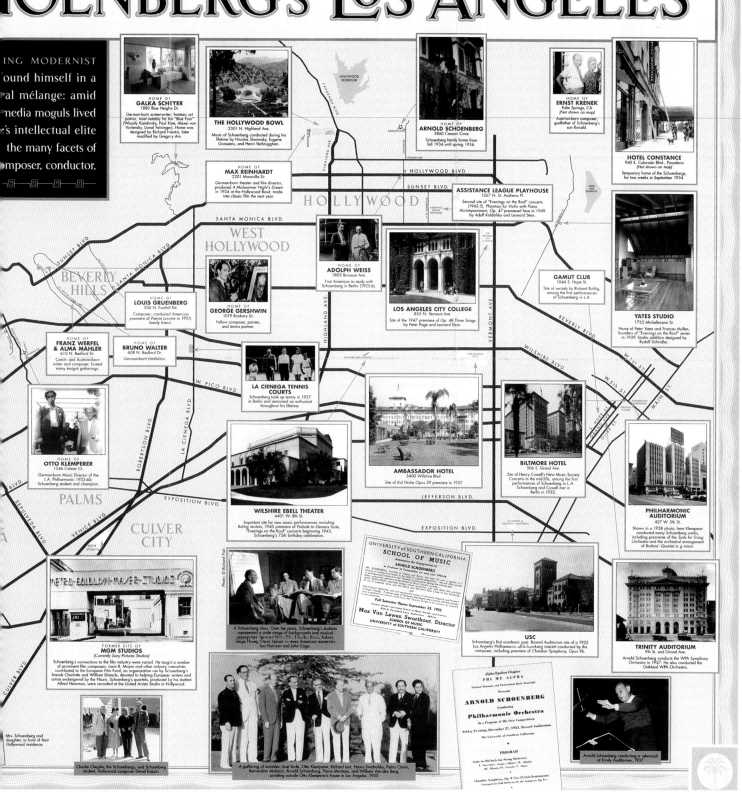

ING MODERNIST ound himself in a al mélange: amid nedia moguls lived 's intellectual elite the many facets of mposer, conductor,

HOME OF GALKA SCHEYER
1880 Blue Heights Dr.
German-born screenwriter; hostess; art patron, most notably for the "Blue Four" (Wassily Kandinsky, Paul Klee, Alexei von Yawlensky, Lionel Feininger). Home was designed by Richard Neutra, later modified by Gregory Ain.

THE HOLLYWOOD BOWL
2301 N. Highland Ave.
Music of Schoenberg conducted during his lifetime by Nicolas Slonimsky, Eugene Goossens, and Henri Verbrugghen.

HOME OF ARNOLD SCHOENBERG
5860 Canyon Cove
Schoenberg family home from fall 1934 until spring 1936.

HOME OF ERNST KRENEK
Palm Springs, CA
(Not shown on map)
Austrian-born composer; godfather of Schoenberg's son Ronald.

HOTEL CONSTANCE
940 E. Colorado Blvd., Pasadena
(Not shown on map)
Temporary home of the Schoenbergs, for two weeks in September 1934.

HOME OF MAX REINHARDT
2201 Maravilla Dr.
German-born theater and film director; produced A Midsummer Night's Dream in 1934 at the Hollywood Bowl; made into classic film the next year.

ASSISTANCE LEAGUE PLAYHOUSE
1367 N. St. Andrews Pl.
Second site of "Evenings on the Roof" concerts (1942-5). Phantasy for Violin with Piano Accompaniment, Op. 47 premiered here in 1949 by Adolf Koldofsky and Leonard Stein.

HOME OF ADOLPH WEISS
1803 Bronson Ave.
First American to study with Schoenberg in Berlin (1925-6).

GAMUT CLUB
1044 S. Hope St.
Site of recitals by Richard Buhlig, among the first performances of Schoenberg in L.A.

YATES STUDIO
1735 Micheltorena St.
Home of Peter Yates and Frances Mullen, founders of "Evenings on the Roof" series in 1939. Studio addition designed by Rudolf Schindler.

HOME OF LOUIS GRUENBERG
506 N. Foothill Rd.
Composer; conducted American premiere of Pierrot Lunaire in 1923; family friend.

HOME OF GEORGE GERSHWIN
1019 Roxbury Dr.
Fellow composer, painter, and tennis partner.

LOS ANGELES CITY COLLEGE
855 N. Vermont Ave.
Site of the 1947 premiere of Op. 48 Three Songs by Peter Page and Leonard Stein.

HOME OF FRANZ WERFEL & ALMA MAHLER
610 N. Bedford Dr.
Czech and Austrian-born writer and composer; hosted many émigré gatherings.

HOME OF BRUNO WALTER
608 N. Bedford Dr.
German-born conductor.

LA CIENEGA TENNIS COURTS
Schoenberg took up tennis in 1927 in Berlin and remained an enthusiast throughout his lifetime.

HOME OF OTTO KLEMPERER
1546 Calmer Ct.
German-born Music Director of the L.A. Philharmonic 1933-40; Schoenberg student and champion.

AMBASSADOR HOTEL
3400 Wilshire Blvd.
Site of Kol Nidre Opus 39 premiere in 1937.

BILTMORE HOTEL
506 S. Grand Ave.
Site of Henry Cowell's New Music Society Concerts in the mid-20s, among the first performances of Schoenberg in L.A. Schoenberg and Cowell met in Berlin in 1932.

PHILHARMONIC AUDITORIUM
427 W. 5th St.
Shown in a 1938 photo; here Klemperer conducted many Schoenberg works, including premieres of the Suite for String Orchestra and the orchestral arrangement of Brahms' Quartet in g minor.

WILSHIRE EBELL THEATER
4401 W. 8th St.
Important site for new music performances including Buhlig recitals, 1945 premiere of Prelude to Genesis Suite, "Evenings on the Roof" concerts beginning 1945, Schoenberg's 75th birthday celebration.

Photo: © Richard Fish

A Schoenberg class. Over the years, Schoenberg's students represented a wide range of backgrounds and musical genres, among them Leonard Stein, Dika Newlin, Bruno Raksin, Serge Hovey, Oscar Levant — even American mavericks Lou Harrison and John Cage.

UNIVERSITY of SOUTHERN CALIFORNIA SCHOOL OF MUSIC
Announces the Engagement of
ARNOLD SCHOENBERG
as Professor of Composition
[...]
Fall Semester Opens September 25, 1935
Max Van Lewen Swarthout, Director
SCHOOL OF MUSIC
UNIVERSITY of SOUTHERN CALIFORNIA

USC
Schoenberg's first academic post. Bovard Auditorium site of a 1935 Los Angeles Philharmonic and Schoenberg concert conducted by the composer, including premiere of Chamber Symphony, Opus 9b.

TRINITY AUDITORIUM
9th St. and Grand Ave.
Arnold Schoenberg conducts the WPA Symphony Orchestra in 1937. He also conducted the Oakland WPA Orchestra.

FORMER SITE OF MGM STUDIOS
(Currently Sony Pictures Studios)
Schoenberg's connections to the film industry were varied. He taught a number of prominent film composers. Louis B. Mayer and other industry executives contributed to the European Film Fund, an organization run by Schoenberg's friends Charlotte and William Dieterle, devoted to helping European writers and artists endangered by the Nazis. Schoenberg's quartets, produced by his student Alfred Newman, were recorded at the United Artists Studio in Hollywood.

Mrs. Schoenberg and daughter, in front of their Hollywood residence.

Charlie Chaplin, the Schoenbergs, and Schoenberg student, Hollywood composer David Raksin.

A gathering of notables: José Iturbi, Otto Klemperer, Richard Lert, Henry Svedrofsky, Pietro Cimini, Bernardino Molinari, Arnold Schoenberg, Pierre Montoux, and William Van den Berg, standing outside Otto Klemperer's house in Los Angeles, 1935.

Alpha Epsilon Chapter
PHI MU ALPHA
National Honorary and Professional Music Fraternity
Presents
ARNOLD SCHOENBERG
Conducting
Philharmonic Orchestra
In a Program of His Own Compositions
Friday Evening, December 27, 1935, Bovard Auditorium
The University of Southern California

Arnold Schoenberg conducting a rehearsal at Trinity Auditorium, 1937.

Bell Quadrangle

What might appear to be a garden-variety topo-graphic map of part of southeast Los Angeles County carries two controversial stories from Los Angeles's checkered past. The Bell Quadrangle in 1936 covers a mixture of working-class suburbs like South Gate, Bell, Maywood, and Lynwood but also the aforementioned Simons Brickyard and, little over a mile away, a reservoir once known as Sleepy Lagoon. Both live in particular infamy among the stories of overt racism and the oppression of minorities in the city of angels. They can also be seen as testaments of courage, endurance, the power of family, and even the ethnic pride that eventually defeated such ignorance.

Sleepy Lagoon was just one of two reservoirs used to irrigate the Williams Ranch on the outskirts of Bell. Named "Sleepy Lagoon" after a popular song of the day, it was used as a swimming hole by local kids who were discouraged from using local municipal pools because of their Mexican heritage. On the night of August 1, 1942, there was an altercation between teenagers during a party held nearby that left young Jose Diaz dead in its aftermath. The tragedy was greatly compounded by the xenophobic witch hunt that ensued, with more than six hundred Mexican Americans rounded up by the police and taken into custody, many solely on the style of dress they affected called the "Zoot Suit." The trial and hysteria continued for months, and twelve men were convicted of murder with no compelling evidence except for their membership in a youth gang. The city seemed to be looking for a scapegoat for what was then called "the delinquent problem," and local newspapers added fuel to the fire with articles condemning what they called "boy gangsters."

Just a few months later, with tensions still high and prejudice against the Zoot Suiters boiling, a street fight downtown set off days of mob rule and ruthless beatings by servicemen of Mexican Americans, African Americans, and even Filipinos. Goaded on by the local papers that gave instruction on "de-zooting," young sailors, soldiers, and marines roamed in packs searching for those wearing the clothes that were merely a statement of style rather than rebellion. The Zoot Suit Riots continued for an entire week, the violence spreading to anyone of different ethnicity, and made a blemish on the city's social fabric that has been slow to heal. Most of the injustice of the events was swept under the rug for decades until the groundbreaking play *Zoot Suit* by Luis Valdez brought it all to the surface for reexamination in 1978.

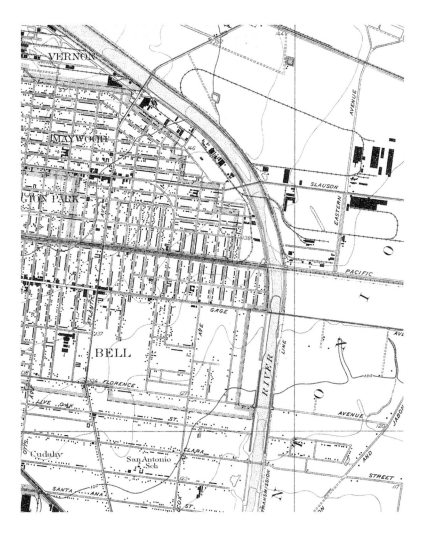

1936
U.S Geological Survey
Printed map
Los Angeles Public Library

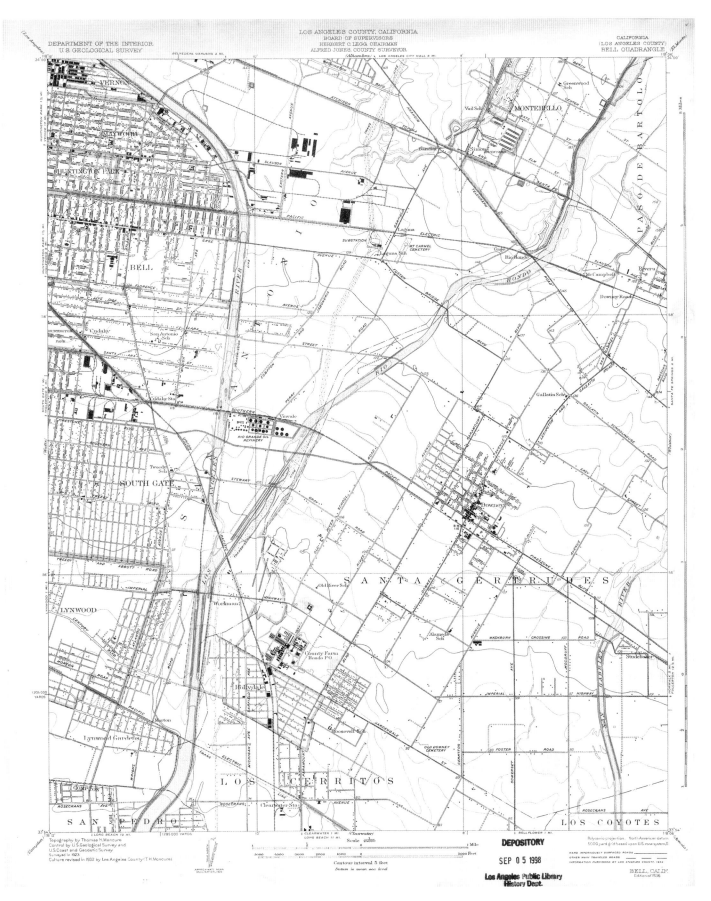

LOS ANGELES COUNTY, CALIFORNIA
BOARD OF SUPERVISORS
HERBERT C. LEGG, CHAIRMAN
ALFRED JONES, COUNTY SURVEYOR

CALIFORNIA
(LOS ANGELES COUNTY)
BELL QUADRANGLE

Topography by Thomas H. Moncure
Control by U.S. Geological Survey and
U.S. Coast and Geodetic Survey
Surveyed in 1923
Culture revised in 1932 by Los Angeles County (T.H. Moncure)

Scale 31500

Contour interval 5 feet
Datum is mean sea level

Polyconic projection. North American datum
5000 yard grid based upon U.S. zone system(s)

HARD IMPERVIOUSLY SURFACED ROADS
OTHER MAIN TRAVELED ROADS
INFORMATION FURNISHED BY LOS ANGELES COUNTY, 1934

BELL, CALIF.
Edition of 1936

Central Avenue

This composite of two sheets from a Sanborn Fire Insurance atlas might seem like a rather mundane couple of blocks in the city, but they actually represent one of the genuine cultural phenomenons of Los Angeles. Central Avenue seen here (at map's bottom) at the end of its heyday in 1950 was a Mecca for music lovers and the heart of the African American community for decades. Although Central Avenue existed as a destination from the 1920s to the '50s, it reached a peak for glamour and excitement during World War II with the city finally coming out from under the Depression and a great influx of black workers arriving in the area to take jobs in the defense industry. In 1920 the African American population was under sixteen thousand, but it more than doubled in each ensuing decade, with 40 percent of those living within blocks of Central Avenue as it stretched from 11th street downtown south past 42nd. Because of restrictive real estate covenants and a pernicious racism that limited opportunities in the county, most African Americans were forced to settle into that narrow strip. However, Central Avenue was an answer to such bigotry, with its self-sufficient black-owned businesses, hotels, insurance companies, restaurants, markets, and entertainment venues that created a city within a city. In many ways this surpassed anything in the rest of Los Angeles. The streets were "safe, friendly and very lively at all hours of the day."

People flocked to the area in the evenings to visit the many night clubs and hear jazz or rhythm and blues played by the finest musicians around, including native son Dexter Gordon, Big Jay McNeely, Charles Mingus, Art Farmer, Art Tatum, Dizzy Gillespie, and for a short time Charley Parker. Within two blocks there were six major clubs where top artists performed and strolled back in forth between sets to hear other stars play. The Club Alabam, one of the best known, is on these sheets along with the one-hundred-room Dunbar Hotel, where huge celebrities like Duke Ellington, Louis Armstrong, Billie Holiday, Cab Calloway, Ella Fitzgerald, Paul Williams, Bill Robinson, Joe Louis, and Jackie Robinson stayed or just performed in splendorous surroundings. The Memo, the Downbeat, the Last Word, Bird in the Basket, and the Turban Room were all nearby clubs with great music. Because of the twenty-four-hour-a-day production in wartime factories, many of the clubs operated a swing shift set from 2 a.m. to dawn, and stars like Mae West, Lana Turner, Orson Welles, and Ava Gardner came out from Hollywood to get in on the action. Many early jazz or rhythm and blues hipsters were drawn to Central Avenue, like the teenaged Art Pepper who played at Club Alabam and its eighty-foot-long bar. Of course, the street was not all fun and games, and these Sanborn maps also show the other sides of the neighborhood, where the Golden State Mutual Life Insurance offices toiled, Racers Auto Works repaired cars, the Alabama Cleaners pressed suits, or Federal Plumbing fixed sinks. Down 43rd Place the *Los Angeles Sentinel* published just one of three newspapers, a short stroll led to Sonny's Billiard Parlor or Lena Torrence's Phonograph Records, and across the street from the Dunbar Hotel, the People's Funeral Home, years after Central Avenue lost its luster, was the sad place of soul singers at Sam Cooke's funeral.

Insurance Maps of Los Angeles, California, Volume 4
1950
Sanborn Map Company
Atlas sheets 479 and 480
California State University Northridge

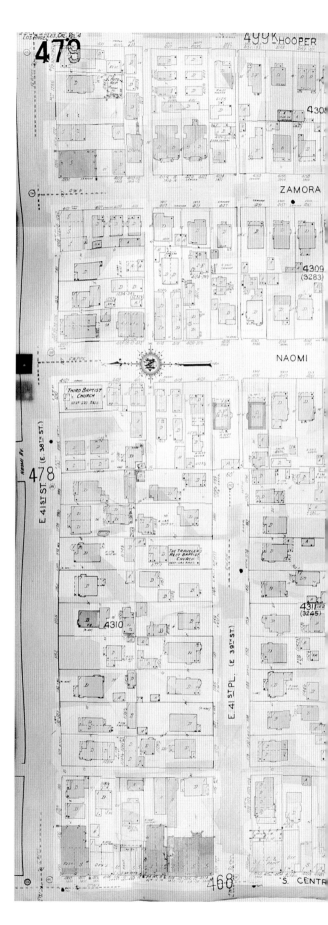

Wrigley Field

Atlases created to determine fire risk for insurance underwriters date back to the early nineteenth century, and many cartographers took on the task in cities throughout North America as the population moved closer and closer into the cities. The Sanborn Company was started by D. A. Sanborn, a young surveyor from Massachusetts who used his experience with Aetna Insurance to create his own company in New York after the end of the Civil War. The maps became invaluable, and when Sanborn died in 1883 the company continued on to become the country's preeminent provider of such maps, with more than seven hundred employees and three main offices in New York, Chicago, and San Francisco. The maps are hand colored, meticulously created by cartographers at fifty feet to one inch, and issued in very small lots on single sheets. Much later they were bound into books that, in the case of Los Angeles, reached forty-two volumes. It was not until the 1920s that the company moved into loose-leaf sheets to accommodate changes, and as neighborhoods evolved, clerks placed pastings over the sites to reflect new buildings or structures being torn down. The colors signify building information ranging from construction materials to the location of hydrants, skylines, elevators, porches, and even garages marked as auto houses. The Sanborn Company covered Los Angeles from 1888 and to contemporary times, but few could foresee the importance of these detailed atlases in the study of urban history. The greatest single collection of the hard-copy atlases is in the Library of Congress, but California State University at Northridge maintains the best existing West Coast collection, with an archive of 1,631 towns in pristine condition.

One of the many uses of the atlases is the study of historical ballparks, and the maps are used with great success by baseball researchers all over the world. Here, on sheet 437 of a Sanborn atlas from 1956, is a little slice of nostalgia called Wrigley Field. It was one of the last glory years for a minor-league baseball franchise that once was the toast of the town, and the place was a lightening rod of local baseball excitement and later of great controversy.

Los Angeles has been a sports-loving town since the days of the Plaza, and particularly a baseball town, as evidenced by some sixteen ballparks that existed around the city. The game was played as early as the eighteenth century from the open land near St. Vincent's College downtown, to 1st street on the east side, to industrial Vernon, to Venice where the American pastime was enjoyed by the Pacific Ocean. In the beginning, the continual fine weather permitted the game almost year round, and baseball was played by the pros in barnstorming tours throughout the winter. In 1903, at the time of its founding, the Pacific Coast League welcomed the Los Angeles Angels as one of six teams that played on the West Coast in seasons that could last from February to December because of the climate. The Angels were the darlings of the city during those years and won the pennant eight times playing at Washington Park (also Chutes Park), which was at the end of a short trolley ride from the center of the city.

In 1921 the team was purchased by chewing gum magnate William K. Wrigley, who owned the big league Chicago Cubs and used the Angels as his farm team, training them for some years on Catalina Island, which he also owned. The Angels needed a new home, and they got it in 1925 with the beautiful Wrigley Field at 41st and Avalon in South Central Los Angeles. As seen on this Sanborn sheet, Wrigley was an intimate, 21,000-seat stadium supposedly modeled after Cubs Park in the Windy City. Ironically, the ballpark in Los Angeles was the first to be called Wrigley Field. While the description is simple, the map shows the fireproof steel girders holding up the stadium (and blocking the view of some fans) and the grandstand wrapping around the diamond and bleachers out in right center field, a lengthy 412 feet from home plate. For many years the park was shared with the rival Hollywood Stars until 1939, when they left for their own Gilmore Field. Old-timers swear that the Pacific Coast League was almost as good as the big leagues and certainly the Angels were as popular as any team in the country. The year this map was published marked the last time the team won the PCL with Big Steve Bilko leading the way, but when the major leagues came west their days were numbered.

When the Dodgers came to Los Angeles the Angels left Wrigley behind, but Walter O'Malley purchased the stadium for approximately three million dollars and swapped the old ballpark for the land in Chavez Ravine, where Dodger Stadium stands today. While there is much controversy about the misplacement of many families who lived in the area, the city had originally taken the land to build public housing, which failed for political reasons. While the Dodgers did not actually evict the families, their grand baseball stadium put an end to the era of the Pacific Coast League and the communities of Chavez Ravine.

Insurance Maps of Los Angeles, California
1956
Sanborn Map Company
Volume 4, sheet 437
Colored lithograph
17″ x 9″
California State University, Northridge Library

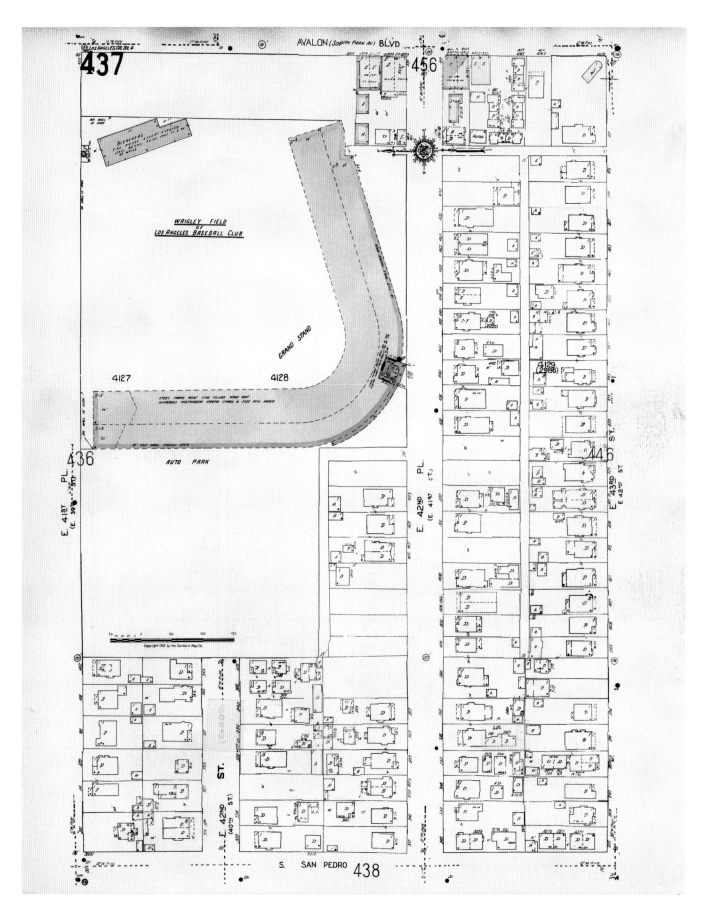

AVALON (SOUTH PARK AV) BLVD

437

456

BLEACHERS

WRIGLEY FIELD
OF
LOS ANGELES BASEBALL CLUB

GRAND STAND

4127   4128

436

AUTO PARK

E. 41ST PL.
(E. 39TH ST.)

E. 42ND PL.
(E. 41ST ST.)

E. 43RD ST.
(E. 42ND ST.)

446

4129
(2986)

Copyright 1953 by the Sanborn Map Co.

ST.

E. 42ND
(40TH ST.)

S. SAN PEDRO   **438**

The Goez Map Guide to the Murals of East Los Angeles

The story of the Goez studio and the creation of this map parallel a reassertion of Hispanic pride in the city. The map illustrates a neighborhood brimming with creativity and the decoration of the East Los Angeles homeland with the art of murals inspired by Mexican and Spanish traditions. The Goez gallery began when John and Joe Gonzalez realized a life-long dream of celebrating the Chicano art movement that had been growing throughout the 1960s. They wanted to "beautify the area and preserve cultural and historical heritage of the Chicano," so the brothers and some fellow artists physically transformed a dilapidated meat processing plant to a center of inspiration and great creativity for more than three hundred artists by the mid-seventies. The choice of the east side and the transformation of the site, along with a powerful Chicano art community, fueled a drive toward the expression of stories that were significant in the founding of the city and the development of the area of east Los Angeles.

One of the first examples of the direction and aesthetic of the gallery was a mural, *The Birth of Our Art*, undertaken to distinguish the building housing the Goez gallery at 3757 East 1st street. This auspicious beginning and a positive reaction from the art community at large led to the gallery's transformation into a remarkable oasis of Chicano culture. One of its main activities was the planning and painting of murals across the urban landscape. Inspired by Mexican wall painting, murals seemed the perfect artistic solution to a disenfranchised area of the city. The mural was a unique form of open expression that truly reached the people at a street level and was egalitarian without sacrificing ideals. While the themes communicated were contemporary, the works done in brilliant hues and bold strokes were often inspired by pre-Columbian, Aztec, and Mayan art.

The murals listed on this invaluable map actually catalog and describe hundreds of art works, including many that have faded from sight. Yet the Goez map shows places given color and distinction that were never considered art-worthy before. Murals appeared on the walls of public housing, on neighborhood markets, on recreation buildings and freeway underpasses where they could be seen by thousands of people. At the time of this map's publication, the Goez gallery had tracked 271 murals in 107 different locations, a staggering number for any metropolitan area in the world. The mapmakers dedicated the map to "the heritage of our ancestors," but they also preserved East Los Angeles as it looked in this transformational period, with the neighborhood framed by the modern freeways as the inscription suggests but retaining the old street names, as old as the city of Los Angeles itself.

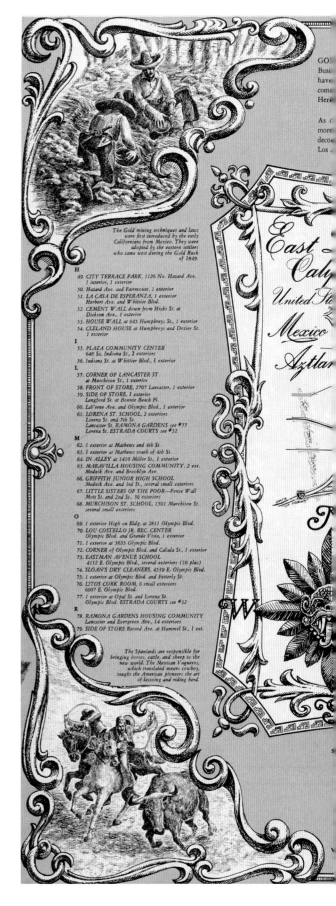

1975
John D. Gonzalez, David Botello,
and Robert Arenivar
Goez Publishing Company
Paper mounted on linen
Los Angeles Public Library

all the ARTISTS,
c Organizations who
beautification of our
cate this map to the
ors.

GOEZ has recorded
al murals and wall
ate locations in East

1st
1. *GOEZ ART STUDIOS & GALLERY*
   3757 E. 1st St., 1 exterior
2. *THE FIRST STREET STORE*, 1 interior
   3640 E. 1st St., 19 exterior
3. *THE PAN AMERICAN BANK*
   3626 E. 1st St., 3 exterior
4. *ZAPATERIA GUADALAHARA SHOES*
   1st St. and Hicks St., 1 exterior
5. *ANA MARIA RESTAURANT*
   3451 E. 1st St., 2 interior
6. 1st St. and Indiana, 1 long exterior
7. 1st St. at Commonwealth, 1 exterior
8. *EL MERCADO* (Parking Lot), 2 exterior
   1st St. and Lorena St.
9. 1st St. at Fresno, 2 exterior
10. 2301 E. 1st St., 1 interior

11. 1946 E. 1st St., 2 exterior
12. *SLOANS' DRY CLEANERS*
    3852 E. 1st St., 1 exterior
13. 1st St. at Dickerson, 1 exterior
14. *McDONNELL AVE. SCHOOL*
    4335 E. 1st St., 1 interior
15. *RIGGIN SCHOOL*
    4865 E. 1st St., several exterior

2nd
LITTLE SISTERS OF THE POOR see #67

3rd
16. 3636 E. 3rd St., 1 exterior
17. *SANCTUARY OF OUR LADY OF GUADALUPE CHURCH*, 3rd St. at Sutol Dr., 1 exterior

4th
18. *SEGOVIA MARKET*, 3459 E. 4th St., 1 exterior

In Europe all Roads lead to Rome, In Southern California all Freeways lead to East Los Angeles

Angeles

erica

Boyle
eights

El Sereno Hills

City Terrace

Belvedere

East Los Angeles

Monterey Park Hills

The Californios enjoyed a tranquil, romantic, and prosperous life. They spent much leisure time playing music and creating unusual sporting events.

6th
19. 6th St. and Grande Vista, 1 exterior
20. 6th St. at Bonnie Beach Pl., 1 exterior

A
21. *WALL IN FRONT OF HOUSE*
    1310 Alma Ave., 1 exterior

B
22. *WALL on 3105 Beverly Blvd.*, 1 exterior
23. *STATE SERVICE CENTER, E.L.A. YOUTH CLINIC*, Bonnie Beach Pl. and Fairmount, 1 interior
24. Breed at Brooklyn Ave., 1 exterior
25. *E.L.A. COMMUNITY YOUTH CENTERS*
    3630 E. Brooklyn Ave., 2 exterior
26. *EAST LOS ANGELES COLLEGE-AUDITORIUM*
    Brooklyn Ave. and Woods, 1 exterior

C
27. *ALLEY behind 4125 City Terrace Dr.*, 1 exterior
28. *PASEO DE LOS BARRILES*, Pathway off Comly St. at Eastern Ave., 1 exterior
29. *HOUSE WALL 655 Concord St.*, 1 exterior

D
30. *GARAGE WALL IN ALLEY off Drucker St. at Lansdowne Ave.*, 1 exterior

E
31. *SIDE OF STORE*, 1720 Eastern Ave., 1 exterior
32. *ESTRADA COURTS*, Olympic Blvd. and Lorena St., 39 exteriors—more in progress
33. *FREEWAY WALL* Eugene St. at Humphrey, 1 exterior
34. *ON SIDE OF WAREHOUSE*, Esperanza and Whittier Blvd., 1 exterior
35. *SIDE OF RESTAURANT* Evergreen and 4th St., 1 exterior

F
36. *E.L.A. PUBLIC LIBRARY*
    248 Fetterly Ave., 1 interior
37. *WALL ON CORNER* Floral Dr. and Record Ave., 1 exterior
38. *SIDE WALL OF BUILDING*
    2811 W. Floral Drive, 1 exterior

G
39. *GARAGE DOOR & SCULPTURED WALL*
    Gage Avenue at Blanchard
40. *LOS COMPADRES*
    Gage Ave. and Hammel St., 3 exteriors
41. 1 interior at 112 No. Gage Ave.
42. *WALL ON CORNER* of Geraghty Ave. and Beaulah Ave., 1 exterior
43. *PROGRESS FOR YOUTH ORGANIZATION*
    SAN FELIPE CHAPEL, Geraghty Ave. and Folsom St., 3 exteriors
44. Gifford Ave. No. of Brooklyn Ave., 1 exterior
45. Gifford Ave. So. of Brooklyn Ave., 1 exterior
46. Grande Vista at 4th St., 1 exterior
47. *DACOTAH ST. SCHOOL*, 1 exterior
    Grande Vista and Hunter St.
48. Grande Vista and Union Pacific, 1 exterior

With the creation of the mission system, and the great ranchos, the Mexicans introduced farming, ranching, and irrigation—which gave California its first great orchards and grape vineyards.

Tierra Por Libertad

THE **GOEZ**
MAP GUIDE TO THE MURALS
OF EAST LOS ANGELES
FIRST EDITION
• EARLY CALIFORNIA SERIES •

CREATED and LAYOUT by JOHN D. GONZALEZ
DESIGN and DRAWING BY DAVID BOTELLO
STORY ILLUSTRATIONS BY ROBERT ARENIVAR

ORE, 900 Soto St., 3 exteriors
n Soto St. and Brooklyn, 1 ext.
n Soto St. and Brooklyn, 1 ext.
EIGHBORHOOD CENTER
d Michigan, several large murals
Soto St.
SCHOOL, 1 exterior
bittier Blvd. and 7th St.
L—LUNCH AREA
2 large exteriors
RK IN BANDSTAND
St.

. and Boca Ave., 1 exterior

RTISING INC.
alifornia

90. *WABASH RECREATION CENTER*
    2765 Wabash Ave., several exterior, 3 walls
91. *BANK OF AMERICA*
    3051 Wabash Ave. at Sentinel, 1 exterior
92. *MOE'S HARDWARE STORE*
    3044 Wabash Ave., 1 exterior
93. *SIDE OF BLDG.*, at 2409 Whittier Blvd., 1 exterior
94. *WALL OF BUILDING*, 2519 Whittier Blvd., 1 ext.
95. *LA QUEBRADITA GROCERY*, 2 large murals on sides of Bldg., 3451 Whittier Blvd.
96. Corner of Whittier Blvd. and Eastman Ave., 1 ext.
97. *MECHICANO ART CENTER*, several walls and sidewalk, 4030 Whittier Blvd., 6 individual exterior
98. 1 exterior at 4045 Whittier Blvd.

99. *EAST LOS ANGELES DOCTORS HOSP.*
    4060 Whittier Blvd., 5 interior, 6 exterior
100. *THE DIP BAR*, 1 large, 2 sided mural exterior
    4433 W Whittier Blvd.
101. *DON'S MONTEREY ROOM*, 1 exterior
    Whittier Blvd. and Fraser St.
102. *LAUSD EAST CLASSIFIED PERSONNEL OFFICE*
    4982 Whittier Blvd., 3 exterior
103. 1 exterior at Whittier Blvd. and Clela Ave.
104. *CENTRO JOAQUIN MURIETA DE AZTLAN*
    5226 Whittier Blvd., 1 exterior
105. *EL REY AZTECA RESTAURANT*, 1 exterior
    5372 Whittier Blvd.
106. *AYUDATE*, 6140 Whittier Blvd., 1 ext. 3 int.
107. *MARY'S MARKET*, 3301 E. Winter St., 1 exterior

GOEZ PUBLISHING CO.
3757 East First Street, Los Angeles, CA 90063

©1975 GOEZ PUBLISHING CO.

The Literary Map of Los Angeles

Though visiting pundits take shots at the place as lacking culture, Los Angeles has been home to many great writers and the scene of an abundance of memorable works of fiction. *The Literary Map of Los Angeles* underlines this fact. While the map does expand the geographical view of the area stretching from Dana Point in the south to Ventura in the north, it keeps L. A. in the middle as the artistic center.

This work of cartography is notable not so much for the lines on the map but the research poured into the details of each numbered dot on the landscape. Even natives of the city of the angels might be surprised to learn that such literary lights as Theodore Dreiser, Robinson Jeffers, Aldous Huxley, or Zane Grey figure in local literary output. Of course, many writers were drawn by the lure of film studio money that enabled them to enjoy the Southern California good life, understanding that maybe later they would write their true masterpieces or finish their days in the sunshine.

Writers who dot this literary landscape include great artists like Thomas Mann (Pacific Palisades), Arthur Miller (Beverly Hills Hotel), John Steinbeck (Eagle Rock), Ray Bradbury (Cheviot Hills), and even L. Frank Baum, who started his own production company unsurprisingly called "Oz." As well, the map demonstrates that writers of mystery and detective fiction were drawn to the city. While Raymond Chandler is among its best known, he is joined many others, including James Cain, Earl Stanley Gardner, Dashiell Hammett, Ross MacDonald, and contemporary greats Walter Moseley, James Ellroy, and Michael Connelly. Some individual works are noted as archetypal Los Angeles stories, like John Fante's *Ask the Dust* set on Bunker Hill or Nathaniel West's *Day of the Locust* in Hollywood and Joan Didion's *Play It as It Lays*, which is literally set on the freeways.

Other literary eccentrics, curmudgeons, visionaries, and luminaries who called the area for some time home include Edgar Rice Burroughs of Tarzan fame, William Faulkner, historians Will and Ariel Durant, Charles Bukowski, F. Scott Fitzgerald, Christopher Isherwood, Hubert Selby, Krishnamurti, Malcolm Lowry, Anita Loos, Norman Mailer, Henry Miller, John O'Hara, Dorothy Parker, Katherine Anne Porter, Damon Runyan, William Saroyan, Dalton Trumbo, Gore Vidal, and Herman Wouk, to mention just a few. Even Ogden Nash had time to stop and pen the verse "Yes it is true, Los Angeles is not only erratic, not only erotic / Los Angeles is crotchety, centrifugal, vertiginous, esoteric, and exotic."

1987
Illustrator: Linda Ayriss
Graphic Artist: Susan Lewis
Cartographers: Molly Maguire and Aaron Silverman
Aaron Blake Publishing, Los Angeles
Printed wall map, 27" x 21"
Los Angeles Public Library

The
Literary Map
of
Los Angeles

SAN FERNANDO VALLEY

HOLLYWOOD
FRANKLIN
LOS FELIZ BLVD
ALTADENA
PASADENA

LAUREL CYN BLVD
HOLLYWOOD BLVD
HOLLYWOOD

BEVERLY

CANON
SUNSET
SANTA MONICA
HIGHLAND
ROSSMORE AVE
VANESS
WESTERN AVE

GLEN
RODEO DR
LA CIENEGA
FAIRFAX
LA BREA
BEVERLY
GOLDEN STATE

DR BLVD
DR
WILSHIRE AVE
BLVD

PICO
ST
FIGUEROA
DOWNTOWN
SAN PEDRO
CENTRAL

FREEWAY
BROADWAY

SANTA MONICA
YORBA LINDA

SAN DIEGO FREEWAY
FREEWAY

LA HARBOR

DANA POINT

179

Los Angeles Area Freeway System

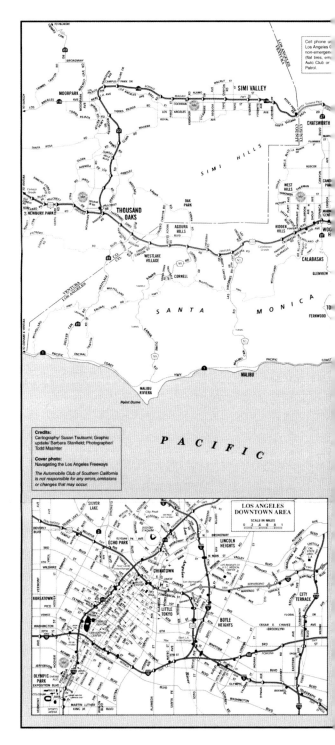

The much-cursed landscape of automotive Los Angeles is best described in its entirety by this current cartographic bible by the Automobile Club of Los Angeles. Seen all at once, the freeway system appears orderly and understandable, but close-up it can be a source of much weeping and gnashing of teeth. Dating back to the Arroyo Seco Parkway, finished in 1940, the freeways spread across the southland in every direction, including some of the most traveled roads in the world. There are 527 miles of roadway within the county alone. As early as the 1930s the city seemed to be turning toward automobiles, and by 1947 the California Department of Public Works laid out a plan to connect all the suburban dots in the county and beyond, eventually creating the Collier-Burns Highway Act. The very same Auto Club that provides road assistance and maps like this one for drivers to this day did much of the planning and studies for that system.

One by one, the four-lane highways were carved out along well-traveled roads, old streetcar paths, or early routes used even by the indigenous Tongva Indians. The Pasadena (110) was followed by the San Bernardino (10), Santa Ana/Golden State (5), Hollywood/Ventura (101), Foothill (210), Long Beach (710), Glendale (2), San Diego (405), and many more. There is a generational quirk about freeways in Los Angeles and how they are referred to by the locals. Older Angelinos tend to call them by their original place-names, such as the "Santa Ana Freeway," the "Santa Monica," or "San Diego," but later generations always precede the number with "the," thus "the 210," "the 405," "north on the 605," "the 10 east," or "take the 5 to the 110 north to the 101." There is even a vocabulary for the features of the freeways as listed on the map: "the Downtown slot," the "Cahuenga Pass" "the Glendora Curve," and others that are identified in the traffic reports and fill the airwaves. Many of the freeways follow historical routes that were just natural paths through the Southern California landscape. "The 60" freeway follows the Pomona Mission Road; "the 5 south" speeds along a kind of Portola expedition path; "the 210" takes the "old stage road to San Bernardino"; "the 110 south" follows Phineas Banning's rail line to San Pedro; and "the 101" takes the revered "El Camino Real" following the trail of the mission northward. Some freeways follow the rivers, including "the 710" along the Los Angeles, "the 91" along the Santa Ana, "the 5 north" again along the Los Angeles River, and "the 605" along the San Gabriel.

This Auto Club map makes the system look logical and perfectly planned, but there has been controversy on every mile of road, including the modern debate over fossil fuels and pollution versus mass transit. Los Angeles is probably still the most automobile-reliant city in America. At the center of this map is the famous cloverleaf interchange where "the 10" and "the 110" intersect over land that once held rooming houses, mom-and-pop markets, bakeries, schools, and even a famous receiving hospital.

2008
Susan Tsutsumi
Graphic update by Barbara Stansfield
Foldout map
Automobile Club of Southern California

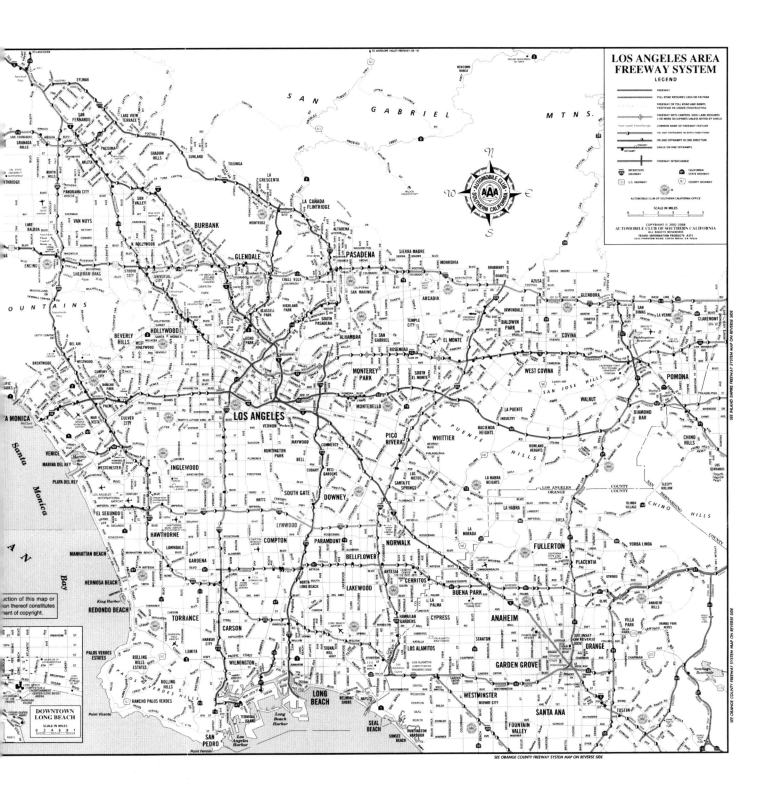

LOS ANGELES AREA
FREEWAY SYSTEM
LEGEND

DOWNTOWN
LONG BEACH

SEE INLAND EMPIRE FREEWAY SYSTEM MAP ON REVERSE SIDE

SEE ORANGE COUNTY FREEWAY SYSTEM MAP ON REVERSE SIDE

SEE ORANGE COUNTY FREEWAY SYSTEM MAP ON REVERSE SIDE

Interactive Map of the Chinatown Area of Los Angeles

I t might seem like the future of mapping is in the digital realm, with data acquired and arranged to produce maps showing aspects of the terrain determined by the viewer's needs. The utilitarian construct works for most applications but does not produce much in the way of aesthetic appeal. Looking at the pictorial works in this book and admiring the artistic depictions of the Los Angeles landscape might cause one to long for those golden days when maps were very much an art form.

However, the link between mapmakers and artists that has survived since Ancient Egypt remains unbroken, with visionaries seeing new ways to understand the landscape using hybrids that bridge the disciplines. Such is the technique created by planner and artist James Rojas in Los Angeles, using a model base map and allowing participants to create their own cityscapes with found objects and pure imagination. The shape changes constantly but the space remains the same as it was when the pobladores first put down roots on the banks of the Porciuncula River in 1789. Appropriately, Rojas chose to depict the Chinatown neighborhood with adjoining "cornfields" where the original pueblo was laid out. You can see where the crucial Zanja Madre wandered away from the river and through the settlement, along with the landmark bluffs of Fort Moore Hill and the city's first cemeteries. The byways are there but no longer called Grasshopper, Eternity, Bull, Wasp, or Virgin. Using Rojas's concept, the names are secondary to the space, as they should be. The interactive city model encourages a relationship to the space Angelinos take for granted and coaxes surprising creativity from those who ponder how the city has changed and how it will look in the near future.

People from all walks of life and ages try out their own architectural plans while discovering how it all must coexist with the rest of the environment. Shown here is a portion of the perpetually unfinished product that will take Los Angeles from the pueblo to today, heading in the north-south direction that seemed to be determined by the river originally and then by routes of rail and commerce. The artist will add more of the city as the model grows toward the modern civic center, increasing its size from a four-by-eight-foot model to a miniature city that reflects the people's dream of Los Angeles. In many ways Rojas's art brings greater insight than all the data flitting through the computers of the city of the angels.

2009
James Rojas
4' x 8' model
Photograph by Rebecca Scott
Courtesy of the artist and Fifth Floor Gallery

Downtown Los Angeles

Cartifact's minutely detailed 2008 map of the revitalized downtown brings us back full circle from the Ord Survey of 1849, when the nerve center of Los Angeles was the old plaza at the center of the original four square leagues. This map is part of a project to lay current geographical data on top of historical cartography and gain perspective on the huge canvas shown here. This hard copy version is a hybrid of satellite imagery, aerial photography, cartography, and graphic art that illustrates the continuing redevelopment of downtown as the true center of the city. While the metropolis is defined by the four automobile-age freeways that encircle the skyline, the map takes pains to demarcate the neighborhoods where residents live and work. After bottoming out in the 1950s and '60s, downtown—and the urban soul of L.A.—was dismissed as dead and gone. However, blood began trickling back into the heart of the area in the 1970s, then pumping in the 1980s, and pretty much gushing in the twenty-first century. This map shows the present and future Los Angeles, with an actual street-level vitality and the continuing evolution of the city as a genuine destination for tourists and those seeking nightlife and entertainment. Downtown once had the commercial center of Spring Street, the motion picture and theater draw of Broadway, the government centers on 1st Street, department stores, cafeterias, and hotels on virtually every thoroughfare. Now the map shows the new move to residential conversions of all manner of building, along with galleries, theaters, restaurants, and genuine cultural centers like Central Library, where lectures, exhibits, and performances draw visitors in great numbers.

There might be layers of concrete on top of this history, but the old streets have stories to tell. Traversing these historic grounds today, visitors can see such great architecture as the Disney Concert Hall, which rises dramatically at the place where Bunker Hill could once be reached by the funicular railway of Angel's Flight. Within walking distance are the beautiful Cathedral of Our Lady of the Angels, the Music Center with two nationally renowned theaters, and the excellent Museum of Contemporary Art. Dodger Stadium in the northwest quadrant once was a Shangri-La of three communities in Chavez Ravine and before that the Stone Quarry Hills. Young people sipping cocktails at the rooftop bar of the trendy Standard Hotel at 6th and Flower while gazing at the city lights might not realize they are looking out at history from a place where the Normal School once trained teachers. Ingloriously, underneath the Hollywood Freeway near the Patsouris Transit Plaza is the spot where the Tongva Indians once settled their village, called Yang-na, and met beneath the giant council tree called El Aliso. At Santa Fe and 1st, near the new metro rail tracks, there are stories to be told of the hopefuls who arrived at the Santa Fe Depot, "Le Grande Station," looking for a piece of the dream called the City of Angels. Some reminders still exist, like the modern Pershing Square, which marks the place where Teddy Roosevelt spoke at the turn of the century and soapbox orators gave opinions in the 1950s. The Pacific Electric Building remains at 6th and Los Angeles from back when the city's streetcars were the envy of the world, and the Pico House survives down at the Plaza. The great movie palaces still stand in varying manifestations on Broadway, some exhibiting classic films, others mutated into swap meets or churches. The Morrison Hotel, once famous for its rock 'n' roll clientele, may be more valued today for the street parking to nearby Staples Center. And where locals once watched bloody bullfights there is now a very green public park and art project called "the Cornfields." There is a high school now where the Los Angeles oil fields once roused the local economy, and at the corner where Chutes Park once provided magical recreation to an entire city there is the Blue Line subway platform for a line that takes contemporaries out to the suburbs. Dazzling popular-culture destinations like the Staples Center, the Nokia Theater, and the Vegas-like LA Live call out to Angelinos from all over Southern California and can be seen on this Cartifact map, which may show today's Los Angeles but has not forgotten the people, places, and memories that have come before.

2009
Cartifact
Printed map
Los Angeles Public Library

CHAVEZ RAVINE

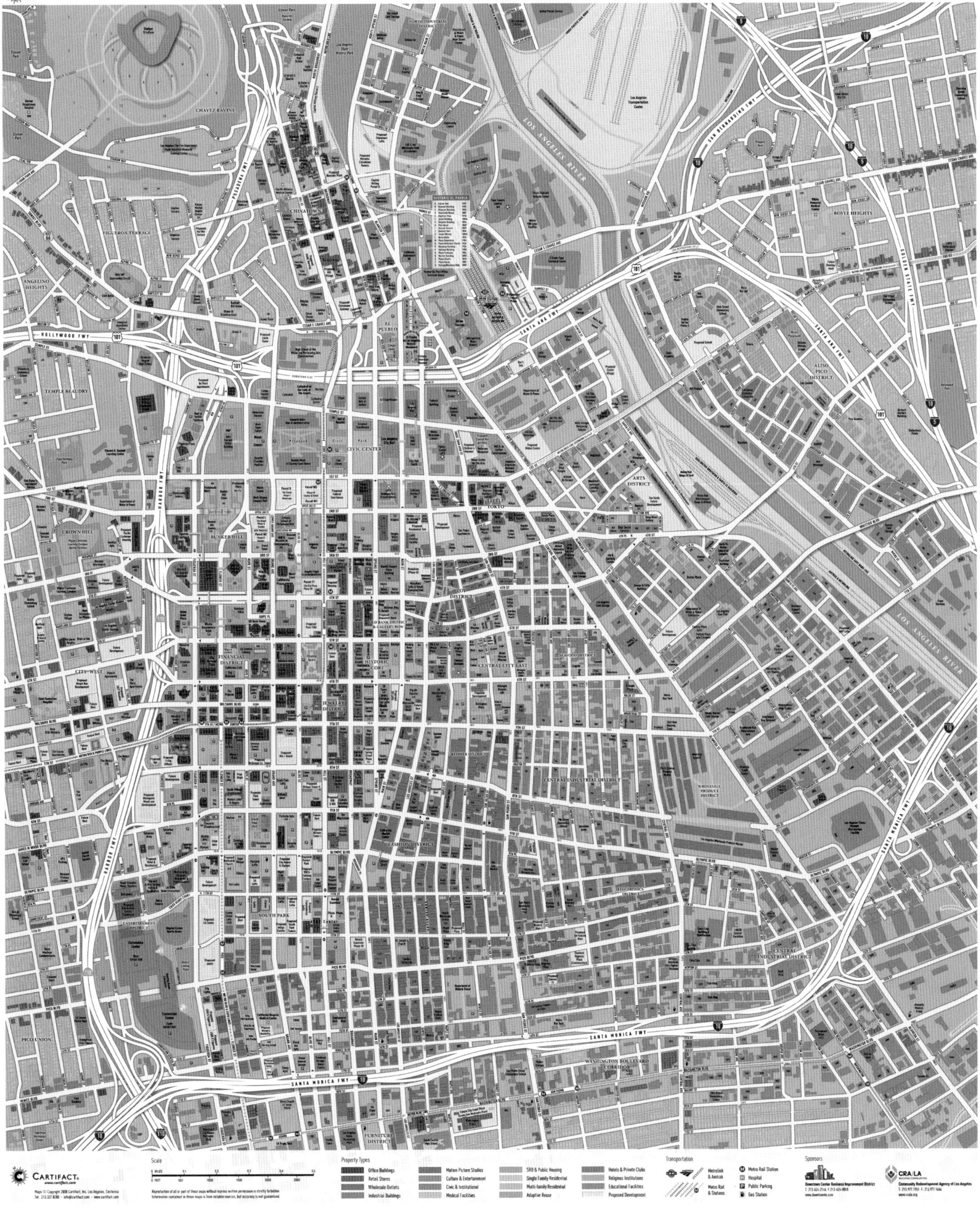

FIGUEROA TERRACE

CHINATOWN

ANGELINO HEIGHTS

BOYLE HEIGHTS

HOLLYWOOD FWY

TEMPLE BEAUDRY

ALISO PICO DISTRICT

EL PUEBLO

CIVIC CENTER

ARTS DISTRICT

LITTLE TOKYO

CROWN HILL

BUNKER HILL

CITY WEST

DISTRICT

CENTRAL CITY EAST

FINANCIAL DISTRICT

JEWELRY DISTRICT

WHOLESALE PRODUCE DISTRICT

CENTRAL INDUSTRIAL DISTRICT

FASHION DISTRICT

OLYMPIC BLVD

SOUTH PARK

ENTERTAINMENT DISTRICT

CENTRAL INDUSTRIAL DISTRICT

PICO UNION

SANTA MONICA FWY

WASHINGTON BOULEVARD CORRIDOR

SANTA MONICA FWY

FURNITURE DISTRICT

LOS ANGELES RIVER

LOS ANGELES TRANSPORTATION CENTER

SAN BERNARDINO FWY

GOLDEN STATE FWY

SANTA ANA FWY

DODGER STADIUM

Map of Los Angeles Neighborhoods

Dorothy Parker quipped that Los Angeles was 72 suburbs in search of a city but she probably would not have had that opinion if she left the Garden of Allah on Sunset Boulevard and took some drives around town. Los Angeles, very much like New York or Chicago, is a city of neighborhoods, some distinctive and some just a few blocks within the city. Hundreds of such enclaves have come and gone over the past century and a half. Very few of the old neighborhoods had any official boundary and those that did were once small independent cities that eventually gave in to the big metropolis and were annexed.

Finally, led by two intrepid reporters from the *Los Angeles Times*, Doug Smith and Maloy Moore, the *Times* data team set out to finally delineate all of these little satellites into one great city map beginning this daunting task in 2009. The project called "Mapping L.A." used census tract data as a baseline but adjusted lines to reflect historical, geographical, and economic factors on the ground. Local historians have battled with setting boundaries of these areas for decades but this undertaking let the residents of the neighborhoods participate and adjust the lines as they were drawn and offered online. Furthermore the use of digital technology allowed the map to have multiple layers and information that no hard copy version could produce. Times staff researchers have made over one hundred boundary changes and have settled on 114 neighborhoods at this point in time.

Even with cutting edge technology and the tremendous resources of the powerful *Los Angeles Times*, setting neighborhood boundaries can still be like eating Jell-O with chopsticks. Locals will argue about street corners between East L.A. and Boyle Heights or Mid-Wilshire and Koreatown with passionate conviction, as seen sometimes on the comments section of "Mapping L.A." Yet, at long last, modern technology and some highly creative journalists have actually placed a handle on the conundrum that may always make for discussion between locals. Places called Glassell Park, Toluca Lake, Beverlywood, Shadow Hills, Elysian Park, Valley Glen, Century City, Vermont Square, University Village, or Cheviot Hills may be quibbled about ad aeternum but the *Times* has finally put the matter up for public cartographical debate. Neighborhoods have come and gone over the past one hundred and sixty years, names like Sonora Town, Florence, Mesmer City, Montezuma, or Zelzah may have vanished from the maps but not from the collective memory of the people of Los Angeles.

2010
Doug Smith and Maloy Moore
Los Angeles Times

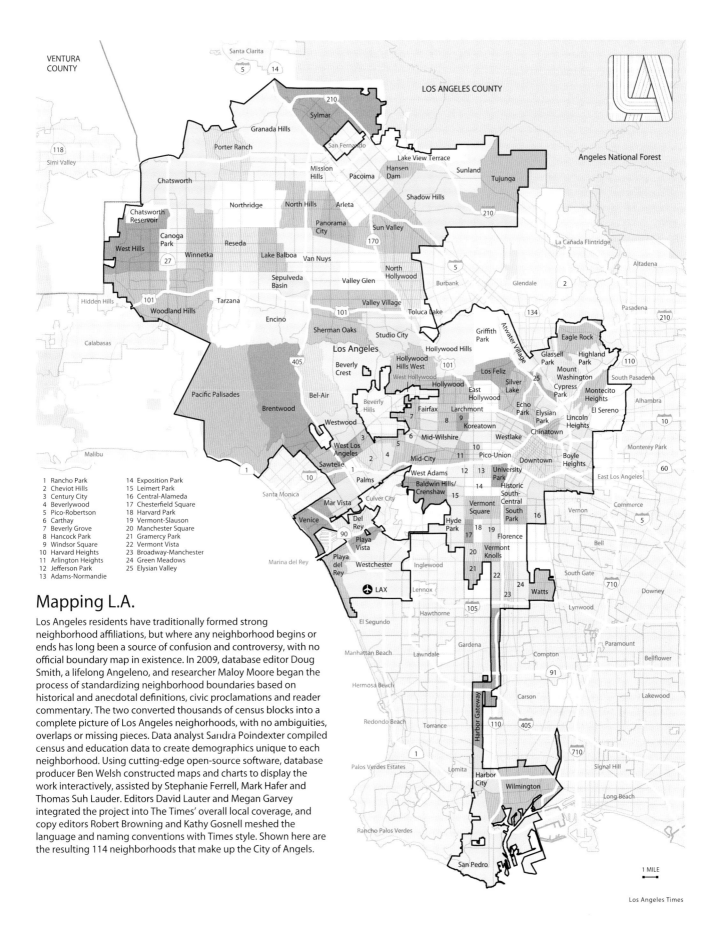

VENTURA
COUNTY

LOS ANGELES COUNTY

Angeles National Forest

Santa Clarita

Sylmar

Granada Hills

Porter Ranch

San Fernando

Lake View Terrace

Chatsworth

Sunland

Mission Hills

Pacoima

Hansen Dam

Tujunga

Northridge

North Hills

Arleta

Shadow Hills

Simi Valley

Chatsworth Reservoir

Canoga Park

Winnetka

Reseda

Panorama City

Sun Valley

La Cañada Flintridge

Altadena

West Hills

Lake Balboa

Van Nuys

Hidden Hills

Sepulveda Basin

Valley Glen

North Hollywood

Burbank

Glendale

Pasadena

Tarzana

Woodland Hills

Encino

Valley Village

Toluca Lake

Calabasas

Sherman Oaks

Studio City

Griffith Park

Atwater Village

Eagle Rock

Los Angeles

Hollywood Hills

Glassell Park

Highland Park

Beverly Crest

Hollywood Hills West

Los Feliz

Mount Washington

South Pasadena

Pacific Palisades

West Hollywood

Hollywood

East Hollywood

Silver Lake

Cypress Park

Montecito Heights

Alhambra

Bel-Air

Beverly Hills

Fairfax

Larchmont

Echo Park

Elysian Park

El Sereno

Brentwood

Westwood

Mid-Wilshire

Koreatown

Chinatown

Lincoln Heights

Malibu

West Los Angeles

Sawtelle

Mid-City

Pico-Union

Westlake

Downtown

Boyle Heights

Monterey Park

Palms

West Adams

University Park

East Los Angeles

Commerce

Santa Monica

Mar Vista

Culver City

Baldwin Hills/Crenshaw

Historic South-Central

Vernon

Venice

Del Rey

Hyde Park

Vermont Square

South Park

Bell

Playa Vista

Vermont Knolls

Florence

Marina del Rey

Playa del Rey

Westchester

Inglewood

South Gate

Downey

LAX

Lennox

Watts

Lynwood

Hawthorne

El Segundo

Paramount

Manhattan Beach

Lawndale

Gardena

Compton

Bellflower

Hermosa Beach

Lakewood

Redondo Beach

Carson

Torrance

Harbor Gateway

Palos Verdes Estates

Lomita

Signal Hill

Long Beach

Harbor City

Wilmington

Rancho Palos Verdes

San Pedro

1 Rancho Park
2 Cheviot Hills
3 Century City
4 Beverlywood
5 Pico-Robertson
6 Carthay
7 Beverly Grove
8 Hancock Park
9 Windsor Square
10 Harvard Heights
11 Arlington Heights
12 Jefferson Park
13 Adams-Normandie

14 Exposition Park
15 Leimert Park
16 Central-Alameda
17 Chesterfield Square
18 Harvard Park
19 Vermont-Slauson
20 Manchester Square
21 Gramercy Park
22 Vermont Vista
23 Broadway-Manchester
24 Green Meadows
25 Elysian Valley

Mapping L.A.

Los Angeles residents have traditionally formed strong
neighborhood affiliations, but where any neighborhood begins or
ends has long been a source of confusion and controversy, with no
official boundary map in existence. In 2009, database editor Doug
Smith, a lifelong Angeleno, and researcher Maloy Moore began the
process of standardizing neighborhood boundaries based on
historical and anecdotal definitions, civic proclamations and reader
commentary. The two converted thousands of census blocks into a
complete picture of Los Angeles neighorhoods, with no ambiguities,
overlaps or missing pieces. Data analyst Sandra Poindexter compiled
census and education data to create demographics unique to each
neighborhood. Using cutting-edge open-source software, database
producer Ben Welsh constructed maps and charts to display the
work interactively, assisted by Stephanie Ferrell, Mark Hafer and
Thomas Suh Lauder. Editors David Lauter and Megan Garvey
integrated the project into The Times' overall local coverage, and
copy editors Robert Browning and Kathy Gosnell meshed the
language and naming conventions with Times style. Shown here are
the resulting 114 neighborhoods that make up the City of Angels.

1 MILE

Los Angeles Times

Bibliography

Bell, Horace. *Reminiscences of a Ranger: Early times in Southern California*. Los Angeles: Anderson, 1965.

Bowman, Lynn. *Los Angeles Epic of a City*. Berkeley, CA: Howell-North Books, 1974.

Cho, Jenny. *Chinatown in Los Angeles*. Charlotte, SC: Arcadia Publications, 2009.

Cox, Bette Yarbrough. *Central Avenue: Its Rise and Fall (1890 – c.1955)*. Los Angeles: Beem Publications, 1993.

Davis, Mike. *City of Quartz*. New York: Verso, 1990.

Demeestere, Helene. *Pioneers and Entrepreneurs: French Immigrants in the Making of Los Angeles*. Charleston, SC: Arcadia Press, 2008.

Deverell, William. *Whitewashed Adobe*. Berkeley, CA: University of California Press, 2004.

Dumke, Glenn. *Boom of the Eighties in Southern California*. San Marino, CA: Huntington Library, 1944.

Estrada, William David. *The Los Angeles Plaza: Sacred and Congested*. Austin, TX: University of Texas Press, 2008.

Guinn, J.M. *History of California and an Extended History of Los Angeles and Environs*. Los Angeles: Historic record company, 1915.

Gumprecht, Blake. *The Los Angeles River: Its Life, Death and Possible Rebirth*. Baltimore: Johns Hopkins University Press, 1999.

Hancock, Ralph. *Fabulous Boulevard*. New York: Funk and Wagnalls, 1949.

Harlow, Neil. *Maps and Surveys of the Pueblo Lands of Los Angeles*. Los Angeles: Dawson's Bookshop, 1976.

Heimann, Jim. *Out With the Stars*. New York: Abbeville Press, 1985.

Henstell, Bruce. *Sunshine and Wealth: Los Angeles in the Twenties and Thirties*. San Francisco: Chronicle Books, 1984.

Herman, Robert D. *Downtown L.A.: a Walking Guide*. Claremont, CA: City Vistas Press, 1997.

Lord, Rosemary. *Los Angeles: Then and Now*. San Diego: Thunder Bay, 2002.

Makower, Joel. *The Map Catalog*. New York: Vintage Books, 1992.

McGroarty, John Steven. *California of the South*. Chicago: S.J. Clarke Publications, 1935.

McWilliams, Carey. *Southern California Country: An Island on the Land*. New York: Books for Libraries Press, 1946.

Morrison, Patt. *Rio L.A.: Tales from the Los Angeles River*. Santa Monica, CA: Angel City Press, 2001.

Newmark, Harris. *Sixty Years in Southern California: 1853–1913*. Los Angeles: Zeitlin and Ver Brugge, 1970.

Pagan, Edwardo Obregon. *Murder at the Sleepy Lagoon*. Chapel Hill, NC: University of North Carolina Press, 2003.

Palmer, Edwin O. *History of Hollywood*. Hollywood: Edwin O. Palmer, 1938.

Poole, Jean, and Bruce and Tevvy Ball. *El Pueblo the Historic Heart of Los Angeles*. Los Angeles: Getty Publications, 2002.

Rasmussen, Cecilia. *Curbside L.A.* Los Angeles: Los Angeles Times, 1996.

Rios-Bustamante, Antonio. *Mexican Los Angeles*. Mountain View, CA: Floricanto Press, 1990.

Robinson, W.W. *Maps of Los Angeles From Ord's Survey of 1849 to the End of the Boom of the Eighties*. Los Angeles: Dawson's Bookshop, 1966.

———. *Panorama: A Picture History of Southern California*. Los Angeles: Title Insurance and Trust Company, 1953.

Roderick, Kevin. *The San Fernando Valley: America's Suburb*. Los Angeles: Los Angeles Times Books, 2001.

Romo, Ricardo. Los Angeles: History of a Barrio. Austin, TX: University of Texas Press, 1983.

Shippey, Lee. *Los Angeles Book*. Boston: Houghton Mifflin, 1950.

Sklar, Anna. *Brown Acres: an Intimate History of the Los Angeles Sewers*. Santa Monica, CA: Angel City Press, 2008.

Ulin, David, Jim Heimann and Kevin Starr. *Los Angeles: Portrait of a City*. Cologne, Germany: Taschen, 2009.

Waldie, D. J. *Where We Are Now: Notes from Los Angeles*. Santa Monica, CA: Angel City Press, 2004.

Wannamaker, Mark. *Hollywood: 1940–2008*. Charleston, SC: Arcadia Press, 2009.

Williams, Gregory Paul. *Story of Hollywood*. Los Angeles: BL Press, 2005.

Wurman, Richard Saul. *Access L.A.* New York: Access Press, 2009.

Zimmerman, Tom. *Paradise Promoted: The Booster Campaign that Created Los Angeles, 1870–1930*. Santa Monica: Angel City Press, 2008.

Index

Page numbers in italics refer to illustrations.

Abel Stearns Ranchos map, 14, 30, *30–31*
Ackerman, Fremont, 17, 86, *86–87*
African Americans, 20, 170, 172
Agricultural Park, 48, 56
Aguilar, Cristobal, 36, 62
Alanis, Jose Maximo, 82
Albright City, 164
All Year Club of Southern California, 19, 142
Alvarado, Juan B., 26
Anaheim, 36
Angeleno Heights, 17, 60; map, 17, 84, *84–85*
Annexation Map, 16, 64, *64–65*
Arenivar, Robert, *176–77*
Arguello, Jose, 98
Arnold Schoenberg's Los Angeles, 168, *168–69*
Arroyo Seco, 76
Arroyo Seco Parkway, 120, 180
Artland Club, 164
Atwood, Mary Hall, 148, *148–49*
Automobile Club of Southern California, 18, 21, 114–20, 124, 180
axonometric map, 17, *72–73*
Ayriss, Linda, *178–79*

Baist, G. William, 21, 74, *74–75*
Baist's Real Estate Atlas of Surveys of Los Angeles, 17, 20, 74, *74–75*
Baker, George H., *30–31*
Baldwin, E. J. "Lucky," 58
Baldwin Hills, 164
Bancroft and Thayer firm, 38
Bandini, Arcadio, 30
Banning, Phineas, 43, 110
Barham, Frank, 142
Barnes, Al G., 164
Barnes City, 162; map, 20, 164, *164–65*
Barratt, Nathan F., 86
baseball, 20, 160, 174
Beaudry, Prudent, 84, 92
Behrend, Sam, 21
Bell, Horace, 68
Bell Quadrangle, *168–69*, 170
Benton, Arthur, 84
Beverly Hills, 64, 150
Bilko, Steve, 174
bird's-eye maps, 16, 42–43, 56, 60
Bird's-Eye View of Los Angeles, 16, 42–43, *44–45*
Board of Harbor Commissioners, 16, 112, *112–13*
Boles, John, 162
Botello, David, *176–77*
Boyle, Andrew, 36, 74
Boyle Heights, 17, 36, 48, 74, 76
Branch Library map, 17, 76, *76–77*
Bray, George, 20, 162, 164
Brent, J. Lancaster, 38
Brentwood, 168
Brown, Karl J., *146–47*
Bunker Hill, 17, 36, 43, 60, 84, 184
Business Property Map of Los Angeles, 17, *72–73*, *72–73*

cadastral maps, 16, 58
Cahuenga, 76
Calabasas, 64
California Department of Public Works, 180
Calle de los Negros, 40
Capone, Al, 112
Carrillo, Leo, 146
Cartifact, 184, *184–85*
Catalina Island, 50, 52, 56, 58, 174; nautical map, 20, 166, *166–67*
Celis, Eulogio de, 88
Central Avenue, 20, 172, *172–73*
Central Park, 60, 62
Chadwick, James P., 16, 110, *110–11*
Chaffee, Adna R., 95

Chandler, Harry, 142
Chaplin, Charlie, 86
Chatsworth, 64
Chavez, Julian, 160
Chavez Ravine, 174, 184; map, 20, 160, *160–61*
Chevalier, Maurice, 86
Chicano art movement, *20*, 176
Chinatown, 60, 70; interactive map, 182, *182–83*
city limits maps, 16, 78, 110
Cleaves, Gail, 76, *76–77*
Coate, Roland, 86
Colegrove, 64
Collier, John, 34
Collier-Burns Highway Act, 180
Consolidation Act, 110
Corbett, Cooper, 86
Crespi, Juan, 98
Crosby, Bing, 151
Cummings, Wilbur, 86
Cundiff, Willard, 124, *124–25*
Curtis, Charles, 148

Dakin Atlas, 17, 70, *70–71*
DeLongpre, Paul, 128
DeMille, Cecil B., 86, 130
Diaz, Jose, 170
Dickson, Edward, 142
digital maps, 182
Disney Studio, 50
Dodd, William J., 86
Dodger Stadium, 160, 184
Doheny, Edward L., 16, 126
Dominguez, Jose, 28
downtown area, 13, 17, 62, 184; maps, *72–73*, 78, 184
Downtown Los Angeles, 184, *184–85*
Dresel, Emil, 34, *34–35*
Durbin, Deanna, 86

Eagle Rock, 64
earthquakes, 120
East Hollywood, 64
East Los Angeles, 48, 176
Eaton, Frederick, 15, 94–95, 102, *102–3*
Echo Park Reservoir, 38, 48, 50, 60, 92, 104
Eddy, Gerald, *28–29*
Edendale, 60
Edison, Thomas, 130
Elliot, H. B., 16, *52–53*
Elysian Park, 36, 50, 52, 60, 160
Evergreen Cemetery, 50, 74
Exposition Park, 54, 142, 148

Fages, Pedro, 28
Fairbanks, Douglas, 130, 151
Fairfax District, 64
Fernandeño Indians, 14
Fields, W. C., 86
Filipino Americans, 170
film studio maps, 19, 130, *130–31*, 134, *134–35*
Fletcher, Ed, 146
flood control, 98, 99, 120
Ford, John Anson, 146
Forncrook, Clarence Samuel, 16, 126, *126–27*
Forncrook, Edna Marie, 16, 126, *126–27*
Forncrook, George, *164–65*
Fort Hill Tract map, 17, 68, *68–69*
Fort Moore Hill, 15, 52, 182
freeways, 18, 180, 184

Gable, Clark, 151
Gabrielino Indians, 14, 24
Gardena, 110
Garland, William May, 62, *62–63*, 148

Garland Atlas of Los Angeles, 62, *62–63*
Gates, Worthington, 60, *60–61*
geological surveys, 104, 170
Glendale, 64
Glover, Eli S., 16, 42, *44–45*
Goez Map Guide to the Murals of East Los Angeles, 20, 176, *176–77*
golf courses, 140
Gonzalez, Joe, 176
Gonzalez, John, 176, *176–77*
Gower Gulch, 19
Grant, Cary, 86
Greater Los Angeles: The Wonder City of America, 19, 140, *140–41*
Griffith Park, 16, 56, 58, 64, 142, 148
Guthrie, Woody, 142

Hall, E. E., 84
Hall, Jessica, 98
Hancock, George Allen, 38, 166
Hancock, Henry, 21, 26, *26–27*, 38, *38–39*
Hancock Survey Official Map No. 2 of Los Angeles City, 14–15, 36, *36–37*
Hansen, George, 36, *36–39*, 38, 92
Hansen Map, 38, *38–39*
harbor, 16, 110–13
Harbor Gateway, 64
Harriman, William R., 24, *24–25*
Heart of Los Angeles, 17, 78, *78–79*
Hering, Rudolph, 102
Hermanson, Ron G., *138–39*
Highland Park, 48, 64
Highland View, 48
Historic Roads to Romance, 19, 146, *146–47*
Historical and Recreational Map of Los Angeles (Mora), 19, 144, *144–45*
Holabird, 64
Hollywood, 17, 19, 64, 104; maps, 17, 19, *128–35*
Hollywood Cemetery, 130
Huntington, Collis P., 106
Huntington, Henry, 18, 106
Huntington Beach, 126
Hutton, William Rich, 32

infrastructure, 15, 102–5
insurance atlases, 14, 20, 70, 172, *172–73*, 174
Ivanhoe, 50

Jacobs and Rock Map of Southern Portion of Los Angeles County, 20, 156, *156–59*
Jansen, Frank, 20, 166, *166–67*
Jewish residents, 74
Jones, E. G., *88–89*
Jones, Lowell, *134–35*
Jones, Wilson, 82

Kaufman, Gordon B., 86
Kelleher, Michael, 15, 40, 90, *90–91*
King, John, 36
Kinney, Abbot, 20, 154, *154–55*
Kirkman, George W., 21, 24, *24–25*
Kirkman-Harriman Pictorial and Historical Map of Los Angeles County, 14, 18, 24, *24–25*
Knott, Walter, 146
Kocher, Theo. G., *82–83*
Koeberle, Theo. G., 15, 50, *50–51*
Kuchel, Charles Conrad, 34, *34–35*
Kuchel and Dresel's California Views, 16, 34, *34–35*

La Ballona Improvement Association, 164
Lake, Martha, *152–53*
Lake, Wesley G., 150, *152–53*
Land Act of 1851, 30
land case maps, 26
Land Ordinance, 104
land title maps, 28, 30, 38

Lankershim, Isaac, 58
Lankershim Ranch Land and Water Company, 17, 88
Lasky, Jesse, 130
Lasky Studios, 130
Lasuen, Fermin, 88
Laughlin, Homer, 86
Laughlin, Homer, Jr., 86
Laughlin Park Tract Number 2099, 17, 86, 86–87
Lawrence, Francis, 60, 60–61
Laws of the Indies, 10
Lazard, Solomon, 34
LeCouvreur, Frank, 40
LeCouvrier, Robert, 102
Leimert Park, 64
Leuschner, K. M., 140, 140–41
Lewis, Susan, 178–79
libraries, 17, 76
Lick, James, 86
Lincoln Heights, 76
Lippincott, Joseph Barlow, 94–95
Literary Map of Los Angeles, 178, 178–79
Lombard, Carole, 86
Los Angeles 1909, 60, 60–61
Los Angeles and Independence Railroad, 43
Los Angeles and San Bernardino Land Association, 30
Los Angeles and Santa Monica Land and Water Company, 17, 82
Los Angeles Angels, 20, 174
Los Angeles Aqueduct, 72, 92, 94; topographic map, 15, 94–95, 96–97
Los Angeles Area Freeway System, 18, 180, 180–81
Los Angeles Bureau of Water Works, 92
Los Angeles Canal and Reservoir Company, 92
Los Angeles City Water Company, 90, 92
Los Angeles County Engineer's Office, 99, 100–101
Los Angeles Dodgers, 174
Los Angeles Harbor, 110, 112
Los Angeles Harbor and Vicinity, 16, 112, 112–13
Los Angeles in 1881, scale model, 15, 46, 46–47
Los Angeles neighborhoods map, 186, 186–87
Los Angeles Railway, 78, 108
Los Angeles River, 36, 50, 90, 98; map, 15, 98, 99, 100–101
Los Angeles Terminal Railway, 56
Los Angeles Times, The, 15
Los Angeles Transit Lines fold-out map, 18, 108, 108–9
Los Angeles Water Company, 102
Los Felix Rancho, 86
Lovers Lane map, 17, 66, 66–67
Lummis, Charles, 144

Maguire, Molly, 178–79
Manso, Juan, 88
Manson, Charles, 151
Map of Los Angeles County (1912), 110, 110–11
Map of the City of Los Angeles (Rowan and Koeberle), 15, 50, 50–51
Map of the City of Los Angeles (Stevenson), 15, 48, 48–49
Mar Vista, 164
Marchessault, Damien, 36
Marsh, Robert, 17, 21, 72, 72–73
McPherson, Aimee Semple, 138
Merget, R. L., 16, 64–65
Mesmer City map, 20, 162, 162–63
Mesner, Joseph, 162
Mesner, Louis, 162
Mexican Americans, 20, 74, 156, 170
mines, 122
Miracle Mile map, 17, 80, 80–81
missions, 14, 26–27, 88
Moore, Maloy, 186, 186–87
Moore, William, 15, 21, 36, 66, 90, 92, 92–93
Mora, Jo, 19, 21, 144, 144–45
Moreno, Antonio, 86
Morgan, Julia, 86
Mott, Thomas Dillingham, 36
Mt. Washington, 73
Mulholland, William, 15, 92, 94–95
Muni, Paul, 130
Murnau, F. W., 166
Murrieta, Joaquin, 144

National City Lines, 108
Native Americans, 14, 24–25, 98, 99
nautical maps, 20, 166, 166–67
Neutra, Richard, 160
Neve, Felipe de, 10
Newmark, Harris, 66
Ninth Street Tract, 17, 54, 54–55
Nirenstein, Nathan, 80
Nirenstein Atlas, 17, 80, 80–81
Normark, Don, 160

Official Map of the County of Los Angeles (1898), 16, 58, 58–59
Official Sightseeing Map of Los Angeles City and County, 19, 142, 142–43
oil fields, 122, 140; map, 16, 126, 126–27
Olmstead, David, 146
Olvera, Augustin, 40
Olympics, 20, 62, 78, 138, 140; map, 148, 148–49
O'Malley, Walter, 174
O'Melveny, Henry, 142
Ord, Edward O. C., 14, 21, 32
Ord's Survey, 14, 32, 32–33; 38, 62, 78, 99, 136, 184
Otis, Harris Gray, 106
Owens Valley, 94–95

Pacific Coast Highway, 120
Pacific Electric Railway, 18, 78, 106, 108; transportation map, 18, 106, 106–7
Pacific Electric Subway, 78
Panorama 1891, 16, 52, 52–53
Panoramic Automobile Road Map and Tourist Guide Book, 18, 124, 124–25
panoramic maps, 16, 34, 42–43, 52, 56, 58
Parker, Dorothy, 186
Parkinson, John, 62
Pasadena, 64
Payne, James H., 17, 21, 78, 78–79
Perry, C. N., 16, 58, 58–59
Pershing Square, 48, 62, 184
Pickford, Mary, 150, 151
Pico, Andres, 88
Pico, Pio, 40, 88
Pierce, Bruce Wellington, 16, 21, 54, 54–57, 56
Pierce's Los Angeles, 16, 56, 56–57
plat maps, 15, 36, 38, 48, 50, 122
Plaza, 14–15, 40, 42, 48, 184
Porter, John Clinton, 78
Power, Tyrone, 130
Public Works of Art Project, 76
pueblo, 13, 14, 24, 26, 34, 36, 38, 40
Putnam, Claude, 146, 146–47

railroads, 15, 106–9
Rancho Los Alamitos, 30
Rancho San Jose de Buenos Ayres, 82
ranchos, 14, 28–31, 58, 82, 86
Rathbone, Basil, 86
Reagan, James, 15, 99, 100–101
real estate advertisement maps, 54, 82, 84, 88, 128
real estate atlases, 62, 74, 80
Reese, Michael, 30
Reeve, Sidney B., 19, 130, 130–31
Reid, Hugo, 26
Renie, Jack, 19, 21
Renshaw, Robert, 68–69
reservoir lands map, 15, 92, 92–93
Reynolds, William P., 66, 66–67
Riehm, Filipe, 34
Riley, Bennett C., 32–33
Road Map of Los Angeles and Vicinity (Auto Club, 1937), 18, 120, 120–21
road maps, 18–19, 114–20, 180
Roads to Romance Association, 146
Rojas, James, 21, 182, 182–83
Roosevelt, Theodore, 95, 122
Rose, Henry, 95
Route 66, 120
Rowan, Thomas E., 50
Rowan, Valentine James, 15, 21, 50, 50–51
Rowland, John, 26
rubber manufacturers, 140
Rueger, Henry, 122
Rueger's Automobile and Miner's Road Map of Southern California, 18, 122, 122–23
Ruxton, A. G., 40, 40–41
Ruxton Plaza map, 15, 40, 40–41

San Clemente Island, 58
San Fernando Valley, 17–18, 28, 50, 64, 88, 88–89, 104
San Gabriel Mission lands map, 14, 26, 26–27, 104
San Pedro, 16, 42, 64, 110, 148
Sanborn, D. A., 174
Sanborn Company, 70
Sanborn Fire Insurance Atlas: sheet of Central Avenue, 20, 172, 172–73; sheet of Wrigley Field, 20, 174, 174–75
Sanford, William T. B., 82
Santa Fe Railroad, 68, 184
Santa Fe Springs, 126
Santa Monica, 16, 42, 43, 45, 52, 64, 110
Satori, Joseph R., 132
scale models, 15, 46
Schoenberg, Arnold, 168, 168–69

Security Trust and Savings Bank, 132, 132–33
Selig Polyscope Company, 130
Semi-Tropic Homestead Company, 17, 54, 56
sewer system (proposed) map, 15, 102, 102–3
Sexton, Robert H., Jr., 46, 46–47
Shatto, George, 166
Signal Hill, 126
Silver Lake Reservoir, 48, 50
Silverman, Aaron, 178–79
Simons, Walter, 156
Simons Brick Company—Yard No. 3, 20, 156, 156–59, 170
Sisters of Charity Hospital, 66
"Sleepy Lagoon," 20, 168–69, 170
Smith, Doug, 186, 186–87
Smith, George Otis, 104
Smith, William A., 146
Southern California Land Company, 52, 52–53
Southern Pacific Railroad, 15, 18, 43, 48, 88, 106, 110
sports maps, 20
Stahlberg, A. J., 40
Stansfield, Barbara, 180–81
stars' homes, maps to, 19, 137, 142, 142–43, 150–51, 152–53
Stearns, Abel, 30, 34
Stevenson, Henry J., 15, 21, 48, 48–49, 98
Stilson, Fielding J., 17, 84, 84–85
Stilson, W. W., 84
streetcar maps, 18, 106, 108
strip maps, 116–18
subdivisions, 14–15, 82, 86, 88, 154, 164
suburbs, 17, 82–89
Sunset, 17; map, 17, 82, 82–83
Sunset Boulevard, 128
survey maps, 32, 36, 38, 40, 50
Sycamore Grove, 50

Tate, Sharon, 151
Terminal Island, 112
Thomas Guide, The (street atlas), 11, 19
Title Insurance and Trust Company ranchos map, 14, 28
Tongva Indians, 14, 24, 98, 126, 166, 184
topographic maps, 15, 94–95, 104, 156, 170
tourist maps, 19, 134–53
transportation maps, 18, 106–9. *see also* road maps
Travelure Map of Los Angeles and Vicinity, 19, 138, 138–39
Tsutsumi, Susan, 180–81
Tujunga, 64

Union Oil Olympics map, 20, 148, 148–49
United States Board of Land Commissioners, 38
United States Geological Survey, 21
University of California at Los Angeles, 82, 86, 168
University Park District, 64
USGS Topo, 104, 104–5

Valdez, Luis, 170
Valentino, Rudolph, 130
Van Nuys, Isaac Newton, 88
Venice, 64; map, 20, 154, 154–55
Vermont Square, 76
Vernon, 76

Walcott, Charles D., 104
Waring, George E., 102
Warren, Althea, 76
water, 15, 36, 90–97
Water Department of the City of Los Angeles, 15
Weathers, Anita L., 138–39
Welton, Vivienne, 150
Westlake Park, 56
Westwood, 17, 64
Whitlock, Laura, 18, 106–7, 108
Wilcox, Horace Henderson, 17, 19, 128, 128–29, 130
Wilkinson, Frank, 160
Wilmington, 36, 43, 44, 64, 110
Wilshire Boulevard, 62
Wilson, Benjamin "Don Benito," 26, 82
Winslow, Carleton, 86
Wolfskill, John, 82
Wolfskill, William, 82
Woodman, Frederick, 99
Workman, William H, 26, 74, 102
Wright, E. T., 58, 58–59
Wright, Frank Lloyd, 86
Wrigley, William, Jr., 166, 174
Wrigley Field, 20, 174, 174–75

Yangna, 14, 24

Zanja Madre, 40, 48, 66, 90, 98, 182
zanja system, 94, 98, 99, 102; map, 15, 90, 90–91
Zoot Suit Riots, 170

Contributor Biographies

Glen Creason is Map Librarian at Los Angeles Public Library and co-curator of the landmark exhibition *L.A. Unfolded: Maps from the Los Angeles Public Library.*

Dydia DeLyser is Associate Professor of Geography at Louisiana State University. Her work focuses on landscape and social memory, with a regional emphasis on the American West. She is the author of *Ramona Memories: Tourism and the Shaing of Southern California.*

Joe Linton is an artist, writer, and activist, living in Koreatown, Los Angeles. He is the author and illustrator of *Down by the Los Angeles River: Friends of the Los Angeles River's Official Guide.* He contributes to the blog "L. A. Creek Freak" at www.lacreekfreak.wordpress.com

Julie Shafer is a Southern California native who lives and works in Los Angeles. She is an exhibiting artist working with photography and video, and teaches photography at several Southern California schools including CSUF, CSUSB, and Chaffey College.

D. J. Waldie is the author of *Holy Land: A Suburban Memoir, Where We Are Now: Notes from Los Angeles, Close to Home: An American Album*, and *California Romantica.*

William J. Warren, a retired engineer, is past-President of the California Map Society and edits their quarterly newsletter. His written work on maps and exploration has been published widely in such places as *Mercator's World* magazine.

Morgan P. Yates is the archivist for the Automobile Club of Southern California in Los Angeles. He contributes regularly to *Westways*, the Auto Club's member magazine and has co-curated numerous Club sponsored exhibitions. He holds graduate degrees in public history and education and lives in Claremont, C.A.

Acknowledgments

Writing about maps of the city took a village and I have much gratitude for those who guided my way. Douglas Woods and his wife Allegra took the first steps and especially Douglas Curran of Rizzoli who calmly saw it through. The research was the greatest struggle and there was great help from peers: first and foremost the Los Angeles Public Library and especially the reference librarians of the History and Genealogy department; Christina Rice, Glenna Dunning, and Mary McCoy, who checked the facts and took up the slack. Also Anne Connor, webmaster Matthew Mattson, photo archivist Carolyn Cole, Michael Kirley, Cynthia McNaughton, Emma Roberts, Kim Creighton, Toria Aiken, Sheila Nash, Kent Brinkmeyer, Lisa Falk, Molly Snider, Bettye Ellison, David Strother, Dan Dupill, Cheryl Funada, Frank Louck, the late Dorothy Mewshaw, Roy Stone, Betty Gay Teoman, Helene Mochedlover, Billie Connor, Bob Timmermann, Pat Spencer, Gene Estrada, Helen Haskell, Jim Sherman, Diane Olivo, Nelson Torres, and the entire excellent staff of the Los Angeles Library Foundation, led by Carolyn Wagner. At the Seaver Center Betty Uyeda for research and support along with John Cahoon and Sojin Kim. The amazing James Rojas at the MTA and the Fifth Floor Gallery in Chinatown. At the Huntington Library Rare books: Alan Jutzi and map maven Bill Warren. The friendliest map library in the West: at California State University at Northridge, Kris Tacsik. For the Los Angeles City Archives: Jay Jones and Todd Gafkowski. At UCLA Rare Books: Jeff Rankin and Carol Nishijima. The Automobile Club of Southern California, with the two local history treasures, Matt Roth and Morgan Yates. Generous private collectors: Barry Ruderman and Jim Heiman, who gave advice and maps. Author Derek Hayes, preservationist Mitch Browning, and archivist Peter Hiller of the Jo Mora trust, all gave wisdom. Others who were efficient and helpful include: UC Berkeley's Bancroft Library and the great Library of Congress. The best resource on-line at the California Map Society, the online archive of California, David Rumsey, and Callisphere. And the Yoda of all map librarians, Mary Larsgaard. A special thanks to Photographer Julie Shafer, who took impossible tasks and turned them into beautiful illustrations, bless her.

Special thanks to my family who always kept me a place at the table: my wonderful daughter, Katya, who inspired me from start to finish. My father, Ben Creason, who made all of this possible. Then brother, Stephen, sisters Cheryl and Christine, and their families in California and Colorado. Friends and scholars who gave support: my muse and my moon Teresa Mons, Romo, Nastassja and Fred Chernoff, Andree Matton, Greg Sheehy, Lissy Ziesing, Lori Levine-Yonan, Freya Reisman, Bob Brian, Paula Weiner, Pat and Diana Bell, Nancy Reppert, Tim Balderama, Francesca Smith, Perla Batalla, Claud Mann, Eva Batalla-Mann, Ry Cooder, Bobby Vega, Billy Hogan, Will Tefft, Lucinda Wehrkamp, Robert Kanner, Anne McNeil, Eve Luckring, Joshua Hale Fialkov, Chris Nichols of Los Angeles Magazine, Elizabeth Gadbois, Hynden Walch, Bonnie Tone, Ed Carroll, Derrick Garbell, Niall White, Nancy Hemme, Susan J.Stone, Ed and Kathleen Sheehy, Wendy Lambo, Roberta Martinez, Kevin P. Smith, Michael Sheehy, Richard Sheehy, Nick Caskey, Katherine Miller, the Strange Heads Softball team, the Ziesing family, the Knowlton family, the Barth family, and the thousands of library patrons who taught me thousands upon thousands of lessons.

—G. C.

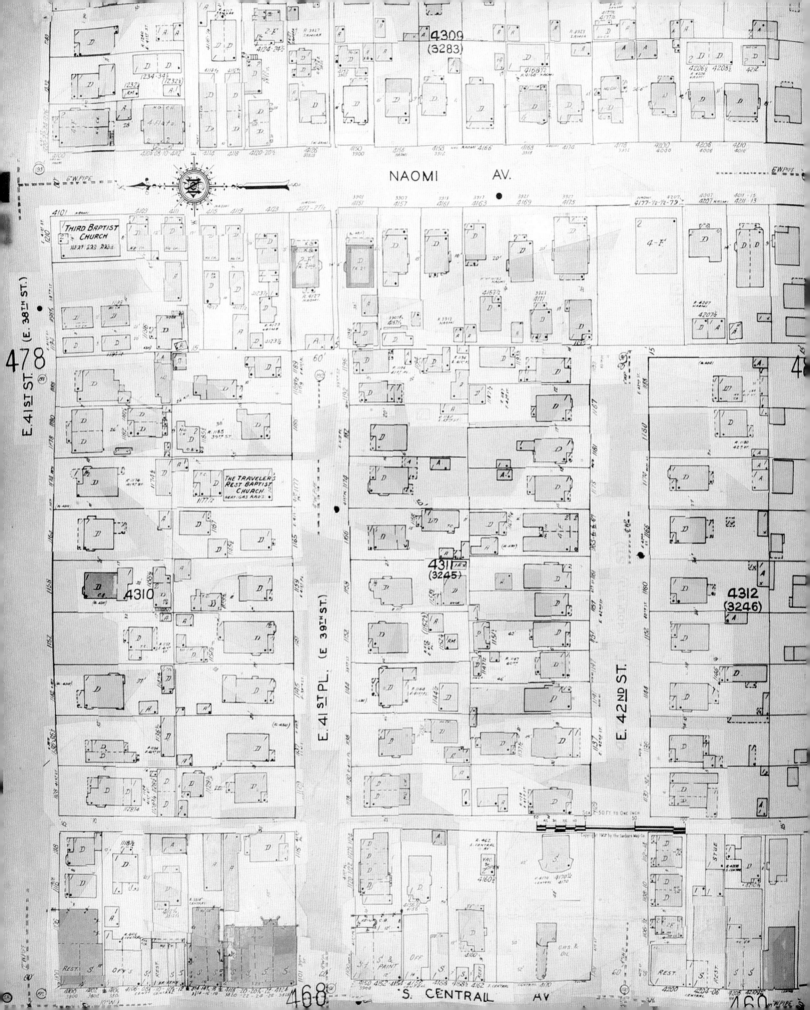